THE BRITISH ARMY GUIDE 2012–2013

Editor – Charles Heyman

ISBN 978 1 84884 107 9

Price £9.99

Pen & Sword Books Ltd
47 Church Street
Barnsley S70 2AS

Telephone: 01226-734222   Fax: 01226-734438
www.pen-and-sword.co.uk

The information in this publication has been gathered from unclassified sources.

Front Cover: Soldiers from The Rifles on patrol in Afghanistan (Copyright MoD 2011)

Rear Cover: The Royal Welsh in Afghanistan (Copyright MoD 2011)

CONTENTS LIST

CHAPTER 1 – OVERVIEW
GENERAL INFORMATION

Population – European Union – Top Five Nations

(2011 Eurostat estimates)

Germany	81.8 million
France	64.7 million
United Kingdom	60.9 million
Italy	60.3 million
Spain	45.9 million

Total European Union population is estimated at 501 million.

Finance – European Union – Top Five Nations

(2010 IMF Estimates)

	GDP (US$)	GDP (Euros)	GDP (£)	Per Capita Income
Germany	US$3,300 bn	€2,390 bn	£2,062 bn	£25,207
France	US$2,550 bn	€1,847 bn	£1,593 bn	£24,621
UK	US$2,250 bn	€1,630 bn	£1,406 bn	£26,290
Italy	US$2,030 bn	€1,471 bn	£1,268 bn	£21,028
Spain	US$1,350 bn	€ 978 bn	£ 843 bn	£21,307

Global Comparison

	Population	GDP	Per Capita Income (nominal)
USA	309 m	US$14,700 bn	US$47,572
China	1,330 m	US$ 5,800 bn	US$ 4,360
EU (27 nations)	501 m	US$16,100 bn	US$32,135

Note:
1. Conversion rates: €1 = US£1.38; £1 = US$1.60
2. GDP (Gross Domestic Product) is an annual figure that values all of the goods and services produced by a country in that year. GDP is a very simple indicator of national wealth.
3. Per Capita Income is the most basic indicator of individual wealth. In this case the figure for GDP has been divided by the size of the population.

UK Population

England	51.1 million
Wales	2.98 million
Scotland	5.14 million
Northern Ireland	1.75 million
Total	60.97 million

The population split in Northern Ireland is approximately 56% Protestant and 41% Roman Catholic with the remaining 3% not falling into either classification (2001 Census).

The figures above relate to 2007 estimates by the UK office for National Statistics. The census that took place in early 2011 will probably return a population figure of around 62 million.

UK Population Breakdown – Military Service Groups

(2010 estimates)

Age Group	Total	Males	Females
16-29	11.2 million	5.7 million	5.5 million
30-44	13.1 million	6.5 million	6.6 million
45-59	11.6 million	5.7 million	5.9 million

There are about 11.4 million in the 0-15 age group and about 9.75 million in the age group 65+.

UK Area (in square kilometres)

England	130,423
Wales	20,766
Scotland	77,167
Northern Ireland	14,121
Total	242,477

Government

The executive government of the United Kingdom is vested nominally in the Crown, but for practical purposes in a committee of ministers that is known as the Cabinet. The head of the Ministry and leader of the Cabinet is the Prime Minister and for the implementation of policy, the Cabinet is dependent upon the support of a majority of the Members of Parliament in the House of Commons. Within the Cabinet, defence matters are the responsibility of the Secretary of State for Defence. The Secretary of State for Defence has five principal deputies; the Minister of State for the Armed Forces; Minister for International Security Strategy; Minister for Defence Equipment, Support and Technology; Minister for Defence Personnel, Welfare and Veterans plus the Under Secretary of State and Lords Spokesman on Defence.

UK Government Expenditure Plans 2011-2012

Total Government Spending-   £701 billion

Of which some elements include:

Health	£122 billion
Social Security	£123 billion
Education	£84 billion
Defence	£35 billion (Total Resource – depreciation)
Protection	£34 billion
Welfare	£113 billion
Transport	£20 billion
Debt Interest	£43 billion

TOTAL BRITISH ARMED FORCES (AT 1 APRIL 2011 – TRAINED PERSONNEL)

Regular: 176,810; Regular Army 101,300; Royal Navy 35,430 (including 8,000 Royal Marines); Royal Air Force 40,090.

Note:
Army figure includes about 3,800 Gurkhas and small numbers of Full Time Reserve Service (FTRS) personnel deployed overseas.

Volunteer Reserves 37,600 (1 April 2010); Army 33,130; Royal Navy 2,900; Royal Air Force 1,500. There are probably about 150,000 Regular Reserves who could be recalled in a major emergency.

Cadets 133,000 (1 April 2010); Army 75,800; Royal Navy 14,000; Royal Air Force 43,300 (includes Combined Cadet Force).

MOD Civilians 85,000 (Early 2011);

CURRENT FORCE LEVELS

Strategic Forces: 4 x Vanguard Class submarines capable of carrying up to 16 x Trident (D5) Submarine Launched Ballistic Missiles (SLBM) deploying with 40 x warheads per submarine. If necessary a D5 missile could deploy with 12 MIRV (multiple independently targetable re-entry vehicles). Future plans appear to be for a stockpile of 120 operationally ready warheads and 58 missile bodies. Strategic Forces are provided by the Royal Navy.

Current plans appear to be for the Vanguard Class submarines to be replaced in the 'early 2030s'.

Regular Army: 101,300 trained and including about 3,800 Gurkhas; 1 x Corps Headquarters (ARRC); 1 x Armoured Divisional HQ in Germany; 1 x Mechanised Divisional HQ in UK; 3 x Non-deployable divisional type HQ in UK; In Germany – 2 x Armoured Brigade Headquarters and 1 x Logistics Brigade HQ; In UK – 5 x Deployable Combat Brigade HQ and 1 x Logistics Brigade HQ; 10 x Regional Brigade HQ; Major Units: 10 x Armoured Regiments; 36 x Infantry Battalions; 15 x Artillery Regiments; 12 x Engineer Regiments; 12 x Signal Regiments; 5 x Army Air Corps Regiments; 7 x Equipment Support Battalions; 17 x Logistic Regiments; 9 x Medical Regiments/ Field Hospitals.

Territorial Army: 33,130; 14 x Infantry Battalions; 4 x Yeomanry Regiments; 7 x Artillery Regiments; 5 x Engineer Regiments; 2 x Special Air Service Regiments; 5 x Signals Regiments; 2 x Equipment Support Battalions; 17 x Logistic Regiments; 2 x Intelligence Battalions; 1 x Army Aviation Regiments; 13 x Field Hospitals/Medical Regiments.

Royal Navy: 35,430 (including some 8,000 Royal Marines): 4 x Nuclear Powered Ballistic Missile (UK Strategic Deterrent); 9 x Nuclear Powered Submarines (attack type – future total 7); 1 x Helicopter Carrier; 2 x Amphibious Assault Ships; 7 x Destroyers; 17 x Frigates (future combined total of 19); 16 x Minehunters and Minesweepers (future total of 14); 4 x Ocean survey vessels; 1 x Antarctic patrol ship; 4 x Patrol vessels and 16 x Patrol craft (fishery protection and patrol duties).

Fleet Support Ships (Manned by Royal Fleet Auxiliary personnel. Supply fuel, stores and ammunition at sea to fleet units) 1 x Fast fleet tanker; 2 x Small fleet tankers; 3 x Support tankers; 2 x Replenishment ships; 1 x Aviation training ship; 1 x Forward repair ship; 4 x Landing Ships.

Royal Marines: 8,000: 1 x Commando Brigade Headquarters; 3 x Royal Marine Commando (Battalion Size); 2 x Commando Assault Helicopter Squadrons; 1 x Commando Light Helicopter Squadron ; 1 x Commando Regiment Royal Artillery; 1 x Commando Regiment Royal Engineers; 1 x Commando Logistic Regiment; 1 Commando Assault Group (Landing-Craft); 1 x Fleet Protection Group; 4 x Special Boat Service Squadrons.

Royal Air Force: 40,090; 5 x Multi-role Squadrons with about 70 x Typhoon (mid 2011); 4 x Attack Squadrons with about 100 x Tornado GR4); 1 x Reconnaissance Squadron with 4 x Shadow; 2 x Airborne Early Warning Squadrons; 1 x Squadron with 7 x Sentry and 1 x Squadron with 5 x Sentinel R1; 2 x Tanker/Transport Squadrons with 11 x VC-10 and 6 x Tristar; 6 x Transport Squadrons with 35 x C-130 Hercules, 2 x Islander, 3 x Tristar C2, 6 x BAe 125 and 2 x BAe 146; 9 x Support Helicopter Squadrons with 40 x Chinook; 28 x Puma, 25 x Sea King (SAR, 28 x Merlin, 16 x Griffin, 30 x Squirrel; Possibly 5-7 Reaper UAVs; 8 x Ground (Field) Defence Squadrons (RAF Regiment).

Future Personnel Totals: UK Mod sources suggest that by 2020 the Army trained personnel figure will be around 82,000, with both the Royal Navy and Royal Air Forces personnel totals reducing by 5,000 for each service.

BRITISH ARMY EQUIPMENT SUMMARY

Armour: 345 x Challenger 2; 81 x CRARRV; 33 x Trojan (AVRE); 33 x Titan (AVLB); 320 x Scimitar; 620 x Fv 432/430 family; 785 x MCV 80 Warrior (possibly 500 in service); 390 x Spartan;

380 x Bulldog; 300 x Mastiff; 11 x Fuchs (NBC); 400 x Panther; 155 x Ridgeback; 115 x Warthog; 574 x Snatch (including variants; 179 x Vector; 161 x Viking; 73 x Wolfhound; 250 x Husky. **Artillery and Mortars:** 146 x AS 90; 59 x 227 mm MLRS/GLMRS; 142 x 105 mm Light Gun; 340 x 81 mm mortar (including about 100 x self- propelled); 1,000 x 60 mm Light Mortar;

Air Defence: 24 x Rapier C Fire Units; 145 x Starstreak (LML); 84 x HVM (SP on Stormer).

Army Aviation: 99 x Lynx Mk7/Mk9; 115 x Gazelle; 6 x BN–2; 66 x WAH-64D Apache; 4 x A109.

JOINT FORCES

Joint Helicopter Command: 4 x Royal Naval Helicopter Squadrons; 5 x Army Aviation Regiments (already listed in the above Army entry); 7 x Royal Air Force Helicopter Squadrons (including 1 x RAuxAF Helicopter Support Squadron).

Joint Special Forces Group: 1 x Regular Special Air Service (SAS) Regiment; 2 x Volunteer Reserve Special Air Service Regiments; 4 x Special Boat Service (SBS) Squadrons; 1 x Special Reconnaissance Regiment; 1 x Special Forces Support Group; 1 x Joint Special Forces Air Wing.

NBC: Joint Nuclear, Biological and Chemical Regiment.

Defence Medical Services: Ministry of Defence Hospital Units; The Royal Centre for Defence Medicine: The Defence Medical Rehabilitation Centre (Headley Court); Defence Medical Services Training Centre; Defence Dental Services; Defence Medical Postgraduate Deanery.

National Police Forces: England and Wales 125,000. Scotland 14,000, Northern Ireland 11,000.

MILITARY TASKS AND DEFENCE PLANNING ASSUMPTIONS OF THE UK'S ARMED FORCES

The Strategic Defence and Security Review (SDSR) of late 2010 stated that the contribution of the UK Armed Forces to the national security effort is defined by a number of Military Tasks (MT) and Defence Planning Assumptions (DPA).

Military Tasks

The seven military tasks are:

♦ Defending the UK and its Overseas Territories
♦ Providing strategic intelligence
♦ Providing nuclear deterrence
♦ Supporting civil emergency organisations in times of crisis
♦ Defending the UK's interest by projecting power strategically and through expeditionary intervention
♦ Providing a defence contribution to UK influence
♦ Providing security for stabilisation

Defence Planning Assumptions

These assume that in the future the UK Armed Forces will have the size and shape that will enable them to conduct operations of the following type:

♦ An enduring stabilisation operation at around brigade level (possibly up to 6,500 personnel) with maritime and air support as required, while also conducting:
♦ One non-enduring complex intervention (up to 2,000 personnel), and
♦ One non-enduring simple intervention (up to 1,000 personnel):

or alternatively:

- Three non-enduring operations if the UK Armed Forces are not already engaged in an enduring operation:

or

- For a limited time period, and with sufficient warning, committing all the UK's effort to a one-off intervention of up to three brigades with air and maritime support at a level of about 30,000 personnel.

FUTURE FORCE 2020

In general terms the planning framework provided by the Military Tasks and Defence Planning Assumptions provides an outline for structure which the UK Government aims to establish by 2020. The proposal is for the Future Force 2020 to have three main combined service elements:

- The Deployed Force
- The High Readiness Force
- The Lower Readiness Force

The Deployed Force

This will consist of those forces that are actually engaged in operations. Therefore aircraft engaged in operations (including the defence of the UK's airspace), forces involved in operations in the South Atlantic, forces operating in Afghanistan and other expeditionary operations plus the nuclear deterrent will all form elements of The Deployed Force.

The High Readiness Force

This force will consist of a range of maritime, air and land based units capable of deploying at short notice to meet the requirements of the Defence Planning Assumptions. Such forces would enable the UK to react quickly to a range of scenarios that might threaten our national security interests. These force elements would be capable of operating with allies or where necessary on 'stand-alone' UK operations.

The High Readiness Force will include a significantly enhanced Special Forces capability.

The Lower Readiness Force

The Lower Readiness Force would consist of elements that have either recently returned from operations, or those that are preparing and training for inclusion in The High Readiness Force. Many Lower Readiness Force units (especially logistic) would be involved in supporting The Deployed Force on operations.

LAND FORCES

Land force capabilities will be based around six brigades as follows:

Five multi-role brigades each consisting of around 6,500 personnel that are comprised of main battle tanks, armoured reconnaissance units, armoured, mechanised and light infantry elements, plus artillery, engineers, army aviation and a complete range of support units. One brigade would always be part of the High Readiness Force and where necessary these brigades could be self supporting.

16 Air Assault Brigade would be the sixth brigade and would provide parachute and air assault units for rapid intervention operations at very short notice. This brigade would be self supporting for short duration operations.

All of the above could form part of a much larger organisation (possibly divisional size) under the command of a deployable UK divisional headquarters. For multinational operations the headquarters of the Allied Rapid Reaction Corps (HQ ARRC) would be available.

Challenger main battle tank numbers will reduce by about 40% and heavy artillery numbers such as the 155 mm AS90 will reduce by about 35%. There are currently no plans to reduce the number of Infantry Battalion's.

There are plans for all UK Army units to have been withdrawn from their bases in Germany by 2020. It is likely that a large number of major units will be returned to the UK well before that date.

The Royal Marines 3 Commando Brigade (a Royal Naval formation) would be available for Land Force operations as required.

ROYAL NAVY

Under the terms of the Future Force 2020 proposals the Royal Navy will provide a continuous nuclear deterrent system at sea, maritime defence of the United Kingdom and defence of territories in the South Atlantic. Forces assigned to these roles will include:

The Vanguard submarine force equipped with Trident submarine launched inter-continental ballistic missiles. Current plans are for the Vanguard class submarines to be replaced in the early 2030s.

Seven Astute class nuclear powered hunter killer submarines equipped with Tomahawk land attack cruise missiles . Astute class submarines are capable of operating at sea indefinitely.

Two new aircraft carriers, one of which will be kept at extended readiness. The aircraft carrier at sea will be equipped with Joint Strike Fighters and a range of helicopters that (depending on the operational requirement) could include Apache attack helicopters and possibly Chinook and Merlin support helicopters. It is expected that following the fitting of catapult and arrestor systems the first of these new carriers will be in-service from about 2020.

A balanced surface fleet of 19 frigates and destroyers.

Up to 14 mine counter measures vessels to be based on the existing Hunt and Sandown class vessels. In addition there will be an ice patrol ship and an oceanographic survey capability.

The Royal Marine's 3 Commando Brigade will provide an important maritime response capability to the High Readiness Force. 3 Commando Brigade will be able to land significant forces anywhere in the world.

Strategic transport will be provided by a force of up to 6 roll-on, roll-off ferries.

The Royal Fleet Auxiliary will continue to supply and refuel Royal Naval vessels at sea worldwide.

ROYAL AIR FORCE

The Royal Air Force will continue to provide the air defence of the United Kingdom and territories in the South Atlantic. To meet this requirement, in the longer term, a fast jet force of both Eurofighter Typhoon and Joint Strike Fighter aircraft will provide air defence, precision ground attack and combat ISTAR capabilities.

In the short term elements of the Tornado fleet will be retained to support operations in Afghanistan and elsewhere should the operational requirement arise.

The Royal Air Force will also provide a fleet of strategic and tactical airlift aircraft based around approximately 7 x C-17, 22 x A400M and 14 x Airbus A330 tanker and transport aircraft. The Chinook helicopter fleet will be increased by 12 new aircraft and Merlin helicopters will be retained.

ISTAR capabilities will be enhanced to include a range of unmanned air systems that will complement existing manned aircraft. The UK may purchase 3 x KC-135 Joint Rivet signals intelligence aircraft to improve the existing ISTAR capability.

It is likely that the Royal Air Force will become the lead agency in the proposed UK Cyber Operations Group.

MINISTRY OF DEFENCE (MOD)

In 1963, the three independent service ministries (Admiralty, War Office and Air Ministry) were merged to form the present MoD.

The UK MoD is the government department that is responsible for all defence related aspects of national policy. This large organisation, which directly affects the lives of about 400,000 servicemen, reservists, cadets and MoD employed civilians, is controlled by The Secretary of State for Defence and his deputies.

The Secretary of State for Defence has the following principal deputies;

- ♦ Minister of State for the Armed Forces
- ♦ Minister for International Security Strategy
- ♦ Minister for Defence Equipment, Support and Technology
- ♦ Minister for Defence Personnel, Welfare and Veterans
- ♦ Under Secretary of State and Lords Spokesman on Defence.

The Secretary of State is assisted by two principal advisers:

Permanent Secretary: The Permanent Secretary is responsible for policy, finance and administration in the MoD. As the MoD's Principal Accounting Officer he is personally responsible to Parliament for the expenditure of all public money voted to the MoD for Defence purposes.

Chief of the Defence Staff (CDS): The CDS acts as the professional head of the Armed Forces and he is the principal military adviser to the Secretary of State and to the Government.

Both the Permanent Secretary and the CDS have deputies; the Second Permanent Secretary, and the Vice-Chief of the Defence Staff (VCDS).

In general terms defence is managed through a number of major committees that provide corporate leadership and strategic direction. The two most senior of these committees are the Defence Council and the Defence Ministerial Committee.

DEFENCE COUNCIL

The Defence Council is the senior committee that provides the legal basis for the conduct and administration of defence.

```
                        Defence Council
         ┌──────────────────────┼──────────────────────┐
   Admiralty Board          Army Board            Air Force Board
```

The Defence Council is chaired by the Secretary of State for Defence and the composition of the Council is as follows:

> The Secretary of State for Defence
> Minister of State for the Armed Forces
> Minister for International Security Strategy
> Minister for Defence Equipment, Support and Technology
> Minister for Defence Personnel, Welfare and Veterans
> Under Secretary of State and Lords Spokesman on Defence
> Permanent Secretary
> Chief of the Defence Staff
> Vice-Chief of the Defence Staff
> Chief of the Naval Staff and First Sea Lord
> Chief of the Air Staff
> Chief of the General Staff

> Chief of Defence Material
> Chief Scientific Adviser
> Director General Finance
> Second Permanent Secretary

Levene Report 2011

The Levene Report in June 2011 proposed a new 'Defence Board that would be the primary decision making body for non operational matters. This new Board would include many of the functions of the current Defence Council and meet up to ten times a year. There would be sub-committees dealing with Defence Audit, Investment Approvals and Senior Appointments.

Current plans appear to suggest a Defence Board membership of the following:

> Secretary of State for Defence
> Defence Minister (to be decided)
> Permanent Secretary
> Chief of the Defence Staff
> Director General Finance
> Chief of Defence Materiel
> Audit Committee Chair (Non Executive Director)
> Investment Approvals Committee Chair(Non Executive Director)
> Appointments Committee Chair (Non Executive Director)

The longer term relationship of this new Defence Board to the Defence Council is currently (mid 2011) slightly unclear.

Single Service Boards

There are three single service boards: Admiralty Board, Army Board and the Air Force Board all of which are chaired by the Secretary of State for Defence. In general the purpose of the boards is the administration and monitoring of single service performance. Each of these three boards has an executive committee chaired by the single service chief of staff; Navy Board, Executive Committee of the Army Board and the Air Force Board Standing Committee.

DEFENCE MINISTERIAL COMMITTEE

This committee provides a forum where ministers, senior civil servants and senior military officers can engage together and ensure that the whole business of defence is conducted effectively.

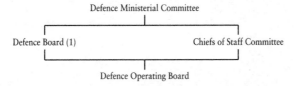

Note:
(1) This is not the 'New Defence Board' as proposed by the 2011 Leven Report but the Board that was in existence prior to June 2011.This Defence Board also has a number of sub committees: Defence Audit Committee; Research and Development Board; Defence Environment and Safety Board; Investments Approval Board; Defence Board Sub Committee for Equipment.

The Defence Ministerial Committee is chaired by the Secretary of State for Defence and the composition of the committee is as follows:

> The Secretary of State for Defence

Minister of State for the Armed Forces
Minister for International Security Strategy
Minister for Defence Equipment, Support and Technology
Minister for Defence Personnel, Welfare and Veterans
Under Secretary of State and Lords Spokesman on Defence
Permanent Secretary
Chief of the Defence Staff
Vice-Chief of the Defence Staff
Chief of the Naval Staff and First Sea Lord
Chief of the Air Staff
Chief of the General Staff
Chief of Defence Material
Chief Scientific Adviser
Director General Finance
Second Permanent Secretary

Other senior officials are invited when the need arises.

Defence Board

This board is chaired by the Permanent Secretary and is the MoD's senior non-ministerial committee. In essence the Defence Board is the MoD's main corporate board providing senior leadership and direction to the implementation of defence policy.

Chiefs of Staff Committee

This committee is chaired by the CDS and is the MoD's senior committee that provides advice on operational military matters and the preparation and conduct of military operations. This is where the CDS seeks the formal advice of the single service Chiefs of Staff.

Defence Operating Board

This board has the responsibility of ensuring that decisions made by the Defence Board and the Chiefs of Staff Committee are acted upon and efficiently discharged. The business of the board is generally conducted in smaller groupings established to implement specific tasks.

CHIEF OF THE DEFENCE STAFF

The Chief of the Defence Staff (CDS) is the officer responsible to the Secretary of State for Defence for the coordinated effort of all three fighting services. He has his own Central Staff Organisation and a Vice Chief of the Defence Staff who ranks as number four in the services hierarchy, following the three single service commanders. The current CDS is General Sir David Richards (May 2011):

General Sir David Richards

General Sir David Richards was born in 1952 and educated at Eastbourne College. He was commissioned into the Royal Artillery in 1971 prior to studying international relations at University College Cardiff. Graduating in 1974 he spent the next nine years at regimental duty in the Far East, Germany and the UK (principally with 29 Commando Regiment RA and C Anti-Tank Battery Royal Horse Artillery) and on the staff of 11th Armoured Brigade in Germany. This period included three tours in Northern Ireland.

After attending the Staff College in 1984, he returned to 11th Armoured Brigade to command a field battery in 47th Field Regiment. From there he spent two years in Berlin as the Chief of Staff of the Berlin Infantry Brigade. Promoted to Lieutenant Colonel, he spent the next three years as an instructor at the Staff College, Camberley, before being appointed to command 3rd Regiment Royal Horse Artillery. This period included another operational tour in Northern Ireland.

In 1994 he was promoted and appointed Colonel Army Plans in the MOD, responsible for the shape and size of the Army. Promoted to Brigadier in 1996, and after attending the Higher Command and Staff course, he became Commander 4th Armoured Brigade in Germany. In 1998 he was posted to the Permanent Joint Headquarters as Chief Joint Force Operations, the UK's default one star commander for short notice expeditionary operations. In this role he was involved in a number of operations, including commanding the UK Contingent in East Timor in 1999, and commanding a UK Joint Task Force in Sierra Leone in 2000.

Promoted to Major General, he was appointed Chief of Staff of the Allied Rapid Reaction Corps in April 2001 before becoming Assistant Chief of the General Staff in September 2002. He assumed the appointment of Commander Allied Rapid Reaction Corps in January 2005, in which role he served as Commander of the International Stabilisation and Assistance Force Afghanistan between May 2006 and February 2007.

On completion of NATO/ISAF expansion across the whole of Afghanistan in October 2006, he was promoted to General for the remainder of his time in Afghanistan. His operational awards include a Mention in Despatches, Commander of the Order of the British Empire, the Distinguished Service Order and Knight Commander of the Order of the Bath.

He became Commander in Chief Land Forces in February 2008 and was appointed as Chief of the General Staff in August 2009. In October 2010 he was appointed as Chief of the Defence Staff.

General Richards is the Honorary Colonel of 3rd Regiment RHA, Colonel Commandant Royal Artillery, Colonel Commandant Brigade of Gurkhas, Chairman of the Gurkha Welfare Trust and President of Army Tennis.

CHAIN OF COMMAND

As previously stated the CDS is the principal service advisor to HM Government and he commands and coordinates the activities of the three services (the three fundamental elements of defence) through the three single service commanders. These single service commanders exercise command of their single services through their respective headquarters.

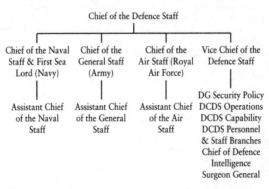

Note: DG – Director General; DCDS – Deputy Chief of the Defence Staff.

The three single services, Royal Navy, Army and Royal Air Force are the fundamental elements of Defence. The single Service Chiefs of Staff (the 1st Sea Lord/Chief of the Naval Staff, the Chief of the General Staff and the Chief of the Air Staff) are the professional heads of their respective services.

However, the complex inter-service nature of the majority of modern military operations, where military, air and naval support must be coordinated has led to the establishment of a permanent tri-service Joint Headquarters. The chain of command resembles the following:

PERMANENT JOINT HEADQUARTERS (PJHQ)

The UK MoD established a Permanent Joint Headquarters (PJHQ) for joint military operations at Northwood in Middlesex on 1 April 1996. This headquarters brought together on a permanent basis, tri-service intelligence, planning, operational and logistics staffs. It contains elements of a rapidly deployable in-theatre Joint Force Headquarters that has the capability of commanding rapid deployment front line forces.

The primary function of the Permanent Joint Headquarters when directed by the CDS is to plan and execute joint, or potentially joint national and UK-led multinational operations conducted outside the UK. PJHQ has operational command of all UK forces assigned for a specific operation.

PJHQ is responsible at the operational level of command for the deployment, direction, sustainment and recovery of a UK Force deployed overseas. Because it exists on a permanent basis rather than being established for a particular operation, PJHQ is involved from the very start of planning for possible operations.

PJHQ, commanded by the Chief of Joint Operations (CJO), (currently a three star officer) occupies existing accommodation above and below ground at Northwood in Middlesex. PJHQ works in close partnership with MoD Head Office in the planning of operations and policy formulation, thus ensuring PJHQ is well placed to implement policy. Having planned the operation, and contributed advice to Ministers, PJHQ will then conduct such operations. Amongst its many tasks PJHQ is currently (mid 2011) engaged in planning and conducting UK military involvement in Afghanistan and elsewhere.

When another nation is in the lead, PJHQ exercises operational command of UK forces deployed on the operation.

Being a Permanent Joint Headquarters, PJHQ provides continuity of experience from the planning phase to the execution of the operation, and on to post-operation evaluation and learning of lessons.

Principal additional tasks of PJHQ include:

- ◆ Monitoring designated areas of operational interest
- ◆ Preparing contingency plans
- ◆ Contributions to the UK MoD's decision making process
- ◆ Exercise of operational control of overseas commands (Falklands, Cyprus and Gibraltar)
- ◆ Managing its own budget
- ◆ Formulation of joint warfare doctrine at operational and tactical levels
- ◆ Conducting Joint Force exercises
- ◆ Focus for Joint Rapid Reaction Force planning and exercising

Areas where PJHQ is not involved:

- ◆ NATO Article V (General War)
- ◆ Strategic Nuclear Deterrent
- ◆ Defence of the UK Home Base
- ◆ Integrity of UK Airspace and Seaspace
- ◆ Counter Terrorism in the UK
- ◆ Northern Ireland

As of mid 2011 PJHQ has been involved with UK defence commitments in the following areas:

Afghanistan, Albania, Algeria, Angola, Bosnia, Burundi, East Timor, Eritrea, Honduras, Iraq (including operations during 2003), Kosovo, Libya, Montenegro, Montserrat, Mozambique, Sierra Leone, East Zaire, West Zaire (Democratic Republic of the Congo).

PJHQ is commanded by the Chief of Joint Operations (CJO):

Air Marshal Sir Stuart Peach KCB, CBE, BA, MPhil, DTech, FRAeS, RAF (CJO)

Sir Stuart Peach joined the Royal Air Force via a University Cadetship at the University of Sheffield in 1977 from where he graduated in Geography, Economics and Social History. After service with RAF Tornado aircraft he attended the Royal Air Force Staff College Bracknell in 1990 and served as Personal Staff Officer to, in succession, the Deputy Commander Royal Air Force Germany, Commander-in-Chief Royal Air Force Germany and Commander Second Allied Tactical Air Force. Following a Master's Degree in Philosophy at the University of Cambridge, he was Director Defence Studies (RAF) before becoming Assistant Director of the Higher Command and Staff Course at the Joint Services Command and Staff College. He was Commander British Forces (Italy) 1999-2000 and NATO Air Commander (Forward) in Kosovo in 2000 before serving as Commandant UK Air Warfare Centre and Assistant Chief of Staff (Intelligence) Strike Command from 2000 to 2003. He was appointed as Chief of Joint Operations in March 2009.

During September 2011 the MoD announced the creation of a new Joint Forces Command (JFC) and that Air MArshal Peach will become the JFC's first commander. In his new role, Air Marshal Peach will be responsible for commanding and generating allocated joint capabilities from the Royal Navy, Army and Royal Air Force. Air Marshall Peach will take up post in December 2011 on promotion to Air Chief Marshal. His immediate task will be to establish a small headquarters by April 2012 before delivering a full capability during early 2013.

PJHQ in the MoD Chain of Command

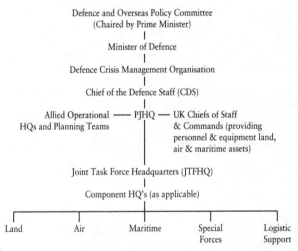

Note:
The Defence and Overseas Policy Committee (DOPC) is responsible for the strategic direction of the UK Government's defence and overseas policy. The DOPC is chaired by the Prime Minister and members include the Secretary of State for Foreign and Commonwealth Affairs (Deputy Chair); Deputy Prime Minister and First Secretary of State; Chancellor of the Exchequer; Secretary of State for Defence; Secretary of State for the Home Department; Secretary of State for International Development; Secretary of State for Trade and Industry. If necessary, other ministers, the Heads of the Intelligence Agencies and the Chief of the Defence Staff may be invited to attend.

PJHQ Headquarters Structure

The PJHQ Headquarters at Northwood brings together about 590 civilian, specialist and tri-service military staff (476 military and 117 civilians) from across the MoD. The headquarters structure resembles the normal Divisional organisation, but staff operate within multidisciplinary groups that are draw from across the headquarters. The headquarters must have the capability of supporting a number of operations simultaneously on behalf of the UK MoD.

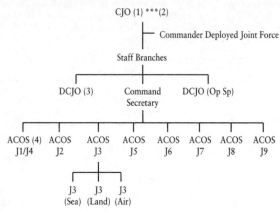

Notes:
(1) CJO – Chief of Joint Operations; (2) *** Denotes the rank of the incumbent (3) DCJO – Deputy Chief of Joint Operations; (4) ACOS – Assistant Chief of Staff.

CJO has a civilian Command Secretary who provides a wide range of policy, legal, presentational, financial and civilian human resources advice.

PJHQ Departments

J1 Personnel and Admin

J2 Intelligence

J3 Operations

J4 Logistics & Medical

J5 Policy and Crisis Planning

J6 Communication and Information Systems

J7 Doctrine and Joint Training

J8 Finance

J9 Policy, Legal and Presentation

The annual PJHQ budget is in the region of £444 million (2009-2010 – Resource DEL). The annual running costs of the Headquarters is estimated at approximately £60 million.

Included in the overall PJHQ budget are the costs of the UK forces in the Falkland Islands, Cyprus and Gibraltar. Major operations such as the ongoing operational commitment in Afghanistan and the ongoing commitment in Libya are funded separately by way of a supplementary budget, and in almost all cases this requires government-level approval. Small operations and the cost of reconnaissance parties are funded from the standard PJHQ budget.

JOINT RAPID REACTION FORCE (JRRF)

The JRRF is essentially the fighting force that PJHQ has immediately available. The JRRF provides a force for rapid deployment operations using a core operational group of the Army's 16th Air Assault

Brigade and the Royal Navy's 3rd Commando Brigade, supported by a wide range of air and maritime assets such as the Joint Helicopter Command.

The force uses what the MoD has described as a 'golfbag' approach with a wide range of units available for specific operations. For example, if the operational situation demands assets such as heavy armour, long range artillery and attack helicopters, these assets can easily be assigned to the force. This approach means that the JRRF can be tailored for specific operations, ranging from support for a humanitarian crisis to missions including high intensity operations.

The 'reach' of the JRRF is enhanced by the Royal Navy's amphibious vessels HMS Albion and HMS Bulwark. Both of these vessels have the ability to carry 650 troops plus a range of armoured vehicles including main battle tanks. A flight deck allows for ship-to-shore helicopter operations.

Responsibility for providing units to the JRRF remains with the single service commands who ensure that units assigned are at an extremely high state of readiness. Units assigned to the JRRF are trained to Joint standards and be committed to NATO, EU, UN or other coalition operations as required.

Under normal circumstances, it would be expected that the Army would ensure the following land forces were available to the JRRF: a brigade sized grouping held at High Readiness and two Strategic Reserves—the Spearhead Land Element (SLE) held at Extremely High Readiness and the Airborne Task Force (ABTF) held at Very High Readiness.

The force commander is the CJRRFO (Chief of the Joint Rapid Reaction Force), who is responsible to the Chief of Joint Operations (CJO) at PJHQ. CJRRFO is supported by the Joint Force Operations Staff at PJHQ, who provide a fully resourced Joint Task Force Headquarters (JTFHQ) at 48 hours notice to move anywhere in the world.

Joint Force Logistics Component

The Joint Force Logistics Component (JFLogC) provides a joint logistic headquarters with force logistics under the command of PJHQ. It delivers coordinated logistic support to the deployed Joint Force in accordance with the commander's priorities. The composition of the JFLogC will be determined by PJHQ during the mission planning stage. Two logistic brigades can be assigned to JFLogC.

DEFENCE EQUIPMENT AND SUPPORT

Following the establishment of PJHQ at Northwood it became important to combine the separate logistics functions of the three Armed Forces. As a result, in 2000 the three distinct separate service logistic functions were fused into one and the Defence Logistic Organisation was formed.

From 1 April 2007 the Defence Procurement Agency (DPA) and the Defence Logistic Organisation (DLO) were merged to form Defence Equipment and Support (DE&S).

The MoD plans for the DE&S to be the engine that delivers 'Through Life' equipment and logistic support, and making sure the whole factory to front line process is seamless and properly integrated.

Some of the DE&S responsibilities to Joint Operations include:

Logistics planning, resource management, contractual support and policy
Global fleet management and land-based equipment
Support of the naval fleet and all naval systems
Communication and Information Systems
Transport and movements
Food and ration packs
Ammunition
Fuel, Oil and Lubricants
Postal Services
Clothing and tentage
Storage for all equipment and materiel

Support is provided through the single service Chiefs of Materiel, a civilian Chief of Materiel (Joint Enablers) and Director General Resources.

With approximately 21,000 personnel, DE&S is one of the largest organisations within the MoD with an annual budget of around £16 billion.

THE UNITED KINGDOM DEFENCE BUDGET

"You need three things to win a war,
Money, money and more money".

Trivulzio (1441-1518)

In general terms defence is related to money. Estimates for the world's top defence budgets for 2010 (in billions of UK£ and US$):

United States	£445 billion	US$ 712 billion
China	£47.8 billion	US$76.5 billion
United Kingdom	£35.9 billion	US$ 57.4 billion
Japan	£33 billion	US$ 52.8 billion
Saudi Arabia	£28.3 billion	US$45.4 billion
France	£26.6 billion	US$ 42.6 billion
Russia	£26 billion	US$41.6 billion
Germany	£25.7 billion	US$ 41.2 billion
India	£24 billion	US$38.5 billion

Note:
Currency conversion rates at £1 : US$1.60.
US figure is the 2011 request.

The figures in the above table are figures derived from £ Sterling, Euro, Rouble and Yen exchange rates during early 2011..

In the 2010–2011 Financial Year (FY) the UK Government has allocated £35.9 billion on defence expenditure with £35 billion allocated for the FY 2011-2012. Actual expenditure in FY 2010–2011 represented about 2.5% of GDP. In 1985 UK defence expenditure represented about 5.2% of GDP.

UK – TOP LEVEL BUDGETS FY2009-2010 (DEPARTMENTAL EXPENDITURE LIMITS – RESOURCE DEL)

Under the early 1990s 'New Management Strategy' the UK defence budget was allocated to a series of 'Top Level Budget Holders' each of whom were allocated a budget with which to run their departments. The money allocated to these Top Level Budgets (TLBs) constitutes the building bricks upon which the whole of the defence budget is based.

Royal Navy Command	£2,211 million
Land Forces	£6,990 million
Air Command	£2,790 million
Permanent Joint Headquarters	£444 million
Defence Equipment & Support	£16,496 million
Central	£1,620 million
Defence Estates	£2,732 million
Science, Innovation & Technology	£466 million

Note: Land Forces TLB includes Service Children's Education; Defence Equipment & Support TLB includes Defence Storage and Distribution Agency; Central TLB includes Defence Vetting Agency, MoD Police and Guarding Agency, People Pay and Pensions Agency and Service Personnel and Veterans Agency.

The Conflict Prevention Resource DEL was £2,682 million and the Capital DEL was £11,536 million. Pay accounted for over £10 billlion.

In addition to the eight major TLBs there are four Trading funds as follows: Met Office, Defence Support Group, Defence Science and Technology Laboratory, Hydrographic Office.

UK MoD Major Investment Decisions

As of late 2010 the UK MoD had some 15 major outstanding projects approximately £67 billion. This figure represents projects where the MoD has taken the decision to invest over the coming years.

Some of the largest contracts are amongst the following:

Typhoon Production and Future Capability	£17,115 million
A400M Transport Aircraft	£2,628 million
Lynx Wildcat Helicopter	£1,901 million
Joint Combat Aircraft	£2,672 million
Queen Elizabeth Class Aircraft Carriers	£4,085 million
Meteor Beyond Visual Range Air-to-Air Missile	£1,240 million
Type 45 Destroyers	£5,000 million
Future Strategic Tanker Aircraft	£12,326 million
Falcon Deployable Communications System	£354 million
Merlin Helicopter Capability Sustainment Programme	£837 million
Watchkeeper UAV	£907 million

The high unit costs of individual items of equipment illustrate the problems faced by defence planners when working out their annual budgets. At 2011 prices the following items cost:

Storm Shadow (Air to Ground) Missile	£500,000
Kinetic Energy Round for Challenger	£3,500 each
155 mm High Explosive Round	£900 each
Individual Weapon (IW)	£800 each (estimate)
5.56 mm round for IW	£1.25
Tomahawk Cruise Missile (Block IV)	£600,000
One Rapier Missile	£60,000
One Challenger 2 MBT	£4.5 million (approx)
Combat High Boot	£95 per pair
Starstreak Missile	£110,000 each
Attack Helicopter	£42 million (region)
Eurofighter	£60 million (estimate)
Merlin Support Helicopter	£34 million
F-35B Lightning II	£90 million (estimate in mid 2011)
Panther CLV	£500,000
Tornado GR4 (cost per flight hour)	£34,000

Defence Budgets – NATO Comparison (2010 Figures)

The nations of the North Atlantic Treaty Organisation (NATO) spent some US$969.6 billion on defence during 2010.

It is probably worth noting that Canada and the European members of NATO spent approximately US$257 billion, while the US spent some US$712 billion. Collectively, Canada and the European members of NATO spent about 36% of the US total.

For ease of conversions from national currencies, amounts are shown in US$.

Country	2010 Budget (billions of US$)
Belgium	3.6
Bulgaria	0.7

Canada	19.9
Czech Republic	2.5
Denmark	3.6
Estonia	0.3
France	42.6
Germany	41.2
Greece	9.66
Hungary	1.35
Italy	20.5
Latvia	0.25
Lithuania	0.3
Luxembourg	0.5
Netherlands	11.3
Norway	5.77
Poland	8.35
Portugal	3.19
Romania	2.14
Spain	10.2
Slovakia	1.1
Slovenia	0.7
Turkey	10.5
United Kingdom	57.4
Other NATO	**257.6**
United States	712.0
Final Total	**969.6**

Note: Iceland has no military expenditure although it remains a member of NATO.

During 2010 the total amount spent on defence by the 27 European Union nations was US$222 billion.

An interesting comparison is made by the total national defence budget divided by the total number of full time personnel in all three services. 2010 figures for the top five world defence spending nations are as follows:

Nation	2010 Defence Budget (US$)	Total Service Personnel	Cost per Serviceman (US$)	
United States	712 billion	1,555,000	457,887	
China	76.5 billion	2,200,000	34,772	Excluding paramilitary
UK	57.4 billion	177,600	323,198	
Japan	52.8 billion	245,000	215,510	
France	42.6 billion	230,000	185,217	Excluding gendarmerie
Germany	35 billion	250,000	140,000	Includes conscripts

BRITISH ARMY STATISTICS

Regular Army (As at 1 April 2011)

	2011	1995	1990
Trained Strength	101,300	104,600	137,200
Untrained Strength	9,140	7,200	15,600
	110,440	**111,800**	**152,800**

Note: Previous years figures are given for comparison purposes. Figures for 2011 include 3,800 trained Gurkhas and 180 untrained Gurkhas.

Regular Army – Requirement Against Strength at 1 April 2011

	Requirement	*Strength*
Officers	12,980	14,120
Other Ranks	89,230	87,180

Regular Army – Intake to the Training Organisation – (During Financial Year 2010/2011)

	(2010/2011)	*(1980/81)*
Officers	740	1,489
Soldiers	7,790	27,382
	8,530	**28,871**

Note: 1980/81 figures are given for comparison.

Regular Army – Outflow – (During Financial Year 2010/2011)

	(2010/11)	*(1990/91)*	*(1980/81)*
Officers	990 (1)	1,860	1,497
Soldiers	10,510 (2)	20,964	20,422
	11,500	**22,824**	**21,919**

(1) Includes 100 untrained officers
(2) Includes 2,760 untrained soldiers

Volunteer Reserves (As at 1 April 2011)

Volunteer Reserves	27,410	(4,250 officers and 23,160 ORs)
NRPS	1,550	(550 officers and 1,000 ORs)
Officer Training Corps	4,140	

NRPS – Non Regular Permanent Staff.

Army Cadet Force

	(1 Apr 2011)	*(1 Apr 1980)*
Total Army Cadets	75,800	74,600

The Army Cadets are run and administered by the MoD. Figures include Combined Cadet Force and Army Cadet Force.

Dogs and Horses

In mid 2011 there were approximately 610 military working dogs and 485 horses in service with the UK Armed Forces. There are a further 419 dogs in service with the Ministry of Defence Police and other guarding agencies.

Full-time trained Strength of the Army (including FTRS*)   Strength (early 2011)

Staff	820	
The Household Cavalry/ Royal Armoured Corps	6,000	
Royal Regiment of Artillery	7,710	
Corps of Royal Engineers	9,660	
Royal Corps of Signals	7,600	
The Infantry	24,750	
Army Air Corps	2,140	
Royal Army Chaplains Department	130	
The Royal Logistics Corps	15,420	
Royal Army Medical Corps	3,010	
Royal Electrical and Mechanical Engineers	10,010	
Adjutant General's Corps (Provost Branch – RMP & MPSC))	1,810	(110 MPSC)
Adjutant Generals Corps (Staff and Personnel Support Branch)	3,750	

Adjutant Generals Corps (Educational and Training Services Branch)	340
Adjutant Generals Corps Royal (Army Legal Service)	120
Royal Army Veterinary Corps	350
Small Arms School Corps	160
Royal Army Dental Corps	370
Intelligence Corps	1,530
Army Physical Training Corps	480
Queen Alexandra's Royal Army Nursing Corps	900
Corps of Army Music	790
Long Service List	340
Unallocated	10
Total trained regular Army and FTRS	98,200
Gurkhas (trained and untrained)	3,800

Note: The overall number of trained personnel differs slightly (about 700) from that given at the beginning of this chapter because of the time-lag between reports being published and the inclusion of FTRS personnel.

*FTRS (Full Time Reserve Service)

Service Personnel Deployed in the UK (April 2010): 166,060

Service Personnel Deployed/Stationed outside the UK mainland (April 2010)

Germany/Belgium/Netherlands	19,710 (majority in Germany)
Cyprus	2,870 (includes 300 UNFICYP)
Gibraltar	270
Other Europe	440
Sierra Leone	30
Middle East	380
Belize/Caribbean	70 (estimate)
South America	10
Oceania	50
Kenya	90 (estimate)
Canada	270
USA	520
Falkland Islands	1,500 (estimate)
Afghanistan	10,000 (estimate)
Brunei	700 (estimate – mainly Gurkhas)

Over 100 Years Ago – Strength of the British Army at 1 Jan 1905

Regular Army	195,000
Colonial Troops or Native Indian Corps	14,000
Army Reserve	80,000
Militia	132,000
Yeomanry (Cavalry)	28,000

Regular forces in India totalled 74,500.

The Indian Army totalled approximately 240,000 all ranks.

Three years previously Regular Army totals by Corps were:

Household Cavalry	1,390
Cavalry of the Line	20,200
Horse Artillery	3,483
Field Artillery	15,509
Mountain Artillery	1,200

Garrison Artillery	18,400
Royal Engineers	7,130
Foot Guards	5,873
Infantry of the Line	132,332
Colonial Corps	5,217
Army Service Corps	3,555
Ordnance Staff	920
Armourers	352
Medical Services	2,993
	218,554

A force reduction was in place due to the drawdown following the end of the war in South Africa.

CHAPTER 2 – ORGANISATIONS

Under the direction of the Defence Council (described in Chapter 1) management of the Services is the responsibility of the Service Boards; in the case of the Army the Army Board is the senior management directorate.

THE ARMY BOARD

The routine management of the Army is the responsibility of The Army Board the composition of which is as follows:

Secretary of State for Defence
Minister of State for the Armed Forces
Minister for International Security Strategy
Minister for Defence Equipment and Support
Minister for Defence Personnel, Welfare and Veterans
Chief of the General Staff
Second Permanent Under-Secretary of State (Secretary of the Army Board)
Assistant Chief of the General Staff
Adjutant General
Quartermaster General
Master General of the Ordnance
Commander-in-Chief Land Forces

Executive Committee of the Army Board (ECAB)

Attended by senior UK Army commanders, ECAB dictates the policy required for the Army to function efficiently and meet the aims required by the Defence Council and government. The Chief of the General Staff is the chairman of the Executive Committee of the Army Board.

Army Board and ECAB decisions are acted upon by the military staff at the various headquarters worldwide.

The Chief of the General Staff (CGS) is the officer responsible for the Army's contribution to the national defence effort and he maintains control through the commanders and the staff branches of each of the various army headquarters organisations.

Chief of the General Staff - General Sir Peter Wall

Educated at Whitgift School (Croydon), General Peter Wall was commissioned into the Royal Engineers in 1974. After a short period of military duties he studied engineering at Cambridge University, before joining airborne forces and going on to serve with the Royal Engineers in Belize and Rhodesia. He was appointed Chief of Staff of 5 Airborne Brigade, before commanding 9 Parachute Squadron, Royal Engineers. He was then appointed Commanding Officer of 32 Engineer Regiment in Germany, deploying on operations to Bosnia.

General Wall was promoted to Brigadier and assumed command of 24 Airmobile Brigade in 1999 where he was responsible for converting the formation into 16 Air Assault Brigade later that year. In 2001 he became Chief of Joint Force Operations at Permanent Joint Headquarters Northwood, and went on to serve as Chief of Staff of the National Contingent HQ in Qatar, overseeing UK operations in Iraq, from January 2003.

In May 2003 General Wall was appointed General Officer Commanding 1st (UK) Armoured Division in which capacity he was responsible for security in Basra in Iraq. In 2005 he became Deputy Chief of Joint Operations at the Permanent Joint Headquarters Northwood and in 2007 he was appointed Deputy Chief of Defence Staff (Commitments).

He was appointed as Commander-in-Chief, Land Forces in August 2009 and appointed Knight Commander of the Order of the Bath (KCB) in the 2009 Birthday Honours.

In September 2010 General Wall succeeded General Sir David Richards as Chief of the General Staff (CGS).

Chain-of-Command (From 1 November 2011)

The Army is commanded from the MoD by the CGS via three subsidiary headquarters and a number of smaller headquarters worldwide. The following simplified diagram illustrates this chain-of-command.

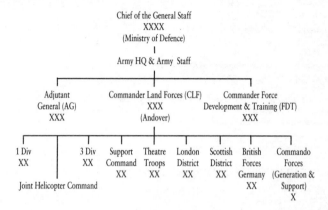

XXX – Denotes the rank of the commander. XXXX – General; XXX Lieutenant General; XX Major General; X Brigadier.

CLF has the responsibility for delivering and sustaining the Army's operational capability, whenever required throughout the world. CLF commands all operational troops in Great Britain, Germany, Nepal and Brunei, together with the Army Training Teams in Canada, Belize and Kenya.

1st Division (1 Div) is currently stationed at Herford in Germany and will return to Edinburgh in the UK at some stage (probably around 2016). 1st Division could then assume the responsibility for Scottish District in addition to serving as a manoeuvre division headquarters.

Support Command (Aldershot) will assume the responsibilities of the now disbanded 2, 4 and 5 Divisions and in the interim command of the 10 x Regional Brigades (described later in this chapter).

British Forces Germany will cease to exist 'towards the end of the decade' as UK Forces are withdrawn to the UK. The size of the headquarters will gradually diminish as troop numbers are reduced.

From Mid 2009 the CLF has been located at Andover in Hampshire having moved from Wilton near Salisbury.

STAFF BRANCHES

The Staff Branches that you would expect to find at every military headquarters from the Ministry of Defence (MoD) down to Brigade level are as follows:

Commander Usually a General (or Brigadier) who commands the formation.

Chief of Staff The officer who runs the headquarters on a day-to-day basis and who often acts as a second-in-command. Generally known as the COS.

G1 Branch	Responsible for administration, personnel matters including manning, discipline and personal services.
G2 Branch	Responsible for intelligence and security.
G3 Branch	Responsible for operations including staff duties, exercise planning, training, operational requirements, combat development and tactical doctrine.
G4 Branch	Logistics and quartering.
G5 Branch	Plans.
G6 Branch	Communications and IT.
G7 Branch	Training.
G8 Branch	Resource Management (finance and contracts).
G9 Branch	CIMIC (Civil affairs and cooperation with other agencies).

Note 1: Current (mid 2011) speculation is that HQ 1st Division will be the operational division title that is retained when the majority of UK troops have returned to the UK – possibly around 2014. This division would probably command the 6 x brigades in the High Readiness Force.

Note 2: HQ 3 Div will probably be the title that is retained for command of the Lower Readiness Force.

JOINT HELICOPTER COMMAND (JHC)

The Joint Helicopter Command's primary role is to deliver and sustain effective Battlefield Helicopter and Air Assault assets, operationally capable under all environmental conditions, in order to support UK's defence missions and tasks. JHC major formations are as follows:

- ◆ All Army Aviation Units
- ◆ RAF Support Helicopter Force
- ◆ Commando Helicopter Force
- ◆ 16 Air Assault Brigade
- ◆ Combat Support Units
- ◆ Combat Service Support Units
- ◆ Joint Helicopter Command and Standards Wing

The Joint Helicopter Command (JHC) is supported by the CLF (through the Deputy Commander Land Forces – DCLF) on a day to day basis. For operations it would be assigned to PJHQ. The Permanent Joint Headquarters (PJHQ) at Northwood in Middlesex has an important input into this chain-of-command and it is almost certain that any operation with which the army is involved will be tri-service and under the overall command of PJHQ.

There is more detail relating to the JHC in Chapter 13.

THEATRE TROOPS (2011)

Commander Theatre Troops (under the Field Army heading) is responsible for the following:

1 Artillery Brigade
16 Regiment RA
1 Signal Brigade
2 (NC) Signal Brigade
11 Signal Brigade
8 Force Engineer Brigade
2 Medical Brigade
1 Reconnaissance Brigade
1 Military Intelligence Brigade

101 Logistic Brigade
102 Logistic Brigade
104 Logistic Brigade
Equipment Support Theatre Troops
HQ RLC TA

LAND EQUIPMENT (LE)

The Land Equipment Directorate (under the command of Defence Equipment and Support) exists to provide front line support and 'through life' equipment solutions for land operations. LE is composed of five major groups with each group having a number of subsidiary teams providing specific support to various group activities. Director Land Equipment (DLE) is responsible for the operations of these major groups which are:

Combat Tracks Group (CTG)

Systems Team (ST); Combat Tracks Group Platforms Team; Armoured Vehicle Support Transformation Team; Artillery Systems Team (AST); Platforms Team (PT); The Medium Armoured Tracks Team (MATT).

Combat Wheels Group (CWG)

Protected Mobility Team (PMT); Manoeuvre Support Team (MST); Utility Vehicle Team (UVT).

General Support Group (GSG)

Battlefield Utilities Unit (BFU); Deployable Support and Test Equipment Team(DS&TE); Expeditionary Campaign Infrastructure (ECI); General Support Vehicles (GSV); Service Provision (SP).

Individual Capability Group (ICG)

Integrated Soldier Systems Executive (ISSE); Dismounted Soldier Systems Team (DSST); Surveillance, Target Acquisition and Night Observation (STANO); Light Weapons, Photographic & Batteries Team (LWPBT).

Joint and Battlefield Trainers; Simulation & Synthetic Environments Group (JBTSE)

Manoeuvre Divisions (2011)

There are two Manoeuvre Divisions: the 1st (UK) Armoured Division, based in Germany, and the 3rd (UK) Division in the United Kingdom. Both of these divisions are earmarked to form part of the Allied Command Europe Rapid Reaction Corps (ARRC), NATO's premier strategic formation; but they also have the flexibility to be employed on rapid reaction tasks or in support of other Defence Roles.

In addition to their operational roles, these divisions also command the Army units in specified geographic areas: in the case of the 1st Division, this area is made up of the garrisons in Germany where the Division's units are based; and in the case of some of the garrison areas in the 3rd Division's area of responsibility in the South West of England.

Due to the 2010 SDSR the situation regarding the future organisation of these divisions is unclear. There will be considerable reorganisation of both of these formations during the next five years.

As explained previously this situation may change with one of these divisional headquarters probably commanding the High Readiness Force and the other headquarters commanding the Lower Readiness Force.

Districts

Two Districts remain: Scottish District and London District. In the short term Scottish District will remain under the command of GOC Scotland but will almost certainly be replaced by the Headquarters of 1 (UK) Division following its return to the UK from Germany

London District is responsible for all Army units within the M25 boundary. The activity for which the Headquarters and the District is most well known is State Ceremonial and Public Duties in the Capital. The district insignia shows the Sword of St Paul representing the City of London and the Mural Crown representing the County of London. The District has its Headquarters in Horse Guards and is commanded by a Major General.

Combat Service Support Group (United Kingdom) consists of a supply regiment, two transport regiments, general support medical regiment which has both Regular and Territorial Army squadrons, three field hospitals, and a field medical equipment depot. For operations, the group may have assigned to it two Territorial Army transport regiments, five Territorial Army field hospitals, and a Territorial Army Royal Electrical and Mechanical Engineers maintenance battalion.

Combat Service Support Group (Germany) consists of a supply regiment; two transport regiments, and a general support medical regiment which has both Regular and Territorial Army squadrons. For operations, the group may have assigned to it a Territorial Army transport regiment, six Territorial Army field hospitals, a Territorial Army field medical equipment depot, and a Territorial Army Royal Electrical and Mechanical Engineers maintenance battalion.

The majority of these units will have returned to the UK by 2016.

Other areas and tasks

Although CLF is not responsible for running operations in Northern Ireland, the Former Yugoslavia, Afghanistan, Sierra Leone, Cyprus, the Falkland Islands and Iraq (a responsibility of PJHQ), it will provide the operational troops for these areas. Some 3,900 troops have been stationed in Northern Ireland since 2008; and a further 15,000 are deployed in Afghanistan, Cyprus, the Balkans, Sierra Leone the Falkland Islands and Iraq.

Some 500 troops are involved at any one time in MoD -sponsored equipment trials, demonstrations and exhibitions. Public Duties in London take up two/three battalions at any one time. All troops not otherwise operationally committed are also available to provide Military Aid to the Civil Authorities (MACA) in the United Kingdom.

1 (UK) ARMOURED DIVISION AND BRITISH FORCES GERMANY (NOV 2011)

The 1st Armoured Division was formed in 1940. Since World War II the Division has been re-titled three times and became the 1st (United Kingdom) Armoured Division in 1993, having successfully fought in the Gulf War of 1991. The Division has its headquarters at Herford in Germany and currently (2011) commands two Armoured Brigades situated throughout North West Germany and is the major component of British Forces Germany.

British Forces Germany (BFG) is the composite name given to the British Army, Royal Air Force and supporting civil elements stationed in Germany. The terms British Army of the Rhine (BAOR) and Royal Air Force Germany (RAFG), until recently were the traditional names used to describe the two Service elements of the British Forces stationed in Germany.

For many years following World War II, and as a result of the confrontation between NATO and the former Warsaw Treaty Organisation, the UK Government had stationed four Army divisions and a considerable part of its Air Force at five airbases in the Federal Republic of Germany. On the whole this level of commitment was maintained until 1992 and although these forces appeared to be solely national, they were in fact closely integrated with the NATO Northern Army Group (NORTHAG) and the 2nd Allied Tactical Air Force (2 ATAF).

As a result of political changes in Europe and the UK Government's 'Options for Change' programme, the British Army's presence in Germany has been reduced to two armoured brigades and a divisional headquarters with logistical support. The majority of the RAF presence has since been withdrawn and the 2010 SDSR announced plans to withdraw all of BFG to bases in the UK by 2020. It is likely that a large number of major units will be returned to the UK well before that date.

Headquarters BFGis moving from Rheindahlen to Bielefeld and this will allow the Rheindahlen Military Complex to close during 2014.

COMPOSITION OF 1(UK) ARMOURED DIVISION

1 (UK) Armoured Division has its headquarters at Herford in Germany (about 50 kms from Hanover) and the two Armoured Brigades under command are located at Bergen-Hohne and Paderborn. This division will return to the UK (Edinburgh) at some stage during the next five years.

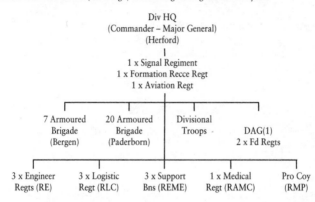

Note: (1) DAG (Divisional Artillery Group) This DAG could be reinforced by Rapier Air Defence and MLRS units from the UK as necessary. (2) Personnel total in Germany is approximately 18,500 with about 17,000 in 1 (UK) Armoured Division. During early 2011 this Division could probably provide the Headquarters (HQs) for up to six Battlegroups.

Estimate of Force Levels in 1 (UK) Armoured Division (1 Jan 2011 – our estimates)

Army Personnel	17,000
Challenger 2 MBT	100
Warrior AIFV	300
Other Tracked Vehicles	900
Helicopters (Army Aviation)	24
Artillery Guns	48
MLRS	0
AVLB	18

It is probable that in the event of hostilities (as was the case in recent operations in Iraq) considerable numbers of officers and soldiers from the Territorial Army (TA) would be used to reinforce this division. These reinforcements would consist of individuals, drafts of specialists, or by properly formed TA units varying in size from Mobile Bath Units of 20 men, to Major Units over 500 strong.

COMPOSITION OF 3 (UK) MECHANISED DIVISION

The 3rd (United Kingdom) Division is the only operational (Manoeuvre) Division in the UK. The Division has a mix of capabilities encompassing armoured and wheeled elements in its brigades.

In the diagram we have shown 16 Air Assault Brigade as being part of 3 (UK) Division purely as an example of how this formation might be deployed. 16 Air Assault Brigade is under the command of the Joint Helicopter Command (JHC). However, the JHC is not an Operational Headquarters and for operations, 16 Air Assault Brigade will probably be detached to under command of HQ Allied Rapid Reaction Corps, PJHQ, HQ 1 (UK) Division or HQ 3 (UK) Division.

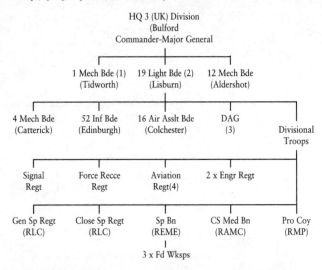

Note: (1) 1 Mechanised Brigade; (2) 19 Light Brigade disbands in 2013. (3) Divisional Artillery Group - Artillery Regiment with Multi Launch Rocket System (if allocated), UAVs, Close Support Artillery plus Rapier and HVM air defence systems when required; (4) Army Air Corps Regiment with helicopters (from Joint Helicopter Command as required). The composition of this division allows the UK MoD to retain a balanced force for out of NATO area operations.

ARMY BRIGADES

The 2010 SDSR stated that five operational brigades plus 16 Air Assault Brigade would be retained and it is likely that the following will be the brigades that survive.

Armoured Brigades: 7 Armoured Brigade; 20 Armoured Brigade

Mechanised Brigades: 1 Mechanised Brigade; 4 Mechanised Brigade; 12 Mechanised Brigade

Air Assault: 16 Air Assault Brigade

At this stage we are uncertain as to the future brigade titles.

Multi-role forces for complex interventions and enduring stabilisations

As stated previously, under the terms of the 2010 SDSR the Army will restructure the Army around five multi-role brigades (plus 16 Air Assault Brigade), keeping one brigade at high readiness available for an intervention operation and four in support to provide the ability to sustain an enduring longer term operation. These brigades will be composed of a number of standard units (building blocks) and brigades can be tailored for specific operations. Plans allow for brigades to be grouped under the command of a (divisional) headquarters for larger scale operations.

Multi-role Brigades will include:

♦ Main battle tanks providing protection, mobility and firepower
♦ Reconnaissance forces to gain information even in high-threat situations
♦ Infantry operating from a range of protected vehicles both tracked and wheeled

Mullti-role Brigades will have their own artillery, engineer, communications, intelligence, logistics and medical support under command. Territorial Army personnel will be fully integrated into the new structures.

The sixth Brigade is 16 Air Assault Brigade which is a high-readiness, short-duration intervention capability, organised and trained for parachute and air assault operations. This Brigade with its own supporting units is trained and equipped to be at high readiness for intervention in any new   conflict.

Possible Multi-role Brigade (Mixed Brigade) Organisation

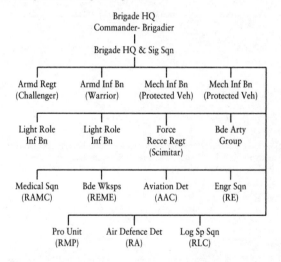

Note:
In this Brigade we are showing five infantry battalions of various types – the longer term reality may be different.

A further brigade - 3 Commando Brigade (Royal Marines) is available for operations. Although this formation is under the command and control of the Royal Navy it includes some major army units such as 1 Rifles, 29 Commando Regiment Royal Artillery and 24 Commando Regiment Royal Engineers.

16 AIR ASSAULT BRIGADE

Nearly 10,000 personnel form the personnel component of 16 Air Assault Brigade. The following diagram shows a possible configuration for 16 Air Assault Brigade during significant operations:

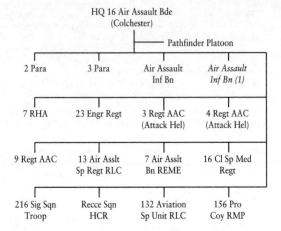

Note:
(1) In this diagram we are showing a fourth air assault battalion something that we expect to happen post 2012.

The Brigade capitalises on the combat capabilities and experience of the former 24 Airmobile Brigade and 5 Airborne Brigade. The introduction of the Apache attack helicopter has provided a new generation of weapons systems bringing major improvements in military capability. This brigade is under the command of the JHC (Joint Helicopter Command) and would be detached to other formations for operations.

In mid 2011 there is speculation regarding the future of the Parachute Regiment. Some reports suggest that only one company in the Brigade will be parachute trained, with a corresponding fall in the numbers parachute trained personnel in the supporting units.

Support helicopters are provided by the RAF (from the Joint Helicopter Command) and the Brigade would normally expect to operate with 18 x Chinook and 18 x Puma. An air assault infantry battalion can be moved by 20 x Chinook equivalents lifts. Each air assault infantry battalion has a personnel strength of 687 and a battalion has 12 x ATGW firing posts.

REGIONAL BRIGADES

During early 2012 the three Regenerative Divisions, the 2nd Division with its Headquarters at Edinburgh, the 4th Division with its Headquarters at Aldershot, and the 5th Division with its Headquarters at Shrewsbury were disbanded. These Regenerative Divisions were responsible for the Regional Brigades within their boundaries have been replaced by a single HQ Support Command in Aldershot.

These Regional Brigades are:

♦ 15 (North East) Brigade, with its HQ in York, responsible for units in the North East of England.
♦ 8 (Irish) Brigade with HQ at Lisburn in Northern Ireland.
♦ 42 (North West) Brigade, with its HQ at Preston in Lancashire.

- ◆ 51 (Scottish) Brigade, with its HQ in Stirling, responsible for all units north of Stirling including Shetland and the Western Isles.
- ◆ 2 (South East) Brigade based at Shorncliffe in Kent.
- ◆ 43 (Wessex) Brigade at Exeter in Devon.
- ◆ 145 (South) Brigade at Aldershot in Hampshire.
- ◆ 49 (East) Brigade at Chilwell in Nottinghamshire.
- ◆ 143 (West Midlands) Brigade based at Shrewsbury in Shropshire.
- ◆ 160 (Wales) Brigade based at Brecon in Wales.

At some stage each of these Regional Brigades will be re-subordinated under one of the two manoeuvre divisions for aspects of training training and some personnel matters.

Logistics Brigades

There are three Logistic Brigades - 101 Logistic Brigade, 102 Logistic Brigade and 104 Logistic Brigade. The late 2011 future of these logistic brigades is uncertain.

The operational role of a Logistic Brigade is to receive both troops and equipment into the theatre of operations, and be responsible for movement to the forward areas, ensuring that the combat formations have the combat supplies necessary to achieve their aim. 102 Logistics Brigade is also responsible for the establishment of Field Hospitals and the evacuation of casualties to the UK.

In general terms a logistic brigade would consist of the following:

Supply Regiment RLC
2 x Transport Regiment RLC
General Support Medical Regiment RAMC
Regiment RMP
Military Dog Support Unit RAVC
Signals Squadron R Signals

The Battlegroup

A division usually consists of two or three brigades. These brigades are further sub-divided into smaller formations known as battlegroups. The battlegroup is the basic building brick of the fighting formations.

A battlegroup is commanded by a Lieutenant Colonel and the infantry battalion or armoured regiment that he commands, provides the command and staff element of the formation. The battlegroup is then structured according to task, with the correct mix of infantry, armour and supporting arms.

The battlegroup organisation is very flexible and the units assigned can be quickly regrouped to cope with a change in the threat. A typical battlegroup fighting a defensive battle on the FEBA (Forward Edge of the Battle Area), and based upon an organisation of one armoured squadron and two mechanised companies, could contain about 600 men, 16 tanks and about 80 armoured fighting vehicles.

The number of battlegroups in a division and a brigade could vary according to the task the formation has been given. As a general rule you could expect a division to have as many as 12 battlegroups and a brigade to have up to three or four. The following diagram shows a possible organisation for an armoured battlegroup in either 1(UK) Armd Div or 3(UK) Mech Div.

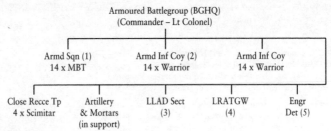

Armoured Battlegroup (BGHQ)
(Commander – Lt Colonel)

Armd Sqn (1)
14 x MBT

Armd Inf Coy (2)
14 x Warrior

Armd Inf Coy
14 x Warrior

Close Recce Tp
4 x Scimitar

Artillery
& Mortars
(in support)

LLAD Sect
(3)

LRATGW
(4)

Engr
Det (5)

Notes:
(1) Armoured Squadron; (2) Armoured Company (in a Mechanised Company the vehicles will be Saxon); (3) LLAD-Low Level Air Defence – HVM; (4) LRATGW - Long Range Anti Tank Guided Weapon; (5) Engineer Detachment.

Company Groups/Task Group

Each battlegroup will operate with smaller organisations called task groups or company groups. These groups which are commanded by a Major will be allocated tanks, armoured personnel carriers and supporting elements depending upon the aim of the formation. Supporting elements such as air defence, anti-tank missiles, fire support and engineer expertise ensure that the company group/task group is a balanced all arms grouping, tailored specifically for the task. In general a battlegroup similar to the one in the previous diagram could be expected to form three company groups.

A possible Company Group/Task Group organisation could resemble the following diagram:

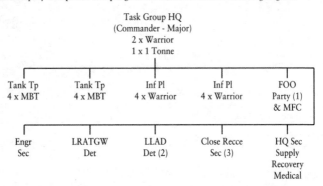

Task Group HQ
(Commander - Major)
2 x Warrior
1 x 1 Tonne

Tank Tp
4 x MBT

Tank Tp
4 x MBT

Inf Pl
4 x Warrior

Inf Pl
4 x Warrior

FOO
Party (1)
& MFC

Engr
Sec

LRATGW
Det

LLAD
Det (2)

Close Recce
Sec (3)

HQ Sec
Supply
Recovery
Medical

Notes: (1) Forward Observation Officer (FOO - usually a Captain) with his party from the Royal Artillery. This FOO will be in direct communication with a battery of six/eight guns and the Artillery Fire Direction Centre. The MFC is usually a sergeant from an infantry battalion mortar platoon who may have up to six mortar tubes on call. In most Combat Teams both the FOO and MFC will travel in close proximity to the Combat Team Commander; (2) Possibly 2 x Spartan with HVM; (3) Possibly 2 x Scimitar.

Northern Ireland

On 1 August 2007, Op BANNER, the military support to the civilian police in Northern Ireland ended and despite recent activity by resurgent Irish Republican factions, the Province remains relatively peaceful.

The worst year for terrorist violence was in 1972, when 131 service personnel were killed and 578 injured. At one stage in 1972 there were over 30,000 service personnel in the Province supported by another 10,000 police. Overall, 763 members of the armed forces and 303 members of the security forces lost their lives as a result of the violence in Northern Ireland.

During early 2011 there were approximately 3,900 UK service personnel in the Province of whom over 96 per cent were from the Army. The core of the peacetime garrison is centred around facilities at Aldergrove, Antrim, Ballykinler, Holywood, Lisburn and Magilligan.

On 1 January 2009 HQ Northern Irend was disbanded and HQ 38 (Irish) Brigade (Thiepval Barracks, Lisburn) became the Province's single headquarters.

Some units stationed in the Province are available for operations worldwide.

Return of UK Troops from Germany

During early 2011 there were just over 18,000 UK Service Personnel stationed in Germany, over 96 per cent of which were army personnel. Since 2009, a number of major units have returned to locations in the UK amongst which were HQ Allied Rapid Reaction Corps (HQ ARRC), 102 Logistics Brigade (102 Log Bde) and 1 Signal Brigade (1 Sig Bde).

During the 2010 SDSR the Secretary of State for Defence announced the return of half of UK personnel from Germany by 2015 and the remainder by 2020.

The estimated cost to the public purse of maintaining and operating bases in Germany in 2010-11 is approximately £250 million. It is believed that the net injection to the German economy from the UK presence in Germany is around £700 million and following the return from Germany, a similar sum will be injected into the UK economy.

CHAPTER 3 – INTERNATIONAL COMMITMENTS

NATO OVERVIEW

The United Kingdom is a member of NATO (North Atlantic Treaty Organisation) and the majority of military operations are conducted in concert with the forces of NATO allies. In 1993, NATO was reorganised from three into two major commands with a further reorganisation of these two commands in 2003. The first is ACT (Allied Command Transformation) with headquarters at Norfolk, Virginia (USA) and the second is ACO (Allied Command Operations), with its headquarters at Mons in Belgium.

NATO operations in which the United Kingdom was a participant would almost certainly be as part of a coalition force under the command and control of Allied Command Operations (ACO).

The current Supreme Allied Commander Europe (SACEUR) is Admiral Stavridis. SACEUR, (a US officer) is responsible for the overall command of NATO military operations and conducts the necessary military operational planning, including the identification of forces required for the mission and requesting these forces from NATO countries, as authorised by the North Atlantic Council and as directed by NATO's Military Committee.

The following nations are members of the NATO Alliance.

Albania, Belgium, Bulgaria, Canada, Croatia, Czech Republic, Denmark, Estonia, France, Germany, Greece, Hungary, Iceland, Italy, Latvia, Lithuania, Luxembourg, Netherlands, Norway, Poland, Portugal, Romania, Spain, Slovakia, Slovenia, Turkey, United Kingdom, United States.

SACEUR – ADMIRAL JAMES STAVRIDIS

Admiral Stavridis is a 1976 graduate of the US Naval Academy and a native of South Florida.

A Surface Warfare Officer, Admiral Stavridis commanded the Destroyer USS Barry from 1993-1995, completing deployments to Haiti, Bosnia, and the Arabian Gulf. USS Barry won the Battenberg Cup as the top ship in the Atlantic Fleet under his command.

In 1998, he commanded Destroyer Squadron 21 and deployed to the Arabian Gulf, winning the Navy League s John Paul Jones Award for Inspirational Leadership. From 2002-2004, Admiral Stavridis commanded Enterprise Carrier Strike Group, conducting combat operations in the Arabian Gulf in support of both Operation Iraqi Freedom and Operation Enduring Freedom.

Ashore, the Admiral has served as a strategic and long range planner on the staffs of the Chief of Naval Operations and the Chairman of the Joint Chiefs of Staff. At the start of the Global War on Terror (GWOT), he was selected as the Director of the US Navy Operations Group, DEEP BLUE. He has also served as the Executive Assistant to the Secretary of the US Navy and the Senior Military Assistant to the US Secretary of Defense. Admiral James Stavridis assumed command of the US Southern Command on October 19, 2006.

Admiral Stavridis earned a PhD and MALD from The Fletcher School of Law and Diplomacy at Tufts University in International Relations in 1984, where he won the Gullion Prize as the outstanding student. He is also a graduate of both the US Naval and US National War Colleges.

He holds various decorations and awards, including the Defense Distinguished Service Medal, the Defense Superior Service Medal and five awards of the Legion of Merit. He is author or co-author of several books on naval shiphandling and leadership, including Command at Sea and Destroyer Captain.

In mid-2009 Admiral Stavridis was appointed as the Supreme Commander Allied Powers Europe.

NATO COMMANDS

There are two major NATO Commands:

- ♦ Allied Command Operations (ACO)
- ♦ Allied Command Transformation (ACT)

ALLIED COMMAND OPERATIONS (ACO)

Allied Command Operations, with its headquarters, SHAPE, near Mons, Belgium, is responsible for all Alliance operations. The levels beneath SHAPE have been significantly streamlined, with a reduction in the number of headquarters. The operational level consists of two standing Joint Force Commands (JFCs) one in Brunssum, the Netherlands, and one in Naples, Italy – which can conduct operations from their static locations or provide a land-based Combined Joint Task Force (CJTF) headquarters, and a robust but more limited standing Joint Headquarters (JHQ), in Lisbon, Portugal, from which a deployable sea-based CJTF HQ capability can be drawn. The current organisation of Allied Command Operations is as follows:

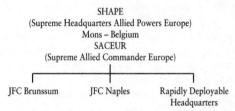

SHAPE
(Supreme Headquarters Allied Powers Europe)
Mons – Belgium
SACEUR
(Supreme Allied Commander Europe)

| JFC Brunssum | JFC Naples | Rapidly Deployable Headquarters |

Component Headquarters at the tactical level

The component or tactical level consists of six Joint Force Component Commands (JFCCs), which provide service-specific land, maritime, or air expertise to the operational level. Although these component commands are available for use in any operation, they will be subordinated to one of the Joint Force Commanders.

Joint Forces Command – Brunssum

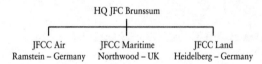

HQ JFC Brunssum

| JFCC Air Ramstein – Germany | JFCC Maritime Northwood – UK | JFCC Land Heidelberg – Germany |

Joint Forces Command – Naples

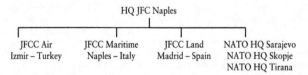

HQ JFC Naples

| JFCC Air Izmir – Turkey | JFCC Maritime Naples – Italy | JFCC Land Madrid – Spain | NATO HQ Sarajevo NATO HQ Skopje NATO HQ Tirana |

Static Air Operations Centres (CAOC)

In addition to the above component commands there are four static Combined Air Operations Centres with two more deployable as follows:

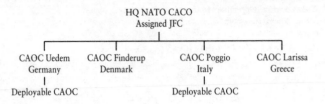

HQ NATO CACO
Assigned JFC

CAOC Uedem	CAOC Finderup	CAOC Poggio	CAOC Larissa
Germany	Denmark	Italy	Greece
Deployable CAOC		Deployable CAOC	

As the deployable CAOCs will need to exercise their capability to mobilise and deploy, the current facilities at Torrejon Air Base in Spain are the primary site for training and exercising in that region. A small NATO air facility support staff is stationed at Torrejon to support this capability.

Deployable Immediate Reaction Forces (IRF) available:

Immediate Reaction Forces (Maritime) – There are four Maritime Immediate Reaction Forces that provide NATO with a continuous naval presence and can be deployed NATO-wide, when required.

ACE (Allied Command Europe) Rapid Reaction Corps (ARRC) – The ARRC is prepared for deployment throughout Allied Command Europe in order to augment or reinforce local forces whenever necessary. The Headquarters of the ARRC are located the UK.

Reaction Forces (Air) Staff – With headquarters at Kalkar in Germany.

ACE Mobile Force (AMF) – With headquarters at Heidelberg in Germany.

Deployable National Corps – These deployable corps are available with headquarters provided by Italy, Turkey, Germany/Netherlands, Spain and Greece.

NATO Airborne Early Warning Force (NAEWF) – The NATO Airborne Early Warning Force provides air surveillance and command and control for all NATO commands. It is based in Geilenkirchen, Germany, and Waddington, United Kingdom.

NATO Programming Centre (NPC) – The NATO Programming Centre maintains NATO Air Command and Control Software and provides system expertise to nations and NATO agencies and headquarters. It is located in Glons, Belgium.

ALLIED COMMAND TRANSFORMATION (ACT)

In the future, Allied Command Transformation, with its headquarters in Norfolk, US, will oversee the transformation of NATO's military capabilities. In doing so, it will enhance training, improve capabilities, test and develop doctrines and conduct experiments to assess new concepts. It will also facilitate the dissemination and introduction of new concepts and promote interoperability. There will be an ACT Staff Element in Belgium primarily for resource and defence planning issues.

ACT commands the Joint Warfare Centre in Norway, a Joint Force Training Centre in Poland and the Joint Analysis and Lessons Learned Centre in Portugal. ACT Headquarters will also supervise the Undersea Research Centre in La Spezia, Italy and the NATO School at Oberammergau in Germany. There will be direct linkages between ACT, Alliance schools and NATO agencies, as well as the US Joint Forces Command. In addition, a number of nationally or multinationally-sponsored Centres of Excellence focused on transformation in specific military fields support ACT.

THE 2003 NATO CONCEPT

Under the 2003 concept, NATO forces are able to rapidly deploy to crisis areas and remain sustainable, be it within or outside NATO's territory, in support of both Article 5 and Non-Article 5 operations. The successful deployments of the Allied Command Europe Rapid Reaction Corps (ARRC) to two NATO-led Balkan operations (the Implementation Force (IFOR) to Bosnia Herzegovina in

1995 and Kosovo Force (KFOR) to Kosovo in 1999) are early examples of non-Article 5 crisis response operations outside NATO territory. The 2011 deployment of coalition assets to the Libyan no-fly zone (in support of a UN Resolution) is a good example of rapid deployment in a crisis situation.

The 2003 concept has its largest impact on land forces. Maritime and air forces are by nature already highly mobile and deployable and often have a high state of readiness. Most of NATO's land based assets, however, have been rather static and have had limited (strategic) mobility. In the new structure, land forces should also become highly deployable and should have tactical and strategic mobility. The mobility requirements will have great impact on the Alliance's transport and logistic resources (sea, land and air based). The need for quick reaction requires a certain amount of highly trained forces that are readily available. Further, interoperability (the possibility of forces to co-operate together with other units) and sustainability (the possibility to continue an operation for an extended period of time) are essential in the new force structure.

Note:
Article 5 operations commit each NATO member state to consider an armed attack against one state to be an armed attack against all states. Non-Article 5 operations are operations that are not concerned with collective defence.

High Readiness Forces and Forces of Lower Readiness

There are forces at two different kinds of readiness posture. First, forces with a higher state of readiness and availability, the so-called High Readiness Forces (HRF) to react on short notice. Second, forces with a lower state of readiness (FLR) to reinforce and sustain. Graduated Readiness Headquarters have been developed to provide these forces with command and control facilities.

High Readiness Forces (Land) Headquarters candidates available:

The Allied Command Europe Rapid Reaction Corps (ARRC) HQ in Gloucestershire with the United Kingdom as framework nation;

The Rapid Deployable German-Netherlands Corps HQ, based on the 1st German-Netherlands Corps HQ in Munster (Germany);

The Rapid Deployable Italian Corps HQ based on the Italian Rapid Reaction Corps HQ in Solbiate Olona close to Milan (Italy);

The Rapid Deployable Spanish Corps HQ based on the Spanish Corps HQ in Valencia (Spain);

The Rapid Deployable Turkish Corps HQ based on the 3rd Turkish Corps HQ near Istanbul (Turkey);

The Eurocorps HQ in Strasbourg (France) sponsored by Belgium, France, Germany, Luxembourg and Spain.

Note: The Eurocorps Headquarters which has a different international military status based on the Strasbourg Treaty has signed a technical arrangement with SACEUR and can also be committed to NATO missions.

Forces of Lower Readiness (Land) Headquarters candidates:

The Multinational Corps HQ North-East in Szczecin (Poland) sponsored by Denmark, Germany and Poland;

The Greek "C" Corps HQ near Thessaloniki (Greece).

High Readiness Forces (Maritime) Headquarters:

Headquarters Commander Italian Maritime Forces on board the Italian Naval Vessel GARIBALDI.

Headquarters Commander Spanish Maritime Forces (HQ COMSPMARFOR) on board of LPD CASTILLA.

Headquarters Commander United Kingdom Maritime Forces (HQ COMUKMARFOR) onboard a UK vessel.

THE ALLIED RAPID REACTION CORPS (ARRC)

The concept of the Allied Rapid Reaction Corps was initiated by the NATO Defence Planning Committee in May 1991. The concept called for the creation of Rapid Reaction Forces to meet the requirements of future challenges within the alliance. The ARRC provides the Supreme Allied Commander Europe with a multinational corps sized grouping in which forward elements can be ready to deploy within 14 days (lead elements and reconnaissance parties at very short notice).

As stated by SHAPE the mission of the ARRC is: "HQ ARRC, as a High Readiness Force (Land) HQ, is prepared to deploy under NATO, EU or coalition auspices to a designated area, to undertake combined and joint operations across the operational spectrum as:

- ◆ a Corps HQ
- ◆ a Land Component HQ
- ◆ a Land Component HQ in command of the NATO Response Force
- ◆ a Joint Task Force HQ for Land-centric operations

These formations will enable support for crisis support management options or the sustainment of ongoing operations."

As NATO's most experienced High Readiness Force (Land) Headquarters the ARRC is actively engaged in the NATO Response Force (NRF) transformation initiative.

Currently the ARRC trains for missions across the spectrum of operations from deterrence and crisis management to regional conflict.

Currently (2011) Headquarters ARRC is located in Innsworth (UK) with a peace-time establishment of about 400 personnel. It comprises staff from all the contributing nations. As the Framework Nation, the UK provides the infrastructure, administrative support, communications and 60 per cent of the staff.

HQ ARRC moved from Rheindahlen (Germany) to Innsworth in the UK during the summer of 2010.

The Commander (COMARRC) and Chief of Staff are UK 3 Star and 2 Star generals and the Deputy Commander is an Italian 2 Star general. The other appointments, as with the training and exercise costs, are shared among the contributing nations.

Outline Composition of the ARRC
(Allied Command Europe Rapid Reaction Corps)

For operations HQ ARRC might have some of the following formations under command:

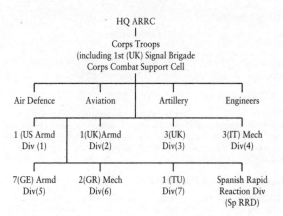

HQ ARRC
|
Corps Troops
(including 1st (UK) Signal Brigade
Corps Combat Support Cell

| Air Defence | Aviation | Artillery | Engineers |

| 1 (US Armd Div (1) | 1(UK)Armd Div(2) | 3(UK) Div(3) | 3(IT) Mech Div(4) |

| 7(GE) Armd Div(5) | 2(GR) Mech Div(6) | 1 (TU) Div(7) | Spanish Rapid Reaction Div (Sp RRD) |

Notes: (1) United States (2) Resident in Germany (3) Resident in the UK (4) IT – Italy (5) GE – Germany (6) GR – Greece (7) TU – Turkey.

The operational organisation, composition and size of the ARRC would depend on the type of crisis, area of crisis, its political significance, and the capabilities and availability of lift assets, the distances to be covered and the infrastructure capabilities of the nation receiving assistance. It is considered that a four-division ARRC would be the maximum employment structure.

The main British contribution to the ARRC is 1 (UK) Armoured Division. This division is stationed in Germany and there are also a considerable number of British personnel in both the ARRC Corps HQ and Corps Troops. In addition, in times of tension 3 (UK) Mechanised Division and 16 Air Assault Brigade could, if required, move to the operational area to take their place in the ARRC's order of battle. In total, we believe that if the need arose some 30,000 British soldiers could be assigned to the ARRC together with substantial numbers of Regular Army Reservists and some formed TA Units.

Command Posts and Deployment

Due to the need to be able to respond flexibly to the whole range of potential operations, HQ ARRC has developed the capability for rapidly deployable and modular HQs. Deployment begins with the despatch of a Forward Liaison and Reconnaissance Group (FLRG) within 48 hours of the order to move being given, which can then be quickly followed up.

Within four days the key enablers from 1 (UK) Signal Bde would be within theatre and three days later HQ ARRC Forward and HQ Rear Support Command (RSC) Forward – as required – could be established. The forward-deployed HQs are light, mobile and C-130 transportable. While there is a standard 'default' setting for personnel numbers, the actual staff composition is 'tailored' to the task and can vary from approximately 50 to 150 staff, depending on the requirement. The 'in-theatre' task would then be supported by the remainder of the staff, using sophisticated 'Reachback' techniques and equipment.

The Early Entry HQs are capable of sustained independent operations if required but can also be used as enablers if it is decided to deploy the full HQ ARRC. This deployment concept has been tested and evaluated on several exercises and has proven its worth. In parallel, HQ ARRC is continuously looking to make all of its HQs lighter and more survivable.

EUROPEAN UNION

The following countries are members of the European Union:

Austria; Belgium; Bulgaria; Cyprus; Czech Republic; Denmark; Estonia; Finland; France; Germany; Greece; Hungary; Ireland; Italy; Latvia; Lithuania; Luxembourg; Malta; Netherlands; Poland; Portugal; Romania; Slovakia; Slovenia; Spain; Sweden; United Kingdom.

Council of the European Union

The Council of the European Union represents the governments of the Union's 27 nations in the legislature of the European Union. Each nation provides one minister whose portfolio includes the subject being discussed. In the case of defence – the ministers responsible would attend (in company with their own National European Commissioner). The other legislative body is the European Parliament.

European Common Security and Defence Policy (CSDP)

The EU CSDP is the successor to what used to be known as the European Security and Defence Policy (ESDP). As such the CSDP is an important component of the EU's Foreign and Security Policy (CFSP) and provides the framework for policy and plans relating to all aspects of European defence and security.

CSDP Objectives – EU Helsinki Headline Goal 2010

The EU has adopted the following illustrative scenarios which form the basis for force planning to meet the EU Helsinki Headline Goal 2010 proposals:

- ♦ Stabilisation, reconstruction and military advice to third world countries
- ♦ Separation of parties by force
- ♦ Assistance to humanitarian operations
- ♦ Conflict Prevention
- ♦ Evacuation Operations in a non-permissive environment

To ensure that the requirements of the CSDP and the objectives of the Headline Goal 2010 are met, the following command and planning elements have been established:

European Political and Security Committee (PSC)

The PSC keeps track of the requirements of the EU's Common Foreign and Security Policy and defines how those requirements can be incorporated into the Common Security and Defence Policy. Reporting to the Council of the EU the PSC is composed of EU Ambassadors who have the responsibility for providing a coherent response to a crisis or emergency.

European Union Military Committee (EUMC)

Under the leadership of its current Chairman, General Hakan Syren (Sweden) the EUMC is composed of the Chiefs of Defence of the EU member nations. Under normal circumstances these Chiefs of Defence are represented by officers seconded to the EUMC from each of the EU member nations. The EUMC provides advice and recommendations on all aspects of EU security and defence matters to the PSC.

Committee for Civilian Aspects of Crisis Management (CIVCOM)

This committee works closely with the EUMC and provides the PSC with information and recommendations relating to all civilian aspects of crisis and emergency management.

CHAIRMAN OF THE EUROPEAN MILITARY COMMITTEE

General Hakan Syren

General Hakan Syren was born on 31 January 1952 in Vaxjo, Sweden. He graduated in 1973 from the Swedish Naval Academy as a Lieutenant in the Coast Artillery. His military education includes the Staff Course and the Command and General Staff Course at the Swedish War College in Stockholm. It also includes the Naval Command Course at the US Naval War College in Newport, USA.

General Syren was appointed as the Chairman of the European Union Military Committee (EUMC) in Brussels in November 2009. Before taking up his present position, General Syrén was Supreme Commander of the Swedish Armed Forces for more than five years. His career also includes four years as Chief of Joint Military Intelligence and Security.

Career

1973-79 – Instructor and Platoon Commander at the Coast Artillery Regiment in Vaxholm (Sweden)

1980-84 – Student at the Swedish War College, Stockholm

1984-88 – Staff Officer at Navy Staff, Stockholm

1988-89 – Student at the Naval War College, Newport, USA

1989-90 – Teacher of Strategy, Swedish War College, Stockholm

1990-92 – Head of Planning Department, Navy Staff, Stockholm

1992-94 – Commanding Officer Marine Amphibious Battalion

1994 – 96 – Commanding Officer Coast Artillery Regiment

1996 – 98 – Head of Operations Planning Department, Swedish Armed Forces Headquarters

1999 – Secretary to the Defence Commission, Ministry of Defence

1999 – 03 – Chief Joint Military Intelligence and Security, Swedish Armed Forces Headquarters

2004 – 09 – Supreme Commander of the Swedish Armed Forces

2009 – Chairman of the European Union Military Committee

In parallel with the positions within the Armed Forces, General Syrén also served as ADC to His Majesty the King of Sweden from 1988 to 1996. He is a member of the Royal Society of Naval Sciences and of the Royal Academy of War Sciences.

General Syren will probably serve as the Chairman of the European Union Military Committee for a period of three years.

European Union Military Staff (EUMS)

Working directly to the Chairman of the EUMC the staff is composed of military and civilian personnel who are responsible for planning and coordination of EU security and defence objectives within the framework of the CSDP.

EU Operations Centre

During January 2007, the EU Operations Centre was established in Brussels. This Headquarters can command a small force of about 2,000 troops (possibly a Battlegroup).

In addition to the EU Operations Centre, there are 5 x national operational headquarters that have been made available for use by the EU. These are:

- ♦ Mont Valerien (Paris)
- ♦ Northwood (London)
- ♦ Potsdam (Berlin)
- ♦ Centocelle ((Rome)
- ♦ Larissa (Greece)

For example: EUFOR's Democratic Republic of the Congo mission uses Potsdam as its Operational Headquarters (OHQ). There is an agreement that where necessary the EU can use NATO capabilities

Civilian Planning and Conduct Capability (CPCC)

Working directly to the Political and Security Committee (PSC) this group is responsible for the command and control of civilian (non-military) elements of CSDP crisis and emergency related operations.

EU DEFENCE BUDGETS

Country	Defence Budget 2010 (Euros)
In billions except where designated in millions (m)	
Austria	2.1
Belgium	2.8
Bulgaria	761 m
Cyprus	450 m
Czech Republic	1.9
Denmark	3.3
Estonia	246 m
Finland	2.7
France	32.1
Germany	31.1
Greece	6.7
Hungary	1.3
Ireland	694 m
Italy	15.5
Latvia	189 m
Lithuania	241 m
Luxembourg	190 m
Malta	42 m
Netherlands	8.5
Poland	6.2
Portugal	1.9
Romania	1.9
Slovakia	900 m
Slovenia	514 m
Spain	11.9
Sweden	4.1
United Kingdom	44
EU-27	**182 billion**

At mid 2011 exchange rates 182 billion Euros is equivalent to £160 billion or US$261 billion

Notes:

(1) The above figures are not authoritative and had been taken from a number of sources. Many EU countries use different accounting systems to show their defence budgets and the above figures should only be treated as a reasonable guide.

(2) Figures are rounded up to the nearest whole number.

(3) All EU Governments are facing financial problems and it would be realistic to assume that almost all of the above defence budgets will fall by at least 10 per cent during 2011/2012.

EUROPEAN DEFENCE AGENCY

The European Defence Agency (EDA) was established in July 2004 following a unanimous decision by European Heads of State and Government. It was established under the Council Joint Action 2004/5 51/CFSP on the basis of Article 14 of the treaty on the European Union (Maastricht).

The purpose of the European Defence Agency is to support the Member States and the Council of Europe in order to improve European defence capabilities in the field of crisis management, and to sustain and develop the European Security and Defence Policy (ESDP).

The EDA has the following tasks:

- ◆ To improve the EU's defence capabilities in the field of crisis management.
- ◆ To promote European armaments cooperation.
- ◆ To strengthen the European defence industrial and technological base and create a competitive European defence equipment market, in consultation with the Commission.
- ◆ To promote research, in liaison with Community research activities, with a view to strengthening Europe's industrial and technological potential in the defence field.

EDA Organisation

In the longer term the EDA will achieve its goals by:

- ◆ Encouraging EU Governments to spend defence budgets on meeting tomorrow's challenges and not, in their words, yesterday's threats.
- ◆ Helping EU Governments to identify common needs and promoting collaboration to provide common solutions.
- ◆ The EDA is an agency of the European Union and therefore under the direction and authority of the European Council, which issues guidelines to, and receives reports from the High Representative as Head of the Agency. Detailed control and guidance, however, is the responsibility of the Steering Committee.

The Steering Committee, the principal decision-making body of the Agency is made up of Defence Ministers from participating Member States (all EU members except Denmark) and a member of the European Commission. In addition to ministerial meetings at least twice a year, the Steering Committee also meets at the level of national armaments directors, national research directors, national capability planners and policy directors.

The EDA's Chief Executive is Claude-France Arnould who was appointed in January 2011. She has more than 20 years' experience in External Relations, Common Foreign and Security Policy and the European Common Security and Defence Policy.

The EDA Headquarters is in Brussels (Belgium) and there is approximately 100 staff.

The Agency had a budget of €31 million (US$£38 million) in 2010.

European Union Institute for Strategic Studies (EU-ISS)

The EU-ISS is based in Paris, was established in 2002 and is an independent think tank that researches issues relevant to EU defence and security. Much of the work is published and the EU-ISS organises conferences and seminars on all aspects of EU related defence and security.

EU MILITARY STRUCTURES

The following table sets out the main multilateral military structures outside NATO that include European Union members. A number of these also include non-EU countries. In addition, there are many other bilateral military agreements between individual EU member states.

Military agreements between other EU members are a matter for those member states' governments.

Structure	EU participants
EAG – European Air Group	Belgium, France, Germany, Italy, Spain, UK
European Airlift Centre	Belgium, France, Germany, Italy, Netherlands, Spain, UK
Sealift Coordination Centre (Eindhoven)	Netherlands, UK
European Amphibious Initiative (including the UK/Netherlands Amphibious Force)	France, Italy, Netherlands, Spain, UK
SHIRBRIG – Stand-by High Readiness Brigade	Austria, Denmark, Finland, Ireland, Italy, Lithuania, Netherlands, Norway, Poland, Portugal, Slovenia, Spain, Sweden. (Observers: Czech Republic, Hungary)
SEEBRIG – South-Eastern Europe Brigade	Greece, Italy, Slovenia
NORDCAPS – Nordic Coordinated Arrangement for Military Peace Support	Finland, Sweden, Denmark
EUROCORPS	Germany, Belgium, Spain, France, Luxembourg
EUROFOR	France, Italy, Portugal, Spain
EUROMARFOR	France, Italy, Portugal, Spain

EUROCORPS

The Eurocorps was created in 1992 and comprises military contributions from its five framework nations: Belgium, France, Germany, Luxembourg and Spain. The Headquarters is located in Strasbourg (France). Austria, Canada, Greece, Italy, Poland and Turkey have military liaison staff co-located at Eurocorps HQ

The Commander Eurocorps (COMEC) is a Lieutenant General (3 stars). The Deputy Commander (DCOM) is a Major General (2 stars). The staff is directed by the Chief of Staff (COS), also a Major General and he is supported by two Deputy Chiefs of Staff (DCOS) for Operations and Support, both of whom are Brigadier Generals (1 star).

The posts of Commanding General and the other general officers as well as some key functions are filled by EU framework nations on a rotational basis. COMEC, DCOM and COS are always of different nationalities. Their tour of duty generally lasts for two years.

In general terms the Eurocorps is at the disposal of the European Union and available for service in support of NATO. The command language is English.

The Eurocorps consists of formations under direct operational control and formations earmarked for assignment during a crisis or emergency:

Under direct operational control:

- ♦ Franco German Brigade (GE-FR Bde)
- ♦ Multinational Command Support Brigade (MNCS Bde)

Formations earmarked for assignment during an emergency:

French Contribution

Etat-Major de Force numéro 3 (EMF3) in Marseille (equivalent to a divisional HQ) composed of:

> 1 x Armoured Brigade
> 1 x Mechanised Infantry Brigade
> Specialised support units

German Contribution

The 10th Armoured Division, with its HQ in Sigmaringen, composed of:

> 2 x Brigades as required
> Specialised support units

Belgian Contribution

> Belgian Operational Command Land, with its HQ in Evere, composed of:

> 1st Mechanised Brigade in Leopoldsburg
> 7th Mechanised Brigade in Marche-en-Fammene
> Support units

Spanish Contribution

1st Land Forces Command its HQ in Burgos, composed of:

> 10th Mechanised Brigade in Cordoba
> 11th Mechanised Brigade in Badajoz
> 12th Armoured Brigade in Madrid

Luxembourg Contribution

Luxembourg assigns a reconnaissance company composed of about 180 personnel. During operations this unit would be integrated into the Belgian contingent.

Operational Experience

During the past decade the Eurocorps HQ has been involved in operations as follows:

> SFOR (Bosnia) 1999-2000

> KFOR III (Kosovo) 2000

> ISAF IV (Afghanistan) 2004-2005

Note: If all earmarked national contributions were committed to operations, the Eurocorps would number approximately 60,000 personnel.

Franco – German Brigade (FGB)

This is a joint formation which consists of both French and German units and under the direct command of the Eurocorps.

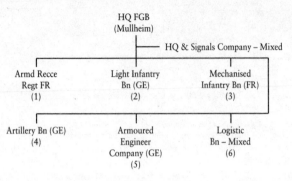

HQ FGB
(Mullheim)

HQ & Signals Company – Mixed

| Armd Recce Regt FR (1) | Light Infantry Bn (GE) (2) | Mechanised Infantry Bn (FR) (3) |

| Artillery Bn (GE) (4) | Armoured Engineer Company (GE) (5) | Logistic Bn – Mixed (6) |

Approximately 5,200 personnel

Notes:

(1) 3e Regiment de Hussars

(2) Jagerbataillon 292

(3) 110e Regiment d'Infanterie

(4) Panzerartilleriebataillon 295

(5) Panzerpionierkompanie 500

(6) Logistic Battalion with: Supply Company; Maintenance Company; Transport Company; Administration & Support Company; HQ & Suport Company.

The Eurocorps was inaugurated in January 1989 and declared operational in October 1991.

The FGB is essentially a wheeled mechanised Brigade. It is the core entry group for Eurocorps operations and in concert with the EU Battlegroups the immediate EU reserve formation.

EU Battlegroups

In the immediate future, the EU plans to be able to provide at least one coherent Battlegroup package at any one time (usually two), to undertake Battlegroup-sized operations in support of the EU Helsinki Headline Goals.

Full Operational Capability (FOC) was reached at the end of 2007 when all Battlegroups became available. The EU now has the capacity to undertake at least two concurrent single Battlegroup-size rapid response operations, including the ability to launch both such operations nearly simultaneously.

There are usually 2 x EU Battlegroups on standby for operations and trained to respond to emerging contingencies at any one time. They would be deployed following a unanimous decision of the European Council of Ministers, with the nations providing the Battlegroup having a veto on any deployment decision.

EU Member States have indicated that they will commit to Battle Groups, formed as follows:

1	United Kingdom
2	France
3	France and Belgium
4	Italy
5	Spain
6	France, Germany, Belgium, Luxembourg and Spain
7	Germany, the Netherlands and Finland (BG 107)
8	Germany, Austria and Czech Republic
9	Italy, Hungary and Slovenia
10	Spain and Italy (Amphibious)

11	Italy, Romania and Turkey
12	Poland, Germany, Slovakia, Latvia and Lithuania
13	Sweden, Finland, Estonia, Ireland and Norway
14	United Kingdom and the Netherlands
15	Greece, Bulgaria, Cyprus, Romania and Slovenia
16	Czech Republick and Slovakia
17	Spain, Germany, France and Portugal

Expect a battle group to have between 1,500 and 2,000 personnel.

Each Battlegroup will have a 'lead nation' that will take operational command, based on the model set up during the EU's peacekeeping mission in the Democratic Republic of the Congo (Operation Artemis). Two non-EU NATO countries, Norway and Turkey participate in the EU Battlegroup program.

Battlegroups would have to be able to deploy within 5-10 days and be sustained initially for 30, but possibly up to 120 days while operating up to 6,000 km from Brussels.

European Rapid Reaction Force

As yet (mid 2011) there is no standing European Rapid Reaction Force (other than the Franco – German Brigade) nor any EU agreement to create one. What has sometimes been referred to as a 'European Rapid Reaction Force' is, in fact, a catalogue of forces that member states could make available to the EU should they choose to participate in a particular EU-led operation. Any contribution to a particular EU-led operation would depend on the operation's requirements, the availability of forces at the time and the willingness of EU members to participate. However, it is likely that this will change during the next five years.

CURRENT EU MILITARY OPERATIONS

EUFOR (Operation Althea)

The EU launched Operation Althea in Bosnia and Herzegovina (BiH) – in December 2004. This follows the decision by NATO to conclude its SFOR mission.

The EU deployed a large force of 6,300 personnel to ensure continued compliance with the Dayton/Paris Agreement and to contribute to a safe and secure environment in BiH.

The key objectives of Operation Althea are to provide deterrence and continued compliance with the responsibility to fulfil the role specified in Annexes 1A and 2 of the Dayton/Paris Agreement (General Framework Agreement for Peace in BiH) and to contribute to a safe and secure environment in BiH, in line with its mandate, and to achieve core tasks in the Stabilisation and Association Process (SAP).

The headquarters of EUFOR is in Sarajevo and in mid 2010 the personnel strength for Operation Althea was in the region of 1,600.

Operation Althea has been authorised by the United Nations Security Council Resolution 1575.

EURONAVFOR (Operation Atalanta)

In December 2008, the EU established operation ATALANTA to protect World Food Programme and other vulnerable shipping transiting through the Gulf of Aden. The UK has provided the Operation Commander and Operation Headquarters at Northwood since its inception and will continue to do so until the end of the mandate, which has recently been extended to December 2012.

EURONAVFOR currently includes warships, support vessels, and the delivery of shipping advice and reassurance from Belgium, Denmark, France, Germany, Greece, the Netherlands and Spain. Maritime Patrol aircraft are provided by Portugal, Spain, Germany, France.

Personnel strength is in the region of 1,290.

EUTM (Somalia)

During January 2010, the EU established a training mission for Somali security forces which commenced during early May. Training actually takes place in Uganda and EUTM has a personnel strength of around 130.

Current EU Civilian Missions (2011)

Mission	Area	Role	Established	Personnel
EUPM	Bosnia	Police Support	2003	281
EULEX	Kosovo	Rule of Law	2008	2,768
EU SSR	Guinea Bissau	Security Reform	2008	16
EUSEC	Congo	Security Reform	2005	46
EUROPOL RD	Congo	Police Reform	2007	51
EUROPOL COPPS	Palestinian Territories	Police Support	2006	96
EUBAM Rafah	Palestinian Territories	Border Assistance	2005	23
EUBAM	Moldova and Ukraine	Border Assistance	2006	200
EUBAM	Georgia	Border Assistance	2008	401
EUPOL	Afghanistan	Police Support	2007	452
EUJUST LEX	Iraq/Baghdad	Legal Training	2005	39

EU Relationship with NATO

In a joint declaration by both the EU and NATO during 2003, a previously slightly confused relationship was clarified under a number of major headings that included partnership, mutual cooperation and consultation, equality and due regard for the autonomy of both the EU and NATO, plus reinforcing and developing the military capability of both organisations.

The 'Berlin Plus Agreement' of March 2003 allows the EU to use NATO structures to support military operations that do not fall within the remit of NATO responsibilities. In addition, there is considerable exchange of information between both organisations and they are EU/NATO liaison cells situated in the headquarters of both organisations.

Because in many cases nations that are members of the EU are also members of NATO, the same forces are often assigned to both EU and NATO missions. It is therefore likely that the EU will only act if NATO first decides that it will not do so.

Afghanistan (Operation HERRICK)

In mid 2011 the UK had approximately 9,500 personnel serving in Afghanistan as part of the international security Assistance Force (ISAF). The security situation varies across the country with over 60% of violent incidents taking part in the southern provinces of Hellmand, Kandahar and Kunar, areas where the population is about 11% of the country's 28 million people. The UK's role is to assist the Afghan government to ensure security, governance, and development.

The International Security Assistance Force (ISAF)

The International Security Assistance Force (ISAF) is mandated under Chapter VII of the United Nations (UN) Charter (Peace Enforcing) by a number of UN Security Resolutions. ISAF exists to help the Afghan people, not to govern them. Additionally, under the UN mandate, the role of ISAF is to assist in the maintenance of security to help the Islamic Republic of Afghanistan and the UN in those areas it is responsible for.

NATO assumed command and control of the ISAF mission on August 11, 2003.

During early 2011 there were approximately 132,000 troops in ISAF with contributions from 48 nations with national contingent strengths changing on a regular basis. Major contributors include:

♦ United States   90,000

◆ United Kingdom	9,500
◆ Germany	5,000
◆ Italy	3,800
◆ France	3,400
◆ Canada	2, 900
◆ Poland	2,500
◆ Turkey	1,800
◆ Romania	1,700
◆ Australia	1,500
◆ Spain	1,500

ISAF is supported by approximately 150,000 personnel from the Afghan National Army (ANA) and about 90,000 personnel from the Afghan National Police (ANP).

UK Forces – Afghanistan Spring 2011 Roulement

As part of the Spring 2011 Roulement 16 Air Assault Brigade were replaced in Helmand by units under the command of HQ 3 Command Brigade. 3 Commando Brigade's planned replacement is the 20th Armoured Brigade who we believe will be deploying in October 2011. Current force levels of around 9,500 troops will probably be maintained.

Formations and units under the command of HQ 3 Commando Brigade will include the following:

3 Commando Brigade Headquarters, Royal Marines
Headquarters, 104 Logistic Brigade
Elements of 7 Armoured Brigade Headquarters and Signal Squadron

Army

29 Commando Regiment Royal Artillery
24 Commando Engineer Regiment
4th Battalion The Royal Regiment of Scotland, The Highlanders
3rd Battalion The Mercian Regiment
2nd Battalion The Royal Gurkha Rifles
1st Battalion The Rifles
2 Close Support Battalion, Royal Electrical and Mechanical Engineers

Elements of: 3rd Regiment Royal Horse Artillery; The Royal Scots Dragoon Guards; 9th/12th Lancers (Prince of Wales's); 5th Regiment Royal Artillery; 12th Regiment Royal Artillery; 16th Regiment Royal Artillery; 26th Regiment Royal Artillery; 32nd Regiment Royal Artillery; 39th Regiment Royal Artillery; 47th Regiment Royal Artillery; 12 (Air Support) Engineer Group; 22 Engineer Regiment; 28 Engineer Regiment; 32 Engineer Regiment; 36 Engineer Regiment; 42 Engineer Regiment (Geographic); 101 Engineer Regiment (Explosive Ordnance Disposal); 170 (Infrastructure Support) Engineer Group; 3rd Division Headquarters and Signal Regiment; 10th Signal Regiment; 14th Signals Regiment (Electronic Warfare); 21st Signal Regiment (Air Support); 22nd Signal Regiment; 1 Regiment, Army Air Corps; 3 Regiment, Army Air Corps; 2 Logistic Support Regiment, The Royal Logistic Corps; 9 Regiment, The Royal Logistic Corps; 11 Explosive Ordnance Disposal Regiment, The Royal Logistic Corps; 17 Port and Maritime Regiment, The Royal Logistic Corps; 23 Pioneer Regiment, The Royal Logistic Corps; 24 Postal Courier and Movement Regiment, The Royal Logistic Corps; 27 Regiment, The Royal Logistic Corps; 29 Postal Courier and Movement Regiment, The Royal Logistic Corps; 7 Air Assault Battalion Royal Electrical and Mechanical Engineers; 101 Force Support Battalion Royal Electrical and Mechanical Engineers; 104 Force Support Battalion Royal Electrical and Mechanical Engineers; 5th Regiment Royal Military Police; 111 Provost Company Royal Military Police;114 Provost Company Royal Military Police; Special Investigations Branch United Kingdom; 1 Military Working Dogs Regiment; 1 Military Intelligence Brigade; Military Stabilisation Support Group (MSSG); 6th Battalion The Royal Regiment of Scotland (Volunteers); 4th Battalion The Mercian Regiment (Volunteers); 6th Battalion The Rifles (Volunteers); 88 Postal and

Courier Regiment (Volunteers), The Royal Logistic Corps; 151 Regiment (Volunteers), The Royal Logistic Corps; 158 Transport Regiment (Volunteers), The Royal Logistic Corps; 162 Postal Courier and Movement Regiment (Volunteers), The Royal Logistic Corps; 166 Supply Regiment (Volunteers), The Royal Logistic Corps; 148 Expeditionary Force Institute Squadron (Volunteers), The Royal Logistic Corps; 383 Commando Petroleum Troop (Volunteers), The Royal Logistic Corps; 395 Air Despatch Troop (Volunteers), The Royal Logistic Corps; 102 Battalion (Volunteers), Royal Electrical and Mechanical Engineers; Military Provost Staff and Military Provost Staff (Volunteers).

Royal Navy

42 Commando Royal Marines including members of the Maritime Reserve
45 Commando Royal Marines including members of the Maritime Reserve
Logistic Regiment, Royal Marines

Elements of: 845 Naval Air Squadron including members of the Maritime Reserve; 846 Naval Air Squadron; 847 Naval Air Squadron; 857 Naval Air Squadron including members of the Maritime Reserve; 854 Naval Air Squadron; Royal Naval Regulating Staff; 30 Commando Information Exploitation Group, Royal Marines; Headquarters Joint Force Support (Afghanistan) including members of the Maritime Reserve; Naval elements forming the in-theatre Medical Regiment and Field Hospital.

Royal Air Force

58 Squadron, Royal Air Force Regiment
617 Squadron, Royal Air Force
31 Squadron, Royal Air Force

Elements of: No 6 Royal Air Force, Force Protection Wing Headquarters; Elements of HQ Royal Air Force Police Wing; the Royal Auxiliary Air Force; 5 (Army Co-Operation) Squadron, Royal Air Force; 18 Squadron, Royal Air Force; 24 Squadron, Royal Air Force; 27 Squadron, Royal Air Force; 28 Squadron, Royal Air Force; 30 Squadron, Royal Air Force; 78 Squadron, Royal Air Force; Tactical Supply Wing, Royal Air Force; 1 Air Mobility Wing, Royal Air Force; 1 Air Control Centre, Royal Air Force; 90 Signals Unit, Royal Air Force; 2 (Mechanical Transport) Squadron, Royal Air Force; 5001 Squadron, Royal Air Force; 3 Mobile Catering Squadron; Tactical Medical Wing; 1 (Expeditionary Logistics) Squadron; 93 (Expeditionary Armaments) Squadron; Tactical Imagery Wing; Joint Ground Based Air Defence;

Volunteer and ex-regular members of the reserve forces will continue to deploy to Afghanistan as part of this integrated force package, and we expect call-out notices to fill some 676 posts. On completion of their mobilisation procedures, the reservists will undertake a period of training and, where applicable, integration with their respective receiving units. The majority will serve on operations for around six months.

The deployment of 3 Commando Brigade and accompanying units will not result in any change to the UK's established and enduring conventional force level of 9,500 personnel.

Afghanistan – Costs

"When the army marches the treasury empties"

Sun Tzu – The Art of War (around 500 BC)

The additional costs for operations in Afghanistan (excluding salaries and ongoing costs that would have happened anyway) are paid for by the Governments Contingency Reserve fund. The next table shows annual costs from 2001 which total to just over £14 billion.

Cost of Operations in Afghanistan 2002-2011

(in million of UK£)

2001-2002	221	
2002-2003	311	
2003-2004	46	
2004-2005	67	
2005-2006	199	
2006-2007	738	
2007-2008	1,504	
2008-2009	2,623	
2009-2010	4,187	Estimate
2010-2011	4,436	Forecast

Supply

Supplies are moved into Afghanistan via Pakistan and countries to the north. However, air supply is a vital ingredient in the support chain and the following table shows the pressure under which the Royal Air Force and civilian supply agencies operate:

	RAF aircraft		Civilian leased aircraft	
	Weight of supplies (in tonnes)	*Number of flights*	*Weight of supplies (in tonnes)*	*Number of flights*
2008	6,709	538	8,817	266
2009	8,225	619	10,675	461
2010	6,971	533	9,568	443

CHAPTER 4 – UNITS OF THE REGULAR ARMY (DURING LATE 2011)

The Cavalry

The cavalry consists of 11 armoured regiments and one mounted ceremonial regiment as follows:

The Household Cavalry

The Household Cavalry Regiment	HCR
The Household Cavalry Mounted Regiment	HCMRD

The Royal Armoured Corps

1st The Queen's Dragoon Guards	QDG
The Royal Scots Dragoon Guards	SCOTS DG
The Royal Dragoon Guards	RDG
The Queen's Royal Hussars	QRH
9th/12th Royal Lancers	9/12L
The King's Royal Hussars	KRH
The Light Dragoons	LD
The Queen's Royal Lancers	QRL
1st Royal Tank Regiment	1 RTR
2nd Royal Tank Regiment	2 RTR

The Infantry

Comprised of 36 battalions.

The Guards Division

1st Bn Grenadier Guards	1 GREN GDS
1st Bn Coldstream Guards	1 COLM GDS
1st Bn Scots Guards	1 SG
1st Bn Irish Guards	1 IG
1st Bn Welsh Guards	1 WG

There are generally three battalions from the Guards Division on public duties in London at any one time. When a Regiment is stationed in London on public duties it is given an extra company to ensure the additional manpower required for ceremonial events is available.

The Scottish Division

The Royal Scots Borderers, 1st Bn The Royal Regiment of Scotland	1 SCOTS
The Royal Highland Fusiliers, 2nd Bn The Royal Regiment of Scotland	2 SCOTS
The Black Watch, 3rd Bn The Royal Regiment of Scotland	3 SCOTS
The Highlanders, 4th Bn The Royal Regiment of Scotland	4 SCOTS
The Argyll and Sutherland Highlanders, 5th Bn The Royal Regiment of Scotland	5 SCOTS

The Queen's Division

1st Bn The Princess of Wales's Royal Regiment (Queen's and Royal Hampshire)	1 PWRR
2nd Bn The Princess of Wales's Royal Regiment (Queen's and Royal Hampshire)	2 PWRR
1st Bn The Royal Regiment of Fusiliers	1 RRF
2nd Bn The Royal Regiment of Fusiliers	2 RRF
1st Bn The Royal Anglian Regiment	1 R ANGLIAN
2nd Bn The Royal Anglian Regiment	2 R ANGLIAN

The King's Division

1st Bn The Duke of Lancaster's Regiment (King's, Lancashire and Border)	1 LANCS
2nd Bn The Duke of Lancaster's Regiment (King's, Lancashire and Border)	2 LANCS
4th Bn The Duke of Lancaster's Regiment (King's, Lancashire and Border)	3 LANCS
1st Bn The Yorkshire Regiment (Prince Of Wales's Own)	1 YORKS
2nd Bn The Yorkshire Regiment (Green Howards)	2 YORKS
3rd Bn The Yorkshire Regiment (Duke of Wellington's)	3 YORKS

The Prince of Wales's Division

1st Bn The Mercian Regiment (Cheshire)	1 MERCIAN
2nd Bn The Mercian Regiment (Worcesters and Foresters)	2 MERCIAN
3rd Bn The Mercian Regiment (Staffords)	3 MERCIAN
1st Bn The Royal Welsh (The Royal Welsh Fusiliers)	1 R WELSH
2nd Bn The Royal Welsh (The Royal Regiment of Wales)	2 R WELSH

The Rifles

1st Bn The Rifles	1 RIFLES
2nd Bn The Rifles	2 RIFLES
3rd Bn The Rifles	3 RIFLES
4th Bn The Rifles	4 RIFLES
5th Bn The Rifles	5 RIFLES

The Brigade of Gurkhas

1st Bn The Royal Gurkha Rifles	1 RGR
2nd Bn The Royal Gurkha Rifles	2 RGR

The Parachute Regiment

1st Bn The Parachute Regiment	1 PARA
2nd Bn The Parachute Regiment	2 PARA
3rd Bn The Parachute Regiment	3 PARA

The Royal Irish Regiment

1st Bn The Royal Irish Regiment 1 R IRISH

Since 2002 there have been four infantry training battalions at the Infantry Training Centre located at Catterick in North Yorkshire.

Under Director Special Forces

The 22nd Special Air Service Regiment 22 SAS

Special Reconnaissance Regiment SRR

Although the SAS cannot be classed as a traditional infantry unit, for brevity the SAS are listed here. Members of the regiment are found from all arms and services of the Army after exhaustive selection tests.

The Royal Regiment of Artillery (RA)

1 st Regiment Royal Horse Artillery	1 RHA
3rd Regiment Royal Horse Artillery	3 RHA
4th Regiment Royal horse Artillery	4 RHA
5th Regiment	5 REGT
7th (Parachute) Regiment Royal Horse Artillery	7 RHA
12th Regiment	12 REGT
14th Regiment	14 REGT
16th Regiment	16 REGT
19th Regiment	19 REGT
26th Regiment	26 REGT
29th Commando Regiment	29 REGT
32nd Regiment	32 REGT
39th Regiment	39 REGT
40th Regiment	40 REGT
47th Regiment	47 REGT

The King's Troop Royal Horse Artillery is a ceremonial unit.

The Corps of Royal Engineers (RE)

21st Engineer Regiment	21 ENGR REGT
22nd Engineer Regiment	22 ENGR REGT
23rd Engineer Regiment (Air Assault)	23 ENGR REGT
24th Commando Regiment	24 CDO REGT
25th Engineer Regiment (Air Support)	25 ENGR REGT
26th Engineer Regiment	26 ENGR REGT
28th Engineer Regiment	28 ENGR REGT
32nd Engineer Regiment	32 ENGR REGT

33rd Engineer Regiment (EOD)	33 ENGR REGT
35th Engineer Regiment	35 ENGR REGT
36th Engineer Regiment	36 ENGR REGT
38th Engineer Regiment	38 ENGR REGT
39th Engineer Regiment (Air Support)	39 ENGR REGT
42nd Engineer Regiment	42 ENGR REGT

There are two training regiments:

1st RSME Regiment	1 RSME REGT
3rd RSME Regiment	3 RSME REGT

The Royal Corps of Signals (R SIGNALS)

1st (UK) Armd Div HQ and Signal Regiment	1 SIG REGT
2nd Signal Regiment	2 SIG REGT
3rd (UK) Div HQ & Signal Regiment	3 SIG REGT
7th Signal Regiment	7 SIG REGT
10th Signal Regiment	10 SIG REGT
11th Signal Regiment (Trg Regt)	11 SIG REGT
14th Signal Regiment (Electronic Warfare)	14 SIG REGT
16th Signal Regiment	16 SIG REGT
18th (UKSF) Signal Regiment	18 SIG REGT
21st Signal Regiment (Air Support)	21 SIG REGT
22nd Signal Regiment	22 SIG REGT
30th Signal Regiment	30 SIG REGT

The Army Air Corps (AAC)

1st Regiment	1 REGT AAC
2nd Regiment (Training)	2 REGT AAC
3rd Regiment	3 REGT AAC
4th Regiment	4 REGT AAC
5th Regiment	5 REGT AAC
7th Regiment (Training)	7 REGT AAC
9th Regiment	9 REGT AAC

THE SERVICES

The Royal Logistic Corps (RLC)

1 Logistic Support Regiment	1 LOG REGT
2 Logistic Support Regiment	2 LOG REGT
3 Logistic Support Regiment	3 LOG REGT

4 Logistic Support Regiment	4 LOG REGT
5 Territorial Army Training Regiment	5 (TRG) REGT
6 Supply Regiment	6 (SUP) REGT
7 Transport Regiment	7 (TPT) REGT
8 Transport Regiment	8 (TPT) REGT
9 Supply Regiment	9 (SUP) REGT
10 (QOGLR) Transport Regiment	10 (TPT) REGT
11 Explosive Ordnance Disposal Regiment	11 (EOD) REGT
12 Logistic Support Regiment	12 LOG REGT
13 Air Assault Regiment	13 REGT
17 Port and Maritime Regiment	17 (PORT) REGT
23 Pioneer Regiment	23 (PNR) REGT
24 Postal, Courier & Movements Regiment	24 (PC&MOV) REGT
25 Training and Support Regiment	25 REGT
27 Transport Regiment	27 (TPT) REGT
29 Postal, Courier & Movements Regiment	29 (PC&MOV) REGT

The Queens's Own Gurkha Logistic Regiment (QOGLR) consists of a Regimental Headquarters and 2 x operational squadrons. 28 Transport Squadron serves with 10 Transport Regiment and 94 Stores Squadron with 9 Supply Regiment.

There are 2 x Combat Service Support (CSS) Battalions. One is with the Royal Marines 3 Commando Brigade and another with 19 Light Brigade.

Royal Electrical and Mechanical Engineers (REME)

1st (Close Support) Bn REME	1 BN REME
2nd (Close Support) Bn REME	2 BN REME
3rd (Close Support) Bn REME	3 BN REME
4th (Close Support) Bn REME	5 BN REME
6th (Close Support) Bn REME	6 BN REME
7th (Air Assault) Bn REME	7 BN REME
101 (Force Support) Bn REME	101 BN REME
104 (Force Support) Bn REME	104 BN REME

Royal Army Medical Corps (RAMC)

1st Close Support Medical Regiment	1 CS MED REGT
3rd Close Support Medical Regiment	3 CD MED REGT
4th General Support Medical Regiment	4 GS MED REGT
5th General Support Medical Regiment	5 GS MED REGT
16th Close Support Medical Regiment	16 CS MED REGT
22nd Field Hospital	22 FD HOSP

| 33rd Field Hospital | 33 FD HOSP |
| 34th Field Hospital | 34 FD HOSP |

Military Bands

Following the 2007 re-organisation of military bands the Regular Army (Corps of Army Music) has 24 bands as follows:

Household Cavalry	70 musicians	2 bands
Grenadier Guards	49 musicians	1 band
Coldstream Guards	49 musicians	1 band
Scots Guards	49 musicians	1 band
Welsh Guards	49 musicians	1 band
Irish Guards	49 musicians	1 band
Royal Artillery	49 musicians	1 band
Royal Engineers	35 musicians	1 band
Royal Signals	35 musicians	1 band
Royal Logistic Corps	35 musicians	1 band
REME	35 musicians	1 band
Adjutant General's Corps	35 musicians	1 band
Army Air Corps	35 musicians	1 band
Royal Armoured Corps	70 musicians	2 bands
Royal Regiment of Scotland	35 musicians	1 band
Queen's Division	35 musicians	1 band
King's Division	35 musicians	1 band
Prince of Wales's Division	35 musicians	1 band
The Rifles	35 musicians	1 band
Parachute Regiment	35 musicians	1 band
Royal Irish Regiment	35 musicians	1 band
Royal Gurkha Rifles	35 musicians	1 band

During early 2011 the Corps of Army Music had 790 personnel.

CHAPTER 5 – THE HOUSEHOLD CAVALRY AND THE ROYAL ARMOURED CORPS

OVERVIEW

The Household Cavalry (HCav) and The Royal Armoured Corps (RAC) are grouped together as one arm and have traditionally provided the tank force and the formation reconnaissance component of the British Army. More recently the RAC have also become responsible for providing the Army element of the Joint NBC Regiment.

The Household Cavalry and the RAC is composed of 12 regular regiments (including the two regiments of the Household Cavalry, discussed below) and the four reserve Yeomanry Regiments with the TA. Apart from the Royal Tank Regiment, which was formed in the First World War with the specific task of fighting in armoured vehicles, the regular element of the RAC is provided by the successors of those regiments that formed the mounted units of the pre-mechanised era. The Yeomanry Regiments are tasked with providing a variety of operational reinforcement tasks in support of the regular RAC.

Although very much part of the RAC as an 'Arm', the Household Cavalry (HCav) is a discrete corps consisting of two regiments. The Household Cavalry Mounted Regiment (HCMR), which is permanently stationed in London has the task of providing mounted troops for state ceremonial functions. The Household Cavalry Regiment (HCR) is stationed in Windsor and is a Force Reconnaissance (FR) Regiment that plays a full role in operational and training activity within the Field Army. Officers and soldiers from the Household Cavalry are posted between the two regiments as needs dictate (For general purposes, in this publication, the term RAC includes the HCav).

Armoured Regiments

Royal Dragoon Guards	Catterick
Kings Royal Hussars	Tidworth
2 Royal Tank Regiment	Tidworth
Scots Dragoon Guards	Fallingbostel (Germany)
Queen's Royal Hussars	Sennelager (Germany)

Under restructuring arrangements we would expect either the Scots Dragoon Guards or the Queen's Royal Hussars to have returned to the UK from Germany by 2015. The remaining Regiment would probably return to the UK shortly after 2015.

Formation Reconnaissance Regiments

Household Cavalry Regiment	Windsor
Queen's Royal Lancers	Catterick
Light Dragoons	Swanton Morley
Queen's Dragoon Guards	Sennelager (Germany)
9/12 Lancers	Hohne (Germany)

Under restructuring arrangements we would expect 9/12 Lancers to return to the UK from Germany by 2015.

Joint CBRN Regiment

1 Royal Tank Regiment	Honington

(with one armoured demonstration squadron at Warminster)

Training

AFV Training Group   Bovington

Ceremonial

Household Cavalry Mounted Regiment   Knightsbridge

Bands

The Heavy Cavalry Band   Catterick

The Light Cavalry Band   Bovington

The total liability for all Household Cavalry and Royal Armoured Corps personnel is 5,778. (2011)

Yeomanry

Royal Yeomanry   London (RHQ)

Queen's Own Yeomanry   Newcastle (RHQ)

Royal Wessex Yeomanry   Bovington (RHQ)

Royal Mercian and Lancastrian Yeomanry   Telford (RHQ)

FORMATION RECONNAISSANCE REGIMENT

During the past decade Formation Reconnaissance was re-organised to provide five regular regiments. Four of these regiments have three sabre squadrons and a command and support squadron, whereas the HCR has a fourth squadron which is specifically affiliated to 16 Air Assault Brigade.

Formation Reconnaissance regiments are usually under the direct command of a formation Headquarters (divisional or brigade). Their more usual task in a defensive scenario is to identify the direction and strength of the enemy thrusts, impose maximum delay and damage to the enemy's reconnaissance forces while allowing main forces to manoeuvre to combat the threat. They would be assisted in such a task by using their own organic long range anti-tank guided weapons and other assets that might be attached such as anti-tank helicopters. In support would be the indirect fire guns (AS90) and Multiple Launch Rocket System (MLRS) of the divisional artillery, and an air defended area (ADA) maintained by Rapier and Stormer HVM air defence missiles.

The basic task of Formation Reconnaissance is to obtain accurate information about the enemy and develop an intelligence picture in their areas of responsibility for their superior commanders in the chain of command, as quickly as possible. However, Formation Reconnaissance Regiments are now capable of providing armour support to infantry on operations in Afghanistan.

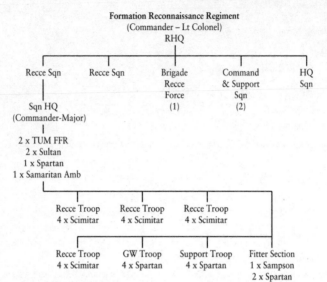

Formation Reconnaissance Regiment
(Commander – Lt Colonel)
RHQ

| Recce Sqn | Recce Sqn | Brigade Recce Force (1) | Command & Support Sqn (2) | HQ Sqn |

Sqn HQ
(Commander-Major)

2 x TUM FFR
2 x Sultan
1 x Spartan
1 x Samaritan Amb

| Recce Troop 4 x Scimitar | Recce Troop 4 x Scimitar | Recce Troop 4 x Scimitar |

| Recce Troop 4 x Scimitar | GW Troop 4 x Spartan | Support Troop 4 x Spartan | Fitter Section 1 x Sampson 2 x Spartan |

A regiment usually operates with 48 x Scimitar.

Notes:

(1) The Brigade Reconnaissance Force (BRF) operates a squadron sized unit using protected vehicles to identify and if necessary strike hostile elements.

(2) Expect the Command and Support Squadron to include a ground surveillance troop, a TACP/FAC party and an NBC protection troop in addition to the normal command and control elements.

(3) Full wartime establishment is approximately 600 all ranks.

(4) In war, each Formation Reconnaissance Regiment could receive an additional reconnaissance squadron from the TA Yeomanry.

ARMOURED REGIMENT

The following diagram shows the current structure of an Armoured Regiment equipped with Challenger 2. A Challenger 2 Regiment with three Squadrons of main battle tanks would have an all up total of 44 tanks when deployed for war.

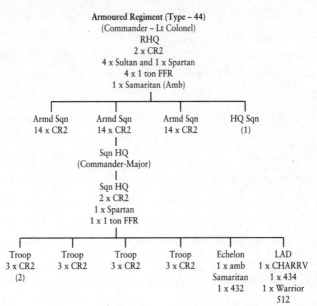

Armoured Regiment (Type – 44)
(Commander – Lt Colonel)
RHQ
2 x CR2
4 x Sultan and 1 x Spartan
4 x 1 ton FFR
1 x Samaritan (Amb)

Armd Sqn 14 x CR2 | Armd Sqn 14 x CR2 | Armd Sqn 14 x CR2 | HQ Sqn (1)

Sqn HQ
(Commander-Major)

Sqn HQ
2 x CR2
1 x Spartan
1 x 1 ton FFR

Troop 3 x CR2 (2) | Troop 3 x CR2 | Troop 3 x CR2 | Troop 3 x CR2 | Echelon 1 x amb Samaritan 1 x 432 | LAD 1 x CHARRV 1 x 434 1 x Warrior 512

Notes:

(1) HQ Sqn has a Reconnaissance Troop with 8 x Scimitar which is under direct control of the CO in the field.

(2) Tank Troop commanded by 2Lt/Lt with Troop Sergeant as 2ic in own tank. The third tank is commanded by a Corporal.

(3) Totals: 44 x CR2, 8 x SCIMITAR, 4 x CHARRV. Total strength for war is approx 550.

(4) A Challenger 2 has a crew of 4 – Commander, Driver, Gunner and Loader/Operator.

JOINT CHEMICAL, BIOLOGICAL, RADIOLOGICSL AND NUCLEAR REGIMENT (JT CBRN REGT)

The Jt CBRN Regt was created in 1999 and is based at RAF Honington, Suffolk. The Regiment is composed of two squadrons from 1 RTR and 27 Sqn RAF Regiment plus supporting staff from other army units. The Jt CBRN Regt fields specialist CBRN defence equipment, specifically the Fuchs nuclear and chemical reconnaissance and survey vehicle, the Integrated Biological Detection System (IBDS) and the Multi-Purpose Decontamination System (MPDS). The Regiment is an essential element for any joint force operation where there is an CBRN threat, enhancing the integral CBRN defence capabilities of the remainder of the force. Not only does the Regiment support Army formations but also other vital assets such as air bases, logistic areas and key lines of communication.

During late 2011 the MoD announced a change of role for 1RTR was planned and that the RAF Regiment would assume responsibility for the JT CBRN Regiment.

Joint CBRN Regiment

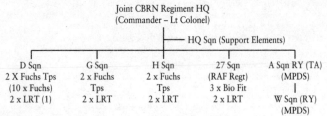

Joint CBRN Regiment HQ
(Commander – Lt Colonel)

—— HQ Sqn (Support Elements)

D Sqn	G Sqn	H Sqn	27 Sqn	A Sqn RY (TA)
2 X Fuchs Tps	2 x Fuchs	2 x Fuchs	(RAF Regt)	(MPDS)
(10 x Fuchs)	Tps	Tps	3 x Bio Fit	
2 x LRT (1)	2 x LRT	2 x LRT	2 x LRT	W Sqn (RY)
				(MPDS)

Note:

(1) The Light Role Team (LRT) consists of specialist personnel with dedicated vehicles and communications equipment plus the required detection systems.

(2) Where appropriate the Direct Application Decontamination System (DADS) is available.

In peace the Army may be asked to provide Military Assistance to the Civil Authorities. In these circumstances, the Joint CBRN Regiment may be called on to deal with radiological, biological or chemical hazards.

The regiment has made a major contribution to almost every UK military operation during the past decade.

Note: 27 Squadron RAF Regiment recently re-roled as a Field Defence Squadron for service in Afghanistan. The Squadron has now returned to the Joint CBRN Regiment.

Joint CBRN Regiment Equipment

Multi-Purpose Decontamination System (MPDS)

MPDS is a diesel driven, high pressure cleaning and decontamination system. It consists of two KARCHER water pumps, capable of spraying water at various temperatures, ranging from cold through to steam, and a 9000 litre water tank mounted on a DROPS flatrack. The system is capable of drawing water (including seawater) from either an open source or Service sources such as bulk water carriers. The system is operated in conjunction with decontaminants. It can be operated mounted on DROPS or dismounted.

Integrated Biological Detection System (IBDS)

IBDS has recently replaced the Prototype Biological Detection System (PBDS) in service with the UK Joint NBC Regiment. This modern system provides an enhanced and automated NBC detection system. Major IBDS elements include:

- ◆ A detection suite, including equipment for atmospheric sampling.
- ◆ Meteorological station and GPS.
- ◆ NBC filtration and environmental control for use in all climates.
- ◆ Chemical agent detection.
- ◆ Independent power supply.
- ◆ Cameras for 360 degree surveillance.

IBDS is installed in a container which can be mounted on a vehicle (standard 4 ton) or ground dumped and can be transported by either fixed wing aircraft or helicopters. IBDS provides the commander in the field with early warning of a chemical or biological warfare attack.

ARMOUR IN THE 21ST CENTURY

Armour has provided battle winning shock action and firepower since the earliest tanks helped to break the stalemate of the Western Front during the First World War. In the same way, armoured reconnaissance, with the ability to penetrate the enemy's forward defences and gain information by using stealth and firepower, has shaped the way in which armour has been used to its best advantage.

Defence represents the best use of ground features in conjunction with engineering and concealed firepower. The ability of armour to overwhelm all but the heaviest defences and deliver a group of highly capable armoured fighting platforms into the combat area remains a battle winning capability embraced by all major armies.

The modern main battle tank weighs between 50 and 70 tonnes, can move at up to 60 kph and can virtually always guarantee a first round hit with its main armament out to 2000 m. Last tested in combat in the Gulf War of 2003, UK armoured forces demonstrated the advantages of armour in a desert landscape. Amongst these was the ability to cover rough terrain quickly and by the use of superior concentrated firepower, create operational level, rather than simple local tactical, advantage. These tanks used the most up to date information systems and state of the art imaging and sighting systems to locate, close with and destroy the enemy. The 2003 Gulf War experience underlined the need for all elements of manoeuvre forces to be able to move swiftly and securely with protection and firepower to maintain a high 'operational tempo'. This includes infantry, artillery and of course the massive logistic supply required.

The argument that 'the days of the tank are over' has been around for many years and certainly since the appearance of the man-portable guided missile in large numbers such as during the Yom Kippur war almost 30 years ago. The advent of the highly capable Attack Helicopter and long-range, smart top-attack precision munitions has only added to this debate. However, tanks remain in the world in large numbers – at least 50,000 by current estimates – and in a surprisingly large number of countries. Whilst the supremacy of armour on the modern battlefield will continue to be challenged by ever more sophisticated anti-armour systems, the requirement for highly mobile, protected direct firepower that can operate in all conditions and climates will remain an enduring requirement to support the infantry. It is this 'endurance' characteristic and the ability to operate in all circumstances which is unique and is not shared by helicopters and aircraft. Every military man will agree that the firepower and flexibility of the main battle tank provides a capability on the battlefield that no other system can match.

It would appear that the UK has decided to retain between 240-250 MBT in service. However, other countries appear to have placed a very high priority on the numbers to be retained in their MBT fleets:

INTERNATIONAL COMPARISON – MAJOR ARMY FORMATIONS AND EQUIPMENT AVAILABLE (ESTIMATE)

Serial	Country	Brigades Available	Main Battle Tanks	Other Armoured Vehicles
(a)	(b)	(c)	(d)	(e)
1	United States (2)	55	6,200	27,500
2	China	136	7,000	6,000
3	Japan	10	800	950
4	Russia (3)	52	21,000	18,000
5	European Union	120	5,000	22,000

Note:

(1) Numbers in column (c) include Armoured, Mechanised, Infantry, Motorised, Airborne, Air Assault and Amphibious Brigades.

(2) Figure for the US includes USMC Brigades and equipment.

(3) Probably about 18,000 Russian MBTs are in store.

(4) Most sources agree on a figure of around 50,000 MBT in world service and available for operations.

(6) Overall numbers in this table are averages over a number of sources that include Jane's Information Group, The International Institute for Strategic Studies (IISS) and the Stockholm Institute for Peace Research (SIPRI).

(7) Russia has stated that they will downsize their MBT fleet during the next 10 years. It is almost certain that large numbers of these vehicles (possibly 18,000 or so) will be sold on to countries in Africa, Asia and South America.

What is certain to change in the future is the shape and size of future tanks. The key is that new technology will allow protection to be delivered in quite different ways. Traditionally, protection has been provided through ballistic armour which, because of its weight, has to be optimised over a relatively narrow frontal arc, with reduced protection on the sides, top rear and belly. Thus full protection is only possible on a small proportion of the total surface area. In the future a more holistic approach is likely to incorporate a wide range of 'survivability' characteristics in view of the three-dimensional and all round threat. These measures include: signature reduction in all aspects – acoustic, visual, thermal, radar cross-section etc; suites of active and passive defensive aids and electro-optic countermeasures; and inherent redundancy in vehicle design and crew i.e. the ability to sustain considerable damage yet be able to continue fighting. The concept is based on a theory of 'don't be detected – if detected, don't be acquired – if acquired, don't be hit – if hit, don't be penetrated – if penetrated, don't be killed'. Such an approach is likely to see future tanks of much smaller design and of significantly lesser weight. In turn, reduced weight and size will improve mobility and enable armour to be deployed more rapidly, strategically if necessary, whilst also reducing the very considerable mobility and logistic support that the heavy 60-70 tonne MBTs of today require.

In terms of firepower, smart, extended range munitions such as fire and forget Gun Launched Anti-tank Guided Missiles, pre-programmable ammunition and other novel natures are all likely to increase the potency of armour. In coming to a balanced view on the future of the tank, the heavy modern tank of today has as much in common with the Mark V tank of 1916 as it will have with its successor in 2030.

Digitisation of the future battlefield has been identified as essential, but base architecture programmes essential for the target data transmission through battlefield management systems is currently running some ten to fifteen years behind schedule. This time lag may enable the tank in its present form to survive for much longer than many analysts had previously predicted.

At the beginning of the 21st Century, we see the major defence orientated countries of the world undergoing a major doctrinal and conceptual rethink based on the information age, embracing new IT and digital technology capabilities. The future, however, always has its roots in the present and while the large fleets of tanks we now have may be more visible from space, and more difficult to protect from remotely fired missiles and guns, the armies who have them will continue to explore and exploit armoured 'stretch' technologies to ensure their armoured capability is credible.

We have no doubt that in both limited and general war the main battle tank is one of the essential systems that will determine the outcome of any battle, and there is also a sound argument to be made regarding the utility of the main battle tank in some counter insurgency operations. Of special interest is the successful use of Leopard MBT in Afghanistan by Canadian, Danish and German forces.

It is impossible to know where the British Army will be and what it will be doing 10 years from now. Experience has taught us that the only thing that we can be sure of is that the current operational requirement, which generally calls for lighter armour will, in the future almost certainly be totally different from what it is today. We firmly believe that the main battle tank will continue to have a major effect on military operations in this difficult and dangerous world for many years to come.

" *The man who looks 10 years out and says he knows what the strategic situation will look like, is quite frankly the Court Jester*"

Gen Sir Richard Dannet KCB, CBE,MC,ADC Gen

CHAPTER 6 – ARMOURED AND PROTECTED VEHICLES

ARMOURED VEHICLES

Challenger 2

(345 available – mid 2011) Crew 4; Length Gun Forward 11.55 m; Height 2.5 m; Width 4.2 m with appliqué armour; Ground Clearance 0.51 m; Combat Weight 62.5 tonnes- MLC 76; Main Armament 1 x 120 mm L30 CHARM Gun; Ammunition Carried max 50 rounds stowed – APFSDS, HESH and Smoke; Secondary Armament Co-axial 7.62 mm Chain Gun; Loaders pintle mounted 7.62 mm GPMG; Ammunition Carried 4000 rounds 7.62 mm; Engine CV12 12 cylinder – Auxiliary Power Unit 4 – stroke diesel; Gearbox TN54 epicyclic – 6 forward gears and 2 reverse; Road Speed 59 kph; Cross-Country Speed 40 kph; Fuel Capacity 1,592 litres usable internal plus 2 x 175 litre external fuel drums.

Challenger 2 was manufactured by Vickers Defence Systems and production was undertaken at their factories in Newcastle-Upon-Tyne and Leeds. At 1999 prices Challenger 2 is believed to cost £4 million per vehicle.

Although the hull and automotive parts of the Challenger 2 are based upon that of its predecessor Challenger 1, the new tank incorporates over 150 improvements which have achieved substantially increased reliability and ease of maintenance. The Challenger 2 turret is, however, of a totally new design. The vehicle has a crew of four – commander, gunner, loader/signaller and driver and is equipped with a 120 mm rifled Royal Ordnance L30 gun firing all current tank ammunition natures plus the new depleted uranium (DU) round with a stick charge propellant system.

The design of the turret incorporates several of the significant features that Vickers had developed for its Mk 7 MBT (a Vickers turret on a Leopard 2 chassis). The central feature is an entirely new fire control system based on the Ballistic Control System developed by Computing Devices Company (Canada) for the US Army's M1A1 MBT. This second generation computer incorporates dual 32-bit processors with a MIL STD1553B databus and has sufficient growth potential to accept Battlefield Information Control System (BICS) functions and navigation aids (a GPS satnav system). The armour is an uprated version of Challenger 1's Chobham armour.

Following the 2010 SDSR it is likely that the majority of the UK' Challenger 2's will be stationed in the UK following the return of British Forces from Germany. We would eventually expect to see 5 x Regiments in the UK with a vehicle fleet of around 240-250 vehicles some of which will be stationed at an overseas training area (possibly Suffield in Canada).

Challenger Repair and Recovery Vehicle (CHARRV)

(80 available – mid 2011) Crew 3; Length 9.59 m; Operating Width 3.62 m; Height 3.005 m; Ground Clearance 0.5 m; Combat Weight 62,000 kg; Max Road Speed 59 kph; Cross Country Speed 35 kph; Fording 1.07 m; Trench Crossing 2.3 m; Crane – Max Lift 6,500 kg at 4.9 m reach; Engine Perkins CV12 TCA 1200 26.1 V-12 direct injection 4-stroke diesel.

Between 1988 and 1990 the British Army ordered 80 Challenger CHARRV in two batches and the contract was completed with the last vehicles accepted into service during 1983. A 'Type 44' tank Challenger 2 Regiment has 4 x CHARRV, one with each sabre squadron and one with the REME Light Aid Detachment (LAD).

The vehicle has a crew of three plus additional space in a separate compartment for another two REME fitters. The vehicle is fitted with two winches (main and auxiliary) plus an Atlas hydraulically operated crane capable of lifting a complete Challenger 2 powerpack. The front dozer blade can be used as a stabiliser blade for the crane or as a simple earth anchor.

MCV – 80 Fv 510 (Warrior)

(785 available – mid 2011) Weight loaded 24,500 kg; length 6.34 m; Height to turret top 2.78 m; Width 3.0 m; Ground Clearance 0.5 m; Max Road Speed 75 kph; Road Range 500 km; Engine Rolls Royce CV8 diesel; Horsepower 550 hp; Crew 2 (carries 8 infantry soldiers); Armament L21 30 mm Rarden Cannon; Coaxial EX-34 7.62 mm Hughes Helicopter Chain Gun; Smoke Dischargers Royal Ordnance Visual and Infra Red Screening Smoke (VIRSS).

Warrior is an Armoured Infantry Fighting Vehicle (AIFV) in service with armoured infantry battalions. The original purchase of Warrior was for 789 units and the vehicle is in service with three armoured infantry battalions in the UK with 3 (UK) Div and four armoured infantry battalions in Germany with 1 (UK) Armd Div.

Warrior armed with the 30 mm Rarden cannon gives the crew a good chance of destroying enemy APCs at ranges of up to 1,500 m and the vehicle carries a crew of three and seven dismounted infantry.

The vehicle is CBRN proof, and a full range of night vision equipment is included as standard. Warrior variants include an Artillery Observation Vehicle and a Repair and Recovery version.

Warrior has seen successful operational service in the Gulf (1991), with British troops serving in the Balkans and more recently in Iraq. The vehicle has proven protection against mines, and there is dramatic BBC TV footage of a Warrior running over a Serbian anti-tank mine during the conflict in the Balkans with little or no serious damage to the vehicle or crew.

The hull and mechanical components of Warrior are exceptional and few other vehicles in the world can match it for reliability and performance. The Warrior armament fire control system and electronics require upgrading if the vehicle is to remain in service to 2025 as intended.

The future Warrior Capability Sustainment Programme (WCSP) will upgrade the current Warrior Infantry Fighting Vehicle to meet current and future operational requirements. The programme is in the early stages of its Acquisition Cycle (2010) and an investment decision is awaited..

WCSP may include a new power pack, vehtronics enhancement, a digital fire control system (FCS) and a modern medium calibre cannon system.

Numbers in UK service are believed to include 482 x Warrior Basic; 59 x Warrior RA; 126 x Warrior Recovery and Repair. The Kuwait MoD has signed a contract for the purchase of 230 Warrior vehicles some of which are Recce vehicles armed with a 90 mm Cockerill gun.

AFV 432 and Bulldog

(Approx 1,100 in service of which about 750 are base line vehicles – models include command vehicles, ambulances, and 81 mm mortar carriers). Crew 2 (Commander and Driver); Weight loaded 15,280kg; Length 5.25 m; Width 2.8 m; Height 2.28 m; Ground Pressure 0.78 kg km squared; Armament 1 x 7.62 Machine Gun; 2 x 3 barrel smoke dischargers; Engine Rolls Royce K60 No 4 Mark 1-4; Engine Power 240 bhp; Fuel Capacity 454 litres; Max Road Speed 52 kph; Road Range 580 km; Vertical Obstacle 0.9 m; Trench Crossing 2.05 m; Gradient 60 degrees; Carries up to 10 men; Armour 12.7 mm max.

In service since the early 1960s the basic 432 armoured personnel carrier is NBC proof and when necessary can be converted for swimming when it has a water speed of 6 kph (if required). Properly maintained it is a rugged and reliable vehicle with a good cross-country performance.

In July 2006 the UK Mod announced the provision, for Iraq, of around 70 uparmoured and upgraded FV430 troop carriers (Bulldog), in addition to the 54 already on contract. Deliveries started in late 2006. In the longer term the MoD expects 900 vehicles to be upgraded to the Bulldog specification and the programme should be complete by late 2011.

For counter-insurgency operations the up-armoured FV430 provides a similar level of protection to Warrior and the vehicle will is able to carry out many of the same tasks, thereby relieving the pressure on heavily committed Warrior vehicles in armoured infantry battlegroups.

Fuchs

(11 available) Road Range 800 kms; Crew 2; Operational Weight 17,000 kg; Length 6.83 m; Width 2.98 m; Height 2.30 m; Road Speed 105 kph; Engine Mercedes-Benz Model OM-402A V-8 liquid cooled diesel; Armament 1 x 7.62 mm MG; 6 x Smoke Dischargers.

Manufactured by the German company Thyssen-Henschel, Fuchs is an armoured vehicle equipped with systems that can detect chemical, radiation, biological and nuclear (CRBN) elements that may have been used during an attack. The vehicle is equipped with a Global Positioning System (GPS) and provides the crew with integral collective protection.

AFV 103 Spartan

(about 500 available) Crew 3; Weight 8,172 kg; Length 5.12 m; Height 2.26 m; Width 2.26 m; Ground Clearance 0.35 m; Max Road Speed 80 kph; Road Range 483 kms; Engine Jaguar J60 No.1 Mark 100B; Engine Power 190 bhp; Fuel Capacity 386 litres; Ammunition Carried 3,000 rounds of 7.62 mm; Armament 1 x 7.62 Machine Gun.

Spartan is the APC of the Combat Vehicle Reconnaissance Tracked (CVRT) series of vehicles, which included Fv 101 Scorpion, Fv 102 Striker, Fv 104 Samaritan, Fv 105 Sultan, Fv 106 Sampson and Fv 107 Scimitar. Spartan is a very small APC that can only carry four men in addition to the crew of three. It is therefore used to carry small specialised groups such as the reconnaissance teams, air defence sections, mortar fire controllers and ambush parties.

Samaritan, Sultan and Sampson are also APC type vehicles, Samaritan is the CVRT ambulance vehicle, Sultan is the armoured command vehicle and Sampson is an armoured recovery vehicle. FV 4333 Stormer (60 available) is an air defence vehicle based on a CVR(T) type chassis.

Spartan, like FV 432 is likely to be replaced in some roles in the future.

Spartan is in service with the following nations: Belgium – 266: Oman – 6: Philippines – 7.

Fv 107 Scimitar

(Approx 320 available) Armament 1 x 30 mm Rarden L21 Gun; 1 x 7.62 mm Machine Gun; 2 x 4 barrel smoke dischargers; Engine BTA 5.9 Cummins diesel; Fuel Capacity 423 litres; Max Road Speed 80 kph; Combat Weight 8,000 kg; Length 4.9 m; Height 2.096 m; Width 2.2 m; Ground Clearance 0.35 m; Road Range 644 km; Crew 3; Ammunition Capacity 30 mm – 160 rounds; 7.62 mm – 3,000 rounds; Main Armament Elevation – 10 degrees to + 35 degrees.

CVR(T) Scimitar is the mainstay reconnaissance vehicle with which all Formation Reconnaissance regiments are equipped as well as all Close Reconnaissance troops and platoons of Armoured and Mechanised Battlegroups. The Scimitar is an ideal reconnaissance vehicle, mobile and fast with good communications and excellent viewing equipment. The vehicle's small size and low ground pressure make it extremely useful where the terrain is hostile and movement difficult.

Scimitar is due to be replaced by the Scout Reconnaissance vehicle, trials of which are expected to start in 2013.

PROTECTED VEHICLES

Panther Command and Liaison Vehicle (Panther CLV)

(Approximately 400 available); Weight 7 tonnes; Armament 1 x 7.62 mm GPMG with Remote Weapon Station.

The UK MoD announced in July 2003 that the BAE Systems Land Systems (formerly Alvis) Multi-role Light Vehicle (MLV) had been selected as the British Army's Future Command and Liaison Vehicle (FCLV). The first procurement contract was signed in November 2003 for an initial 401 vehicles, with an option for up to 400 more. The vehicle has been named the Panther Command and Liaison Vehicle (CLV).

Panther CLV is based on a design by Iveco Defence Vehicles Division of Italy and the vehicles were manufactured during the period 2006 to 2010. Acquisition cost for some 400 vehicles is £193 million spread over five years. The first batch of 50 vehicles was delivered in late 2007.

The vehicle is air transportable, underslung beneath a Chinook helicopter or carried inside C130, C17 and A400M aircraft and is capable of operations in all weathers, day and night using thermal imaging equipment. The vehicles are protected against a range of threats and are fitted with a 7.62 mm weapon system (capable of upgrade to 12.7 mm) which allows the user to operate the machine guns with a camera and joystick from inside the vehicle.

Panther is already is service with units from the 3rd Division and will replace a range of vehicles that are reaching the end of their operational lives, for example some types of Land Rover, Saxon, some FV432 and a number of CVR(T) vehicles. Panther is also entering service with the Royal Air Force Regiment.

Jackal (4 x 4 Patrol Vehicle)

(Approximately 250+ in service – early 2011); Length 5.39 m; Width 2.0 m; Height 1.97 m; Weight 6,650 kg.

During June 2007 the UK MoD announced the purchase of 130 new weapons-mounted patrol vehicles under an Urgent Operational Requirement for troops in Iraq and Afghanistan. The Jackal high mobility weapons platform will deliver a new level of power to the WMIK fleet, with more firepower and a better range and mobility. The vehicle will have a top speed of around 80 mph. Further announcements since 2007 suggest that the over Jackal fleet will reach 300 vehicles by early 2011.

The vehicle can be fitted with a range of firepower including a .50 calibre machine gun or an automatic grenade launcher and a general purpose machine gun, as well as carrying a crew of four soldiers with their personal weapons.

First deployed on operations in 2008 Jackal was designed by Supacat Ltd and manufactured by Devonport Management Ltd (DML) at their facility in Plymouth.

Coyote

The Coyote is a larger version of the Jackal (with six wheels) and mainly used to provide combat support and logistics. Coyote is an element in the Tactical Support Vehicle programme, the other vehicles being Husky and Wolfhound.

Mastiff 2 Force Protection Vehicle (FPV)

(300 available) Height 2.64 m; Width 2,53 m; Length 7.08 m; Top speed 90 kph; All up weight 23,500 kg; Payload 6,350 kg.

Mastiff 2 which replaced the earlier Mastiff 1 (Ridgeback) is a heavily armoured, wheeled , troop carrying vehicle suitable for road patrols and convoys and is the newest delivery in a range of protected patrol vehicles being used for operations. Manufactured by the US Company Force Protection Inc (where it is named Cougar). Mastiff 2 is a 6 x 6 wheel-drive patrol vehicle which carries six people, plus two crew. It has a maximum speed of 90 kph and can be armed with a machine gun, 50 mm canon or 40 mm automatic grenade launcher

The UK MoD purchased some 108 vehicles in an original order worth approximately US$70.1 million (£35 million) and these vehicles were deployed in Iraq during December 2006. During October 2007 the MoD announced the purchase of another 140 Mastiff in a contract worth around £100 million.

Wolfhound

(70 available) This is a variant of the highly successful Mastiff which is generally used for carrying logistic items including extremely heavy loads to the forward troops. The vehicle can also be used by the Royal Artillery to tow the 105 mm Light Gun and carry ammunition. Wolfhound is an element in the Tactical Support Vehicle programme, the other vehicles being Husky and Coyote.

Husky

(250 available) Length; 6.86 m; Width 2.43 m; Height 2.36 m.

Husky is a protected logistic support vehicle designed for a range of missions in Afghanistan that include transporting combat supplies to troops in areas where high-intensity operations are taking place. An ambulance version of the vehicle is also available.

Husky is an element in the Tactical Support Vehicle programme, the other vehicles being Wolfhound and Coyote.

Warthog

(115 available) Length 8.9 m; Front Compartment 2.9 m – crew 3; Rear Compartment 2.3 m – crew 8; Maximum Speed 60 kph; Armament – heavy machine gun.

Capable of operating in a range of operational environments and particularly suited to some of the operational areas to be found in Afghanistan. Warthog is blast protected, armed with a heavy machine gun and provides an excellent platform for infantry operating in a close combat environment. There are four vehicle variants – troop carrier, command vehicle, repair and recovery vehicle and ambulance.

100 vehicles were purchased from Singapore Technologies Kinetics in a contract worth around £150 million. Warthog started to enter service in 2010.

Warthog replaces the earlier Viking vehicles which have now been withdrawn to the UK.

Foxhound

(200 on order) Height; 2.35 m; Length 5.2 m; Width 2.1 m; Weight 7,500 kg; Top speed 110 kph.

Foxhound is a light protected patrol vehicle that was procured under a £180 million contract for 200 vehicles signed in November 2010. Manufactured by Force Protection Europe whose HQ is in Leamington Spa, Foxhound will replace many of the Snatch Land Rovers that have proved vulnerable on recent operations. Light and agile, Foxhound allows for options in operational scenarios that are not available when only heavier armoured is available.

The vehicle has a 'V' shaped hull to protect against blast and its engine can be removed and replaced in around 30 minutes. Crew and passengers sit inside a protective pod, which can be quickly adapted to transform the patrol vehicle into an ambulance or supply truck. It is claimed that Foxhound can drive away from an ambush on only three wheels.

First vehicles were in-service during 2011 with initial operational use in the Spring of 2012. In the longer term there would appear to be a requirement for another 200 vehicles.

FUTURE ARMOURED VEHICLES

Development of the previously named Future Rapid Effects System (FRES) has been recast as three separate medium weight armoured vehicle projects as follows:

Specialist Vehicle

Utility Vehicle

Terrier Engineer Vehicle

Specialist Vehicle (SV):

During Mid 2010 the MoD signed a £500 million with General Dynamics UK (GDUK) for the demonstration phase of seven prototype Scout vehicles and training equipment.

The sophisticated Scout vehicle will provide improved protection against a wide range of threats and bring significant benefits, including greater firepower, improved situational awareness, more protection and enhanced mobility. It will carry three crew and mount both a new type of 40mm cannon and a machine gun. It will replace the Scimitar armoured fighting vehicle.

The Scout design is derived from modifying the ASCOD vehicle, which is already in service with some NATO nations, is well-proven and is suitable for export sales. Work will continue alongside this programme to update existing armoured reconnaissance vehicles in service in Afghanistan, such as the Scimitar, to maintain their operational capabilities.

We believe that it is possible that as many as 600 medium weight Scout armoured reconnaissance vehicles will be built.

Utility Vehicle (UV):

The Ministry of Defence decided to restructure this programme in early 2009 and we expect a resumption of the programme in due course. In the longer term it is expected that the Utility Vehicle will become the core element of the Army's armoured vehicle fleet.

A major UV requirement is that it should be able to be transported in a C-130 Hercules aircraft which will place severe constraints on the platform weight and eventual design. However, experience in Iraq and Afghanistan has underlined the vulnerability of existing vehicles to attack by roadside bombs and rocket-propelled grenades, causing analysts to believe that the UV will be better armoured. As a result, planned weight of the vehicles has risen from about 17 tons to between 20 tons and 27 tons which raises questions over whether they will be too heavy for the RAF's new A400M transport aircraft. It appears likely that the UV will be wheeled.

The Utility Vehicle is expected to replace the FV 432 APC and many variants of the CVR(T) vehicle family.

Terrier Engineer Vehicle:

Terrier is a lightly armoured highly mobile, general support engineer vehicle optimised for battlefield preparation in the indirect fire zone. It will replace the existing FV180 Combat Engineer Tractor, providing mobility support (obstacle and route clearance), counter-mobility (digging of anti-tank ditches and other obstacles) and survivability (digging of trenches and Armoured Fighting Vehicle slots). Terrier is claimed to be faster, more mobile and with more effective armour and mine protection than the FV-180 CET.

The Terrier engineer vehicle programme is currently in the Demonstration and Manufacture Phase. The programme will cost approximately £386 million and the vehicle should be in-service by 2013.

CHAPTER 7 – INFANTRY

REGIMENTS AND BATTALIONS

The British Infantry is based on the well tried and tested Regimental System, which has proved to be repeatedly successful on operations over the years. It is based on Regiments, most of which have one or more regular Battalion and all have associated TA Battalions. The esprit de corps of the Regimental system is maintained in the names and titles of British Infantry Regiments handed down through history, with a tradition of courage in battle. The repeated changing size of the British Army, dictated by history and politics, is reflected in the fact that many of the most illustrious Regiments still have a number of Regular and Territorial Reserve Battalions. For manning purposes, in a number of cases Infantry Regiments are grouped within administrative 'Divisions'. These 'Divisions' are no longer field formations but represent original historical groupings based on recruiting geography.

The 'Division' of Infantry is an organisation that is responsible for all aspects of military administration, from recruiting, manning and promotions for individuals in the Regiments under its wing, to the longer term planning required to ensure continuity and cohesion. Divisions of Infantry have no operational command over their regiments, and should not be confused with the remaining operational divisions, such as 1(UK) Division and 3 (UK) Division.

There are currently 36 Regular Infantry Battalions and the majority of these battalions are now situated in permanent locations.

At the beginning of 2011 we believe that the infantry are located as follows:

United Kingdom	29 battalions (3 Resident in Northern Ireland)
Germany	4 battalions
Afghanistan	3 – 4 battalions on detachment
Cyprus	2 battalions
Falkland Islands	1 company group on detachment
Brunei	1 battalion (Gurkha)

INFANTRY STRUCTURE IN LATE 2011

In 2011 the Administrative 'Divisions' of Infantry are structured as follows:

The Guards Division	5 regular battalions
The Scottish Division	5 regular battalions
The Queen's Division	6 regular battalions
The King's Division	5 regular battalions
The Prince of Wales Division	5 regular battalions

Not administered by 'Divisions' of Infantry but operating under their own similar administrative arrangements are the following:

The Rifles	5 regular battalions
The Parachute Regiment	3 regular battalions
The Brigade of Gurkhas	2 regular battalions
The Royal Irish Regiment	1 regular battalion

Note: 1st Bn The Parachute Regiment forms the core element of the Special Forces Support Group and is not counted in the infantry battalion total.

TA battalions were under the administrative command of the following:

The Guards Division	1 TA battalion
The Scottish Division	2 TA battalions
The Queen's Division	3 TA battalions
The King's Division	2 TA battalions
The Prince of Wales Division	2 TA battalions
The Rifles	2 TA battalions
The Parachute Regiment	1 TA battalion
The Royal Irish Regiment	1 TA battalion
The Royal Gibraltar Regiment	1 composite battalion

In total the British Army has 36 regular battalions available for service and this total combined with the 14 TA battalions (excluding the Royal Gibraltar Regiment) could provide mobilisation strength of 50 infantry battalions.

Outside the above listed Regiments are three companies of guardsmen each of 110 men, who are provided to supplement the Household Division Regiments while on public duties in London. This allows Regiments of the Foot Guards to continue to carry out normal training on roulement from guard duties.

Gibraltar also has its own single battalion of the Royal Gibraltar Regiment comprising one regular and two volunteer companies.

The following listing shows the 2011 infantry structure.

THE GUARDS DIVISION

Regular Bns

1st Bn Grenadier Guards	1 GREN GDS
1st Bn Coldstream Guards	1 COLDM GDS
1st Bn Scots Guards	1SG
1st Bn Irish Guards	1 IG
1st Bn Welsh Guards	1 WG

Territorial Army Bn

| The London Regiment | LONDONS |

THE SCOTTISH DIVISION

Regular Bns

The Royal Scots Borderers, 1st Bn The Royal Regiment of Scotland	1 SCOTS
The Royal Highland Fusiliers, 2nd Bn The Royal Regiment of Scotland	2 SCOTS
The Black Watch, 3rd Bn The Royal Regiment of Scotland	3 SCOTS
The Highlanders, 4th Bn The Royal Regiment of Scotland	4 SCOTS
The Argyll and Sutherland Highlanders, 5th Bn The Royal Regiment of Scotland	5 SCOTS

Territorial Army Bns

| 52nd Lowland, 6th Bn The Royal Regiment of Scotland | 6 SCOTS |

| 51st Highland, 7th Bn The Royal Regiment of Scotland | 7 SCOTS |

THE QUEEN'S DIVISION

The Princess of Wales's Royal Regiment (Queen's and Royal Hampshires)

Regular Bns

| 1st Bn The Princess of Wales's Royal Regiment (Queen's and Royal Hampshires) | 1 PWRR |
| 2nd Bn The Princess of Wales's Royal Regiment (Queen's and Royal Hampshires) | 2 PWRR |

Territorial Army Bn

| 3rd Bn The Princess of Wales's Royal Regiment (Queen's and Royal Hampshires) | 3 PWRR |

The Royal Regiment of Fusiliers

Regular Bns

| 1st Bn The Royal Regiment of Fusiliers | 1 RRF |
| 2nd Bn The Royal Regiment of Fusiliers | 2 RRF |

Territorial Army Bn

| 5th Bn The Royal Regiment of Fusiliers | 5 RRF |

The Royal Anglian Regiment

Regular Bns

| 1st Bn The Royal Anglian Regiment | 1 R ANGLIAN |
| 2nd Bn The Royal Anglian Regiment | 2 R ANGLIAN |

Territorial Army Bn

| 3rd Bn The Royal Anglian Regiment | 3 R ANGLIAN |

THE KING'S DIVISION

The Duke of Lancaster's Regiment (King's, Lancashire and Border)

Regular Bns

| 1st Bn The Duke of Lancaster's Regiment (King's, Lancashire and Border) | 1 LANCS |
| 2nd Bn The Duke of Lancaster's Regiment (King's, Lancashire and Border) | 2 LANCS |

Territorial Army Bn

| 4th Bn The Duke of Lancaster's Regiment (King's, Lancashire and Border) | 3 LANCS |

The Yorkshire Regiment

Regular Bns

1st Bn The Yorkshire Regiment (Prince Of Wales's Own)	1 YORKS
2nd Bn The Yorkshire Regiment (Green Howards)	2 YORKS
3rd Bn The Yorkshire Regiment (Duke of Wellington's)	3 YORKS

Territorial Army Bn

| 4th Bn The Yorkshire Regiment | 4 YORKS |

THE PRINCE OF WALES'S DIVISION

The Mercian Regiment

Regular Bns

1st Bn The Mercian Regiment (Cheshire)	1 MERCIAN
2nd Bn The Mercian Regiment (Worcesters and Foresters)	2 MERCIAN
3rd Bn The Mercian Regiment (Staffords)	3 MERCIAN

Territorial Army Bn

4th Bn The Mercian Regiment	4 MERCIAN

The Royal Welsh

Regular Bns

1st Bn The Royal Welsh (The Royal Welch Fusiliers)	1 R WELSH
2nd Bn The Royal Welsh (The Royal Regiment of Wales)	2 R WELSH

Territorial Army Bn

3rd Bn The Royal Welsh	3 R WELSH

THE RIFLES

Regular Bns

1st Bn The Rifles	1 RIFLES
2nd Bn The Rifles	2 RIFLES
3rd Bn The Rifles	3 RIFLES
4th Bn The Rifles	4 RIFLES
5th Bn The Rifles	5 RIFLES

Territorial Army Bns

6th Bn The Rifles	6 RIFLES
7th Bn The Rifles	7 RIFLES

THE ROYAL IRISH REGIMENT

Regular Bn

1st Bn The Royal Irish Regiment	1 R IRISH

Territorial Army Bn

2nd Bn The Royal Irish Regiment	2 R IRISH

THE PARACHUTE REGIMENT

Regular Bns

1st Bn The Parachute Regiment	1 PARA
2nd Bn The Parachute Regiment	2 PARA
3rd Bn The Parachute Regiment	3 PARA

4th Bn The Parachute Regiment   4 PARA

Note: 1 PARA have formed the core element of the new Special Forces Support Group and as such have been removed from the formal Infantry structure.

THE BRIGADE OF GURKHAS

Regular Bns

1st Bn The Royal Gurkha Rifles   1 RGR

2nd Bn The Royal Gurkha Rifles   2 RGR

LOCATIONS

Regular Infantry Battalion Locations (2011)

1st Bn Grenadier Guards	Wellington Bks, London
1st Bn Coldstream Guards	New Mons Bks, Aldershot
1st Bn Scots Guards	Bourlon Bks, Catterick
1st Bn Irish Guards	Victoria Bks, Windsor
1st Bn Welsh Guards	Lille Bks, Aldershot
1st Bn The Royal Regiment of Scotland	Dreghorn Bks, Edinburgh, Scotland
2nd Bn The Royal Regiment of Scotland	Glencorse Bks, Edinburgh
3rd Bn The Royal Regiment of Scotland	Fort George, Inverness
4th Bn The Royal Regiment of Scotland	St Barbara Bks, Fallingbostel
5th Bn The Royal Regiment of Scotland	Howe Bks, Canterbury
1st Bn The Princess of Wales Royal Regiment	Barker Bks, Paderborn
2nd Bn The Princess of Wales Royal Regiment	Napier Lines, Woolwich
1st Bn The Royal Regiment of Fusiliers	Mooltan Bks, Tidworth
2nd Bn The Royal Regiment of Fusiliers	Trenchard Bks, Celle
1st Bn The Royal Anglian Regiment	Queen Elizabeth Bks, Pirbright
2nd Bn The Royal Anglian Regiment	Dhekelia, Cyprus
1st Bn The Duke of Lancaster's Regiment	Somme Bks, Catterick
2nd Bn The Duke of Lancaster's Regiment	Episkopi, Cyprus
1st Bn The Yorkshire Regiment	Oxford Bks, Munster
2nd Bn The Yorkshire Regiment	Weeton Bks, Preston
3rd Bn The Yorkshire Regiment	Battlesbury Bks, Warminster
1st Bn The Mercian Regiment	Marne Bks, Catterick
2nd Bn The Mercian Regiment	Palace Bks, Belfast
3rd Bn The Mercian Regiment	Lumsden Bks, Fallingbostel
1st Bn The Royal Welsh Regiment	The Dale,Chester
2nd Bn The Royal Welsh Regiment	Lucknow Bks, Tidworth
1st Bn The Rifles	Beachley Bks, Chepstow
2nd Bn The Rifles	Abercorn Bks, Ballykinler
3rd Bn The Rifles	Redford Bks, Edinburgh
4th Bn The Rifles	Kiwi Bks, Bulford
5th Bn The Rifles	Allanbrooke Bks, Paderborn
1st Bn The Royal Irish Regiment	Clive Bks, Tern Hill

2nd Bn The Parachute Regiment	Merville Bks, Colchester
3rd Bn The Parachute Regiment	Merville Bks, Colchester
1st Bn The Royal Gurkha Rifles	Sir John Moore Bks, Shorncliffe
2nd Bn The Royal Gurkha Rifles	Seria, Brunei

INFANTRY STRENGTH

During 2011 the total liability for all infantry personnel was 24,631 which compares with the 2001 liability of 26,740. In general about 90 per cent of infantry personnel are classified as deployable or 'Fit for Task' at any one time.

During an average year we would expect to see about 2,600 recruits joining the infantry. About 400 recruits would join the Guards Division, 2,000 joining the Line Regiments and about 200 joining the Parachute Regiment. In addition we would expect to see about 200 infantry officers leaving Sandhurst.

Force Operations and Readiness Mechanism (FORM)

All Army units, including Infantry Battalions, programme their training and operational commitment activities according to the principles of FORM. This system enables the Army to meet its outputs (force elements ready for both programmed operations and contingent operations/emergency deployments) from within the force structure. The sequence of activity for any one force element, such as an Infantry Battalion, is in five separate six month phases:

> Phase 1 – Recuperation
>
> Phase 2 – Mission specific training
>
> Phase 3 – Unit and battle group hybrid training (where all-arms integrate)
>
> Phase 4 – High readiness
>
> Phase 5 – An operational deployment

Operational units

As explained in Chapter 3, it would be unusual for the Infantry to fight as battalion units especially in armoured or mechanised formations. If the task is appropriate, the HQ of an infantry battalion will become the HQ of a 'battle group', and be provided with armour, artillery, engineers and possibly aviation to enable it to become a balanced Infantry Battle Group. Similarly Infantry Companies can be detached to HQs of Armoured Regiments to make up Armoured Battle Groups.

In the pages that follow, the groupings are based on Unit Establishment figures for peace support operations. For Warfighting a pairing mechanism operates which provides augmentation which allows a unit to meet its role. For example, an Armoured Infantry Regiment will receive additional Manoeuvre Support assets and another Rifle Company to reach its Warfighting Establishment (WFE) of 4 x Companies, 9 x Mortars and 18 x Medium Range Anti-Tank Guided Weapons (ATGW).

Types of Infantry Battalions

Infantry Battalion Armoured	Equipped with Warrior AFV
Infantry Battalion Mechanised	Equipped with Bulldog APC
Infantry Battalion Light Role	Equipped for General Service with protected vehicles
Infantry Battalion Air Assault	Equipped for Air Mobile Operations

Armoured Infantry Battalion

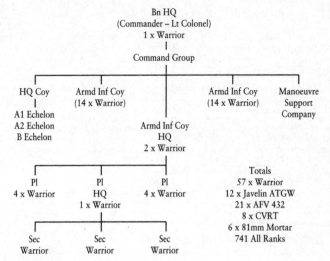

Bn HQ
(Commander – Lt Colonel)
1 x Warrior

Command Group

HQ Coy
A1 Echelon
A2 Echelon
B Echelon

Armd Inf Coy
(14 x Warrior)

Armd Inf Coy
HQ
2 x Warrior

Armd Inf Coy
(14 x Warrior)

Manoeuvre
Support
Company

Pl
4 x Warrior

Pl
HQ
1 x Warrior

Pl
4 x Warrior

Totals
57 x Warrior
12 x Javelin ATGW
21 x AFV 432
8 x CVRT
6 x 81mm Mortar
741 All Ranks

Sec
Warrior

Sec
Warrior

Sec
Warrior

Armoured Infantry Battalion – Manoeuvre Support Company

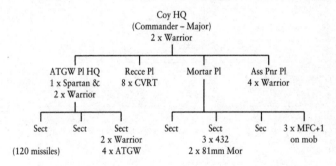

Coy HQ
(Commander – Major)
2 x Warrior

ATGW Pl HQ
1 x Spartan &
2 x Warrior

Recce Pl
8 x CVRT

Mortar Pl

Ass Pnr Pl
4 x Warrior

Sect

Sect

Sect
2 x Warrior
4 x ATGW

Sect

Sect
3 x 432
2 x 81mm Mor

Sec

3 x MFC+1
on mob

(120 missiles)

Mechanised Infantry Battalion

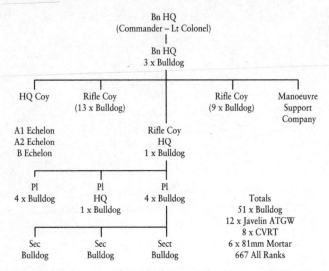

Mechanised Infantry Battalion – Manoeuvre Support Company

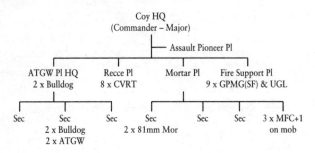

Light Role Infantry Battalion

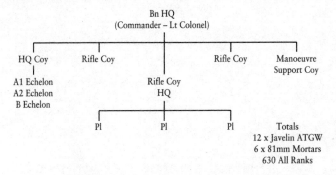

Note: A battalion of this type will usually be equipped with a range of protected vehicles.

Many battalions now have sniper platoons equipped with the Long Range Rifle that has an effective range of up to 1,100 m plus.

Light Role Infantry Battalion – Manoeuvre Support Company

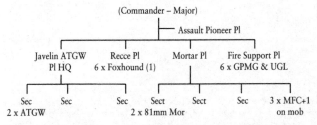

Notes: (1) Foxhound is a Light Protected Patrol Vehicle (LPPV) that should appear in service during 2011. (2) Air Assault Bns have an HMG Pl with 6 x .50 calibre machine guns mounted on TUM.

Platoon Organisation

The basic building bricks of the Infantry Battalion are the platoon and the section.

Under normal circumstances, the whole platoon with the exception of the LMG (Light Machine Gun) gunners are armed with IW – SA80 (Individual Weapon).

In an armoured or mechanised battalion, the platoon vehicles could be either Warrior or AFV 432.

Under normal circumstances expect a British infantry platoon to resemble the organisation in the following diagram:

Armoured or Mechanised Infantry Platoon
Platoon Commander (2/Lt or Lt)
Platoon Sergeant
Radio Operator
51 mm Mortar Operator

Mounted in Warrior or AFV 432 AIFV/APC

Section AIFV/APC	Section AIFV/APC	Section AIFV/APC
Fire Team	Fire Team	Fire Team
Sec Comd (Cpl)	Sec Comd	Sec Comd
Rifleman	Rifleman	Rifleman
Rifleman	Rifleman	Rifleman
LMG Gunner	LMG Gunner	LMG Gunner
Fire Team	Fire Team	Fire Team
Sec 2i/c	Sec 2i/c	Sec 2i/c (Lcpl)
Rifleman	Rifleman	Rifleman
Rifleman	Rifleman	Rifleman
LMG Gunner	LMG Gunner	LMG Gunner

Note: In addition to the above, infantry platoons deploying to Afghanistan have a range of other weapons and systems available to them. It would almost certainly be unwise to list these enhancements here while operations continue.

TA INFANTRY

The current TA Infantry structure has been organised to support and complement the regular regimental structure. There are 14 TA infantry battalions. These provide reinforcement of the regular infantry for up to 14 major units or, where necessary individual or smaller unit reinforcements.

In addition the TA Infantry Structure can provide the manpower to include up to seven Defence Troops for Armoured and Formation Reconnaissance Regiments committed to operations. Restructuring for TA infantry battalions has been conducted on the basis of a minimum of approximately 400 soldiers per battalion.

INFANTRY BATTALION STRENGTHS AGAINST ESTABLISHMENT (LATE 2010)

Division	Battalion	Establishment	Actual strength
Guards	1 Grenadier Guards	575	627
	1 Coldstream Guards	569	529
	1 Scots Guards	639	568
	1 Irish Guards	576	602
	1 Welsh Guards	568	548
Scots	1 Scots	573	523
	2 Scots	566	516
	3 Scots	575	483
	4 Scots	566	478

	5 Scots	591	556
Queens	1 Princess of Wales Royal Regiment	636	645
	2 Princess of Wales Royal Regiment	566	596
	1 Royal Regt Fusiliers	609	614
	2 Royal Regt Fusiliers	569	528
	1 Royal Anglian	609	622
	2 Royal Anglian	571	578
Kings	1 Lancs	609	603
	2 Lancs	555	606
	1 Yorks	571	532
	2 Yorks	566	492
	3 Yorks	637	547
Prince of Wales	1 Mercian	571	504
	2 Mercian	566	509
	3 Mercian	637	598
	1 Royal Welsh	565	520
	2 Royal Welsh	637	592
Rifles	1 Rifles	565	601
	2 Rifles	566	561
	3 Rifles	565	595
	4 Rifles	610	627
	5 Rifles	636	652
Royal Irish	1 Royal Irish	588	589
Para	2 Para	587	598
	3 Para	587	590

In addition to the battalions above, the Guards Division has three incremental companies to assist with public duties.

Company	Establishment	Actual Strength
Nijmegen Coy Grenadier Gds	106	106
7 Coy Coldstream Gds	106	99
F Coy Scots Guards	106	106

Note:
(1) The establishment figures refer to the number of posts within a battalion that may be filled by infantry personnel (officers and soldiers). It excludes posts that are filled by attached personnel of other Arms and Services such as cooks, clerks, etc. Establishments will also vary depending on the particular role of a battalion; for example, armoured infantry battalions have larger establishments than light role infantry battalions.
(2) Figures do not include Gurkhas.

INFANTRY WEAPONS

Javelin LF ATGW

Launch Unit: Weight 6.4 kg; Sight magnification x 4; Missile: Range 2,500 m; Weight 11.8 kg; Length 1.08 m; Seeker – Imaging infra-red; Guidance – Lock on before launch, automatic self-guidance; Missile – Two stage solid propellant with a tandem shaped charge; Weight of Launch unit and missile 22 kg.

The UK version of the US Javelin ATGW system, is a more sophisticated guided weapon with a range of some 2,500 m. A production contract was signed in early 2003 worth over £300 million. Industry sources suggest that up to 5,000 missiles and 300 firing posts were ordered. First deliveries to the UK were made in 2004 and the system has replaced Milan. In UK service Javelin has a number of modifications which include an enhanced Command Launch Unit (CLU) with a wider field of view, and the ability to recognise targets at longer ranges.

Although Javelin has been developed mainly to engage armoured fighting vehicles, the system can also be used to neutralise bunkers, buildings, and low-flying helicopters. Javelin's top-attack tandem warhead is claimed to defeat all known armour systems.

The US Army and Marine Corps have been using Javelin for some years and the system is either in service, or has been selected by Australia, Ireland, Jordan, Lithuania, New Zealand, and Taiwan. Over 7,000 Javelin launchers have been manufactured since 1995. Javelin is planned to be in UK service until 2025.

Figures suggest that in the 12 months to November 2009 some 580 missiles were fired. The cost of each missile is approximately £49,000.

MBT LAW

Max Range: 600 m; Weight 12.5 kg; Calibre 150 mm (warhead – top attack); Length 1016 mm; Guidance Predicted Line of Sight (PLOS).

MBT LAW (formerly NLAW) is a man-portable, short-range anti-armour weapon. It will provide a capability out to a range of 600 m, against main battle tanks and light armoured vehicles; have the ability to be fired from enclosed spaces and defensive positions and be a means of attack against personnel in structures.

The MBT LAW prime contractor is SAAB Bofors Dynamics of Sweden, with Thales Air Defence Ltd as the main UK sub-contractor. Deliveries began in December 2008 and the system replaces LAW 80 and the interim ILAW (Bofors AT-4). The final cost of the MBT LAW contract is in the order of £400 million.

The MBT LAW system has been developed in a collaborative programme with Sweden.

81 mm L16 Mortar

(340 in service including 100 SP) Max Range HE 5,650 m; Elevation 45 degrees to 80 degrees; Muzzle Velocity 255 m/s; Length of barrel 1280 mm; Weight of barrel 12.7 kg; Weight of base plate 11.6 kg; In action Weight 35.3 kg; Bomb Weight HE L3682 4.2 kg; Rate of Fire 15 rpm; Calibre 81 mm.

The 81mm Mortar is on issue to all infantry battalions, with each battalion having a mortar platoon with three or four sections; and each section deploying two mortars. These mortars are the battalion's organic Manoeuvre Support Firepower and can be used to put a heavy weight of fire down on an objective in an extremely short period. Mortar fire is particularly lethal to infantry in the open and in addition is very useful for neutralising dug-in strong points or forcing armour to close down.

The fire of each mortar section is controlled by the MFC (Mortar Fire Controller) who is usually an NCO and generally positioned well forward with the troops being supported. Most MFCs will find themselves either very close to or co-located with a Task Group Commander. The MFC informs the base plate (mortar position) by radio of the location of the target and then corrects the fall of the bombs, directing them onto the target.

Mortar fire can be used to suppress enemy positions until assaulting troops arrive within 200-300 m of the position. The mortar fire then lifts onto enemy counter attack and supporting positions while the assault goes in. The 81 mm Mortar can also assist with smoke and illuminating rounds.

The mortar is carried in an AFV432 or a Truck (Utility Light or Medium) and if necessary can be carried in two, man portable loads of 11.35 kg and one 12.28 kg respectively. In the past, infantry companies working in close country have carried one 81 mm round per man when operating in areas such as Borneo or Aden where wheeled or tracked transport was not available. For Air Mobile and Air Assault operations mortar rounds are issued in twin packs of two rounds per man on initial deployment. These are used as initial ammunition resources until further ammunition loads can be flown in.

The L16A2 81 mm Mortar has undergone a mid life upgrade (MLU) to embrace recent technological developments. The inclusion of the new SPGR (Specialised Personal GPS Receiver) and the LH40C (Laser) combine to make the new TLE (Target Locating Equipment). This generates a significant enhancement in first round accuracy and the ease, and speed with which accurate fire missions can be executed. Additionally, the equipment reduces the number of adjustment rounds which will be used and lead to greater dispersal of mortar barrels, thus increasing protection for the mortar crew soldiers. Plans continue to develop further synergies with The Royal Artillery to improve the existing levels of co-ordination between Artillery and Mortars in fighting the indirect fire battle.

Official figures suggest that in the 12 months to November 2009 some 145,600 81 mm mortar rounds were fired on operations and training. The cost of an 81 mm mortar round varies from between £190 – £890 dependent upon the type of round that is fired. In the main various types of high explosive (HE) and illuminating are used.

60 mm Light Mortar

Max Range 3,800 m; Barrel weight 5.3 kg; Bipod weight 12 kg; Base plate weight 4.8 kg.

Procured under an Urgent Operational Requirement (UOR) in 2007 the M6-895 60 mm Mortar provides the infantry with a light mortar capability out to almost 4 kms in both the direct and indirect fire roles. Capable of firing up to 12 rounds per minute the M6-895 has replaced the 51 mm Mortar in operational service.

Figures suggest that in the 12 months to November 2009 more than 3,500 60 mm mortar rounds were fired on operations and training. The cost of a 60 mm mortar round varies from between £185 – £640 dependent upon the type of round that is fired. In the main high explosive (HE) and illuminating rounds are used.

5.56 mm Individual Weapon (IW) (SA 80 and SA 80A2)

Effective Range 400m; Muzzle Velocity 940 m/s; Rate of Fire from 610-775 rpm; Weight 4.98 kg (with 30 round magazine); Length Overall 785 mm; Barrel Length 518 mm; Trigger Pull 3.12-4.5 kg.

Designed to fire the standard NATO 5.56 mm x 45 mm round, the SA 80 was fitted with an x4 telescopic (SUSAT) sight as standard. The total original buy for SA 80 was for 332,092 weapons. Issues of the weapon are believed to have been made as follows:

Royal Navy	7,864
Royal Marines	8,350
Royal Air Force	42,221
MoD Police	1,878
Army	271,779

At 1991/92 prices the total cost of the SA80 contract was in the order of £384.16 million. By late 1994 some 10,000 SA 80 Night Sights and 3rd Generation Image Intensifier Tubes for use with SA80 had been delivered.

The SA 80 had a mixed press and following some severe criticism of the weapons mechanical reliability the improved SA 80A2 was introduced into service during late 2001.

SA 80A2: Some 13 changes were made to the weapon's breech block, gas regulation, firing-pin, cartridge extractor, recoil springs, cylinder and gas plug, hammer, magazine and barrel. Since modification the weapon has been extensively trialled.

Mean time before failure (MTBF) figures from the firing trials for stoppages, following rounds fired are as follow:

	SA 80A2	LSW
UK (temperate)	31,500	16,000
Brunei (hot/wet)	31,500	9,600
Kuwait (hot/dry)	7,875	8,728
Alaska (cold/dry)	31,500	43,200

The first SA 80A2 were in operational service during early 2002 and these weapons were in service across the Army by late 2004. The cost of the programme was £92 million and some 200,000 weapons were modified by the time the programme ended in May 2006.

The SA80 A2 can be fitted with the Heckler and Koch 40 mm Underslung Grenade Launcher (UGL) which is generally issued on the scale of two per infantry section (or one per four man fire team). This allows an infantry section to lay down HE fragmentation munitions up 350 m in front of their position. With six UGL available to an infantry platoon there is a major enhancement to their operational effectiveness.

5.56mm Light Machine Gun (Minimi)

Effective range 800 m; Calibre 5.56 mm; Weight 7.1 kg; Length 914 mm; Feed 100-round disintegrating belt; Cyclic rate of fire 700 to 1000 rounds per minute.

FN Herstal's Minimi belt fed 5.56mm Light Machine Gun (LMG), has entered service on a scale of one per four-man fire team. The Minimi has been used operationally by British troops in Afghanistan and Iraq and the UK MoD has bought 2,472 weapons. The contract which will boost the firepower within infantry sections was believed to have been completed in late 2007.

The Minimi is in service with the Australian, Canadian and New Zealand Armies as well as the US Armed Forces.

7.62 mm General Purpose Machine Gun (GPMG)

(11,300 in service) Range 800 (Light Role) l,800 m (Sustained Fire Role); Muzzle Velocity 538 m/s; Length 1.23 m; Weight loaded 13.85 kg (gun + 50 rounds); Belt Fed; Rate of Fire up to 750 rpm; Rate of Fire Light Role 100 rpm; Rate of Fire Sustained Fire Role 200 rpm.

An infantry machine gun that has been in service since the early 1960s, the GPMG can be used in the light role fired from a bipod or can be fitted to a tripod for use in the sustained fire role. The gun is also found pintle-mounted on many armoured vehicles. Used on a tripod the gun is effective out to 1,800 m although it is difficult to spot strike at this range because the tracer rounds in the ammunition belt burns out at 1,100 m.

Machine Gun platoons in air assault battalions remain equipped with the GPMG in the sustained fire role. GPMG performance has recently been enhanced by the issue of a Maxi Kite night image intensification sight giving excellent visibility out to 600 m. The GPMG is due to be withdrawn from service in 2015.

12.7 mm Heavy Machine Gun (HMG)

Effective range – up to 2000 m; Calibre 12.7 mm; Weight 38.15 kg (gun only); Length: 1,656 mm; Barrel Length 1,143 mm; Muzzle Velocity 915 m/s; Cyclic rate of fire – 485 – 635 rounds per minute.

The 12.7 mm Heavy Machine Gun (HMG) is an updated version of the Browning M2 'Fifty-cal' – generally recognised as one of the best heavy machine guns ever developed. Currently, the HMG provides integral close-range support from a ground mount tripod or fitted to a Land Rover TUM using a Weapon Mount Installation Kit (WMIK) and a variety of sighting systems. The performance of the HMG has recently been enhanced with a new 'soft mount' (to limit recoil and improve accuracy) and a quick change barrel.

Long Range Rifle (LRR)

(580 available) Effective range 1,100 m plus; Weight 6.8 kg; Calibre 8.59 mm; Muzzle velocity 936 m/s; Length 1,300 mm; Feed 5-round box.

The SA 80 is designed to shoot accurately out to 300 m and be easily handled in combat situations. With the disappearance of the Enfield .303 during the early 1960s the skill of shooting accurately above 400 m has largely died away. The 7.62 Sniper Rifle filled the gap for a while but the vulnerability of the round to wind deflection over longer ranges made it desirable to come up with a weapon which could be fired with some precision in all phases of modern warfare.

The result has been the development by Accuracy International UK of the 8.59 mm (.338) Long Range Large Calibre Rifle L115A3 capable of shooting accurately out to 1100 m and beyond depending on atmospheric conditions. The weapon has been issued to JRRF (Joint Rapid Reaction Force) units on the basis of 14 per battalion, with one per platoon and a small pool for snipers in the battalion recce platoons. The LRR entered service in early 2000.

Reports suggest that in November 2009 a British Army sniper operating near Musa Qala in Afghanistan using a L115A3 rifle shot two Taliban machine gunners at a range of 2,475 m.

Grenade Machine Gun (GMG)

This is a 40 mm high explosive grenade weapon that has a range of up to 1.5 km for point targets and about 2 kms for neutralising/suppressing area targets. Capable of firing up to 340 rounds per minute it is usually mounted on TUM/Land Rover type or Protected Vehicles because of the problems associated with carrying large amounts of ammunition.

CHAPTER 8 – ARTILLERY

BACKGROUND

The Royal Regiment of Artillery (RA) provides the battlefield fire support and air defence for the British Army in the field. Its various regiments are equipped for conventional fire support using field guns, for area and point air defence using air defence missiles and for specialised artillery locating tasks.

The RA remains one of the larger organisations in the British Army with 15 Regiments included in its regular Order of Battle. Early 2011 personnel figures suggest that the RA had a personnel figure of 7,710 officers and soldiers representing just over 100% of its establishment strength.

Before SDSR restructuring, in late 2011 the RA had the following structure in both the UK and Germany.

	UK	Germany
Field Regiments (AS 90 SP Guns)	3	2
Field Regiments (Light Gun)	3 (1)	–
Depth Fire Regiments (GMLRS)	1 (2)	–
Air Defence Regiments (Rapier)	1	–
Air Defence Regiment (HVM)	1	–
Surveillance & Target Acquisition Regiment	1	–
UAV Regiment	2	–
Training Regiment (School Assets Regt)	1	–
The Kings Troop (Ceremonial)	1	–

Note:

(1) Of these three Regiments, one is a Commando Regiment (29 Cdo Regt) and another is an Air Assault Regiment (7 PARA RHA). Either of these Regiments can be called upon to provide Manoeuvre Support Artillery to the AMF (Allied Command Europe Military Force).

(2) A second GMLRS Regiment is now a TA Regt with 12 Launch vehicles in peace uprateable to 18 in war.

(3) Although the artillery is organised into Regiments, much of the Gunner's loyalty is directed towards the battery in which they serve. The guns represent the Regimental Colours of the Artillery and it is around the batteries where the guns are held that history has gathered. A Regiment will generally have three or four gun batteries under command.

(4) The Schools Asset Regiment is not included in the totals given for artillery in Chapter 1.

The Royal Horse Artillery (RHA) is also part of the Royal Regiment of Artillery and its regiments have been included in the totals above. There is considerable cross posting of officers and soldiers from the RA to the RHA, and some consider service with the RHA to be a career advancement.

CURRENT ORGANISATION

In mid 2011 the operational roles of the Regular Regiments of the Royal Artillery were as follows:

Regiment	Role
1 Regiment RHA	155 mm AS 90
3 Regiment RHA	155 mm AS 90
4 Regiment RA	155 mm AS 90
5 Regiment RA	STA & Special Ops (1)
7 (Parachute Regiment) RHA	105 mm Light Gun
12 Regiment RA	HVM & UAV
14 Regiment RA	All School Equipments

16 Regiment RA	Rapier
19 Regiment RA	155 mm AS 90
26 Regiment RA	155 mm AS 90
29 Commando Regiment RA	105 mm Light Gun (2)
32 Regiment RA	UAVs
39 Regiment RA	GMLRS
40 Regiment RA	105 mm Light Gun
47 Regiment RA	UAV
The King's Troop RHA	13-Pounders (Ceremonial)

Notes:

(1) STA – Surveillance and target acquistion.

(2) The Regimental HQ of 29 Commando Regiment with one battery is at Plymouth. The other two batteries are at Arbroath and Poole. Those at Poole provide the amphibious warfare Naval Gunfire Support Officers (NGSFO).

(3) All Regiments equipped mainly with 155 mm AS 90 now have the ability to deploy on operations using the 105 mm Light Gun.

(4) Following the 2010 SDSR there will be considerable changes to the operational roles of many of the above Regiments. Details are awaited.

Royal Artillery Locations (early 2011)

Regiment	*Location*
1 Regiment Royal Horse Artillery	Assaye Barracks, Hampshire
3 Regiment Royal Horse Artillery	Caen Barracks, Hohne
4 Regiment Royal Horse Artillery	Alanbrooke Barracks, Topcliffe
5 Regiment Royal Artillery	Marne Barracks, Catterick
7 (Parachute) Regiment Royal Horse Artillery	Merville Barracks, Colchester
12 Regiment Royal Artillery	Baker Barracks, Hampshire
14 Regiment Royal Artillery	Royal Artillery Barracks, Larkhill
16 Regiment Royal Artillery	St Georges Barracks, North Luffenham
19 Regiment Royal Artillery	Bhurtpore Barracks, Tidworth
26 Regiment Royal Artillery	Mansergh Barracks, Gutersloh
29 (Commando) Regiment Royal Artillery	RHQ 8, 23,79 Batterys, Plymouth
32 Regiment Royal Artillery	Roberts Barracks, Larkhill
39 Regiment Royal Artillery	Albemarle Barracks, Newcastle-Upon-Tyne
40 Regiment Royal Artillery	Thiepval Barracks, Lisburn
47 Regiment Royal Artillery	Baker Barracks, Thorney Island
The King's Troop Royal Horse Artillery	Ordnance Hill, St Johns Wood, London

Note: There are plans for the King's Troop to re-locate at the Artillery Barracks in Woolwich.

TA ARTILLERY

Under the TA Restructuring plans announced in March 2006 the 7x Royal Artillery TA Regiments was restructured as follows:

1 x Observation Post Regiment

1 x STA/MLRS Regiment

1 x Unmanned Air Vehicle/General Support Regiment

1 x Ground Based Air Defence Regiment (HVM)

3 x Close Support Regiments (105 mm Light Gun)

TA Artillery Regiment	Role
HAC	STA and Special Ops
100 Regiment RA (V)	Light Gun
101 Regiment RA (V)	STA/GMLRS
103 Regiment RA (V)	Light Gun
104 Regiment RA (V)	UAVs
105 Regiment RA (V)	Light Gun
106 Regiment RA (V)	HVM

TA Artillery Regimental Locations

Honourable Artillery Company	Finsbury Barracks, London
100th (Yeomanry) Regiment Royal Artillery (Volunteers)	RHQ/201 Bty RA(V), TA Centre, Luton
101st (Northumbrian) Regiment Royal Artillery (Volunteers)	RHQ, Napier Armoury, Gateshead
103rd (Lancashire Artillery Volunteers) Regiment Royal Artillery (Volunteers)	RHQ, Jubilee Barracks, St Helens
104th Regiment Royal Artillery (Volunteers)	Raglan Barracks, South Wales
105th Regiment Royal Artillery (Volunteers)	RHQ, Artillery House, Edinburgh
106th (Yeomanry) Regiment Royal Artillery (Volunteers)	Napier House, Grove Park, London
Central Volunteers Headquarters Royal Artillery and Headquarters Woolwich Station	Royal Artillery Barracks, Woolwich

Training

Artillery recruits spend the first period of recruit training (Phase 1 Training, Common Military Syllabus) at the Army Training Regiment – Pirbright, the Army Training Regiment –Bassingbourn or the Army Foundation College – Harrogate.

Artillery training (Phase 2) is carried out at the Royal School of Artillery (RSA) at Larkhill in Wiltshire. During Phase 2 intensive training is given in gunnery, air defence, surveillance or signals. Soldiers also undergo driver training on a variety of different vehicles. After Phase 2 training officers and gunners will be posted to RA units worldwide, but almost all of them will return to the RSA for frequent career and (Phase 3) employment courses.

ARTILLERY FIRE SUPPORT

The Royal Artillery provides the modern British formation with a protective covering on the battlefield. The close air defence assets cover the immediate airspace above and around the formation, with the artillery assets reaching out to over 50 kms in front, and 60 kms across the flanks of the formation being supported. A formation that moves out of this protective covering is open to immediate destruction by an intelligent enemy.

An armoured or mechanised division has it own artillery under command. This artillery usually consists of three Close Support Regiments, with a number of units detached from the Corps Artillery and could include TA reinforcements from the UK. In war the composition of the DAG will vary from division to division according to the task. The following is a reasonable example of the possible organisation for a DAG.

Armoured Divisional Artillery Group (DAG) – Organisation for War

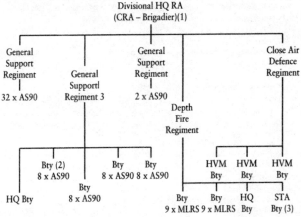

Notes:

(1) This is a diagram of the artillery support which may typically be available to a UK Division deployed with the ARRC. Expect each brigade in the division to have one Close Support Regiment with AS 90. Artillery regiments are commanded by a Lieutenant Colonel and a battery is commanded by a Major.

(2) The number of batteries and guns per battery in an AS 90 Close Support Regiment has changed post SDR 1999 at four batteries of six guns per battery in the UK Regiments, and three batteries of six in the Regiments stationed in Germany. In war plans are for all batteries to have eight guns. AS 90 Regiments now train with 105 mm Light Guns prior to deployment on operations in Iraq or Afghanistan. Following the 2010 SDSR we expect the number of AS90 batterys to be further reduced.

(3) The locating Battery in the Depth Fire Regiment may have a metrological troop with BMETS, a radar troop and a UAV troop. For some operations the radar and UAV component may be enhanced.

(4) Area Air Defence (AAD) is provided by Rapier.

(5) The staff of a UK division includes a Brigadier of Artillery known as the Commander Royal Artillery (CRA). The CRA acts as the Offensive Support Advisor to the Divisional Commander, and could normally assign one of his Close Support Regiments to support each of the Brigades in the division. These regiments would be situated in positions that would allow all of their batteries to fire across the complete divisional front. Therefore, in the very best case, a battlegroup under extreme threat could be supported by the fire of more than 128 guns.

The term Offensive Support Group is the term used when units other than artillery provide fire support:

Artillery Fire Missions

A square brigade (of two infantry battalions and two armoured regiments) will probably have a Close Support Regiment of four batteries in support, and the CO of this regiment will act as the Offensive Support Advisor to the Brigade Commander.

It would be usual to expect that each of the four Battlegroups in the brigade would have a Battery Commander acting as the Offensive Support Advisor to the Battlegroup Commander.

Squadron/Company Groups in the Battlegroup would each be provided with a Forward Observation Officer (FOO), who is responsible for fire planning and directing the fire of the guns onto the target. The FOO and his party travel in equivalent vehicles to the supported troops to enable them to keep up with the formation being supported and are usually in contact with:

(a) The Gun Positions

(b) The Battery Commander at BGHQ

(c) The Regimental Fire Direction Centre

(d) The Company Group being supported.

Having identified and applied prioritisation of targets, the FOO will call for fire from the guns, and he will then adjust the fall of shot to cover the target area. The FOO will be assisted in this task by the use of a Warrior FCLV OP vehicle containing the computerised fire control equipment which provides accurate data of the target location.

Given a vehicle with its surveillance and target acquisition suite the FOO can almost instantly obtain the correct grid of the target and without calling for corrections, order 'one round fire for effect'.

ARTILLERY SYSTEMS

AS 90

(146 available): Crew 5; Length 9.07 m; Width 3.3 m; Height 3.0 m overall; Ground Clearance 0.41 m; Turret Ring Diameter 2.7 m; Armour 17 mm; Calibre 155 mm; Range (39 cal) 24.7 kms (52 cal) 30 kms; Recoil Length 780 mm; Rate of Fire 3 rounds in 10 secs (burst) 6 rounds per minute (intense) 2 rounds per minute (sustained); Secondary Armament 7.62 mm MG; Traverse 6,400 mills; Elevation -89/+1.244 mills; Ammunition Carried 48 x 155 mm projectiles and charges (31 turret & 17 hull); Engine Cumminis VTA903T turbo-charged V8 diesel 660 hp; Max Speed 53 kph; Gradient 60%; Vertical Obstacle 0.75 m; Trench Crossing 2.8 m; Fording Depth 1.5 m; Road Range 420 kms.

AS 90 was manufactured by Vickers Shipbuilding and Engineering (VSEL) at Barrow in Furness. 179 guns were delivered under a fixed price contract for £300 million that started in 1993. These 179 guns completely equipped six field regiments replacing the older 120 mm Abbot and 155 mm M109 in British service. At.the beginning of 2005 three of these Regiments were under the command of 1(UK) Division in Germany and three under the command of 3 (UK) Division in the United Kingdom.

AS 90 equipped with a 39 calibre gun fires the NATO L15 unassisted projectile out to a range of 24.7 kms (Base Bleed ERA range is 30 kms). Funding is available for the re-barreling of 96 x AS 90 with a 52 calibre gun with ranges of 30 kms (unassisted) and 60 to 80 kms with improved accuracy and long range ERA ammunition. However, due to the current inability of the selected bi-modular charge system to meet the requirement for insensitive munitions this program is on hold.

AS 90 has been fitted with an autonomous navigation and gunlaying system (AGLS), enabling it to work independently of external sighting references. Central to the system is an inertial dynamic reference unit (DRU) taken from the US Army's MAPS (Modular Azimuth Positioning System). The bulk of the turret electronics are housed in the Turret Control Computer (TCC) which controls the main turret functions, including gunlaying, magazine control, loading systems control, power distribution and testing.

Artillery has always been a cost effective way of destroying or neutralising targets. When the cost of a battery of guns, (approx £20 million) is compared with the cost of a close air support aircraft, (£40 million) and the cost of training each pilot, (£4 million +) the way ahead for governments with less and less to spend on defence is clear.

105 mm Light Gun

(Approximately 142 available) Crew 6; Weight 1,858 kg; Length 8.8 m; Width 1.78 m; Height 21.3 m; Ammunition HE, HEAT, WP, Smoke, Illuminating, Target Marking; Maximum Range (HE) 17.2 kms; Anti Tank Range 800 m; Muzzle Velocity 709m/s; Shell Weight HE 15.1 kg; Rate of Fire 6 rounds per minute.

The 105 mm Light Gun has been in service with the Royal Artillery for over 30 years, and has received one major upgrade in that time. The enhancement is an Auto Pointing System (APS) which performs the same function as the DRU on the AS 90. The APS is based on an inertial navigation system that enables it to be unhooked and into action in 30 seconds. The APS replaces the traditional dial sight and takes into account trunion tilt without the requirement to level any spirit level bubbles as before.

A touch screen display tells the gun controller when his gun is laid onto the correct target data provided. This enhancement improves the accuracy of the fall of shot to a greater degree of accuracy than possible with the dial sight.

The Light Gun is in service with three regular Artillery Regiments and three TA Artillery Regiments as a go-anywhere, airportable weapon which can be carried around the battlefield underslung on a Puma or Chinook. In addition artillery units deployed to Afghanistan can be equipped with the Light Gun

The gun was first delivered to the British Army in 1975 when it replaced the 105 mm Pack Howitzer. A robust, reliable system, the Light Gun proved its worth in the Falklands, where guns were sometimes firing up to 400 rounds per day. Since then the gun has seen operational service in Kuwait, Bosnia, Afghanistan and Iraq.

During March 2005 the UK MoD placed a contract for an advanced and more effective light artillery shell. This contract for 105 mm Improved Ammunition awarded to BAE Systems led to an initial buy of 50,000 High Explosive shells, and was worth around £17 million.

The new High Explosive munitions are more effective against a range of targets than current shells and incorporate the latest Insensitive Munitions (IM) technology, making them even safer to transport and handle. Under the programme, planned deliveries commenced late in 2006 and will be spread over three years, with possible future buys until 2017.

The Light Gun has been extremely successful in the international market with sales to Australia (59), Botswana (6), Brunei (6), Ireland (12), Kenya (40), Malawi (12), Malaysia (20), Morocco (36), New Zealand (34), Oman (39), Switzerland (6), UAE (50), United States (548) and Zimbabwe (12).

227 mm MLRS/GMLRS

(59 launchers available – 54 operational) Crew 3; Weight loaded 24,756 kg; Weight Unloaded 19,573 kg; Length 7.167 m; Width 2.97 m; Height (stowed) 2.57 m; Height (max elevation) 5.92 m; Ground Clearance 0.43 m; Max Road Speed 64 kph; Road Range 480 km; Fuel Capacity 617 litres; Fording 1.02 m; Vertical Obstacle 0.76 m; Engine Cummings VTA-903 turbo-charged 8 cylinder diesel developing 500 bhp at 2,300 rpm; Rocket Diameter 227 mm; Rocket Length 3.93 m; M77 Bomblet Rocket Weight 302.5 kg; AT2 SCATMIN Rocket Weight 254.46 kg; M77 Bomblet Range 11.5 –32 kms; AT2 SCATMIN Rocket Range 39 kms; One round 'Fire for Effect' equals one launcher firing 12 rockets; Ammunition Carried 12 rounds (ready to fire).

The MLRS launch vehicle is based on the US M2 Bradley (M270) chassis and the system is self loaded with 2 x rocket pod containers, each containing 6 x rockets. The M270 vehicle has a crew of three.

The whole loading sequence is power assisted and loading takes between 20 and 40 minutes. There is no manual procedure. Currently (2011) the MLRS vehicle is used operationally to fire the GMRLS rocket.

Armed with a 200 lb (90 kg) high explosive warhead which carries a payload of 404 Dual Purpose Improved Conventional Munition (DPICM), the improved missile can engage more targets with a lower risk of collateral damage and with a smaller logistical burden.

GMLRS rockets contain Global Positioning System (GPS) elements and the latest advanced computer technology giving them accuracy out to a range of up to 70 kms. The pin-point GMLRS rocket accuracy means that distant targets can be neutralised with a single round. Use of conventional artillery on a similar target would have required the use of a number of guns firing multiple rounds.

The overall programme is worth over £250 million and will see the UK take delivery of several thousand rockets during the next five years. The GMLRS rocket has been developed by a five-nation collaboration of the UK, France Germany, Italy and the US.

Following a series of successful trials the Guided Multiple Rocket Launch System (GMLRS) was declared fit for deployment with UK troops in Afghanistan in mid 2007. Between December 2008 and November 2009 approximately 410 GMLRS rockets were fired on operations in Afghanistan.

There is currently (mid 2011) one Regular and one TA MLRS Regiment. The Regular Regiment operates 18 launcher vehicles and the TA Regiment 12 in peace and 18 in war.

The US Army is currently operating 830 MLRS, the French have 58, the West Germans 154 and the Italians 21.

Starstreak HVM

84 Fire Units on Stormer and 145 on Light Mobile Launcher available; Missile Length 1.39 m; Missile Diameter 0.27m; Missile Speed Mach 3+; Maximum Range 5.5 kms.

Short Missile Systems of Belfast were the prime contractors for the HVM (High Velocity Missile) which continues along the development path of both Blowpipe and Javelin. The system can be shoulder launched by mounting on the LML (lightweight multiple launcher) or vehicle borne on the Alvis Stormer APC. The Stormer APC has an eight round launcher and 12 reload missiles can be carried inside the vehicle.

HVM has been optimised to counter threats from fast pop-up type strikes by attack helicopters and low flying aircraft. The missile employs a system of three dart type projectiles which can make multiple hits on the target. Each of these darts has an explosive warhead. It is believed that the HVM has an SSK (single shot to kill) probability of over 95%.

Under a £72 million contract the HVM Thermal Sighting System (TSS) was procured to enable the HVM to have the capability to operate at night, through cloud or in poor visibility. Some 84 x TSS are believed to have entered service with first units having been equipped during late 2006.

12 Regiment RA is equipped with HVM and there is 1 x TA Artillery Regiment similarly scaled. On mobilisation, 12 Regiment is believed to be configured as follows:

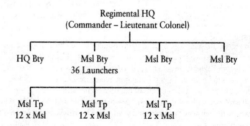

Note: On mobilisation, an HVM Regiment can have up to 108 launchers divided amongst the three missile batteries. An HVM detachment of four personnel is carried in a Stormer armoured vehicle and in each vehicle there are twelve ready to use missiles with a further eight stored inside as reloads.

Rapier (FS'C')

(24 fire units available – possibly 24 in service) Guidance Semi Automatic to Line of Sight (SACLOS); Missile Diameter 13.3 cm; Missile Length 2.35 m; Rocket Solid Fuelled; Warhead High Explosive; Launch Weight 42 kg; Speed Mach 2+; Ceiling 3,000 m; Maximum Range 6,800 m; Fire Unit Height 2.13 m; Fire Unit Weight 1,227 kg; Radar Height (in action) 3.37 m; Radar Weight 1,186 kg; Optical Tracker Height 1.54 m; Optical Tracker Weight 119 kg; Generator Weight 243 kg; Generator Height 0.91 m.

The Rapier system provides area 24 hour through cloud, Low Level Air Defence (LLAD) over the battlefield. The two forms of Rapier in service are as follows:-

Rapier Field standard C (FSC) incorporates a range of technological improvements over its predecessor including an advanced three dimensional radar tracker acquisition system designed by Plessey. The towed system launcher mounts eight missiles (able to fire two simultaneously) which are manufactured in two warhead versions. One of these is a proximity explosive round and the other a kinetic energy round. The total cost of the Rapier (FSC) programme is £1,886 million.

The UK's Rapier air defence capability is held within 16 Regiment Royal Artillery and the capability of 16 Regiment has been enhanced by the creation of a fourth battery. The possible configuration of 16 Regiment on mobilisation will then be four batteries each of two troops with three fire units per troop.

In July 2004 the MoD announced the disbandment of the RAF Regiment Rapier squadrons.

Rapier in all of its versions has now been sold to the armed forces of at least 14 nations. We believe that sales have amounted to over 25,000 missiles, 600 launchers and about 350 radars.

MSTAR

Weight 30 kg; Wavelength J – Band; Range in excess of 20 kms.

MSTAR is a Lightweight Pulse Doppler J – Band All Weather Radar that has replaced the ZB 298 in the detection of helicopters, vehicles and infantry. Powered by a standard army field battery this radar will also assist the artillery observer in detecting the fall of shot. The electroluminescent display that shows dead ground relief and target track history, also has the ability to superimpose a map grid at the 1:50000 scale to ease transfer to military maps. MSTAR can be vehicle borne or broken down into three easily transportable loads for manpacking purposes.

MSTAR is used by Forward Observation Officers. There are believed to be around 100 MAOV (Warrior Mechanised Artillery Observation Vehicles) equipped with MSTAR. MSTAR was believed to cost about £50,000 pounds per unit at mid 1999 prices and in total about 200 MSTAR equipments are in service throughout the British Army.

COBRA

Cobra (Counter Battery Radar) is a 3-D Phased Array Radar that has been developed for West Germany, France and the UK. Cobra came into service with 5 Regt RA in mid 1999. The dominant cost element of the Cobra Radar is the antenna, which probably accounts for about 70% of the unit price. There are believed to be about 20,000 Gallium Arsenide integrated circuits in each antenna. This enables the equipment to produce the locations of multiple enemy artillery at extremely long ranges, and the radar is able to cope with saturation type bombardments. In addition there is a high degree of automated software, with high speed circuitry and secure data transmission to escape detection from enemy electronic countermeasures.

Cobra therefore appears to be an ideal equipment for operation in conjunction with long range artillery assets. 5 Regt is believed to field three Cobra Troops, each Troop consisting of three radars.

MAMBA – Mobile Artillery Monitoring Battlefield Radar (Ericsson ARTHUR)

(possibly 12 available)

In service with 5 Regiment this is an artillery hunting radar which was deployed operationally for the first time in April 2002. MAMBA automatically detects, locates and classifies artillery, rockets and mortars and carries out threat assessment based on weapon or impact position. All acquired data is automatically transmitted to a combat control centre. The equipment also incorporates its own basic command, control and communications system for direct control of counter-battery fire. The contract value is believed to be in the region of £30 million.

Mamba's detection range is 20 km (howitzer) and 30 km (rockets) with a circular error probable (CEP) of around 30 m at extreme range. The system can locate a maximum of eight targets simultaneously.

The system, which is mounted on a tracked vehicle is easily transportable by aircraft or helicopters. Reports from operational areas suggest that this system has been extremely successful.

Sound Ranging

Sound Ranging (SR) locates the positions of enemy artillery from the sound of their guns firing. Microphones are positioned on a line extending over a couple of kilometres to approximately 12 kilometres. As each microphone detects the sound of enemy guns firing, the information is relayed to a Command Post which computes the location of the enemy battery. Enemy locations are then passed to Artillery Intelligence and counter battery tasks fired as necessary. Sound Ranging can identify an enemy position to within 50 m at 10 kms. The only Sound Ranging assets remaining in the Royal Artillery are those with 5 Regt RA at Catterick.

The UK has one battery equipped with Mark 2 HALO ASP (advanced sound ranging system), an acoustic weapons locating equipment specifically for use in out of area or sensitive operations where flying UAVs might be sensitive. The ASP system was deployed in March 2003 and is expected to be in-service until 2017.

BMETS

The Battlefield Meteorological System BMETS came into service in 1999 and replaces AMETS which entered service in 1972 and provided met messages in NATO format. However, with AMETS there was only one system for each division resulting in a high radius of data application and the system was vulnerable because it used an active radar.

With the extreme range of modern artillery and battlefield missiles, very precise calculations regarding wind and air density are needed to ensure that the target is accurately engaged. BMETS units can provide this information by releasing hydrogen filled balloons at regular intervals recording important information on weather conditions at various levels of the atmosphere.

To benefit from current technology BMETS uses commercially available equipment manufactured by VAISALA linked to the Battlefield Artillery Target Engagement System (BATES). It is a two vehicle system with a detachment of five in peace, six in war. It is deployed with all regular field artillery and MLRS regiments.

BMETS can operate in all possible theatres of conflict worldwide where the Meteorological Datum Plain (MDP) varies from 90 m below to 4,000 m above sea level, and can be used with a variety of radiosonde types to sound the atmosphere to a height of up to 20 km. Measurements are made by an ascending radiosonde. This is tracked by a passive radiotheodolite which provides wind data, air temperature, atmospheric pressure and relative humidity from the datum plan for each sounding level, until flight termination. In addition virtual temperature, ballistic temperature and ballistic density are calculated to a high degree of accuracy. Cloud base is estimated by observation. The data is then processed by receiver equipment in the troop vehicles to provide formatted messages to user fire units via the existing military battlefield computer network.

Air Defence Alerting Device (ADAD)

An infra-red thermal imaging surveillance system that is used by close air defence units to detect hostile aircraft and helicopter targets and directs weapon systems into the target area. The air defence missile operators can be alerted to up to four targets in a priority order. This passive system which is built by Thorn EMI has an all weather, day and night capability

Artillery Training Ammunition

Costs of Artillery Training Ammunition During Financial Year 2010-2011

Ammunition type	Quantity
Round 14.5MM Artillery Training Charge 2 L2A1	12,809
Shell 105MM FD HE L31A4 Fuzed L106A4 W/Cart Normal L35A3	15,325
Shell 105MM FD HE L31A4 Fuzed L116A1 W/Cart Normal L35A3	792
Shell 105MM FD BE SMK SCR L52A1 FZD L132A1 W/Cart Nor L35A3	4,189
Shell 105MM FD Illuminating L43A4 Fuzed L132A1	1,683
Cartridge Propelling 105MM FD Normal L35A3	371
Shell 155MM HE L21A2 Plugged	872
Charge Propelling 155MM M3A1	907
Charge Propelling 155MM L8A2 Charge 3 to 7	98
Charge Propelling 155MM L10A2 Charge 8	238
Shell 155MM Smoke BE DM105A2 Fuzed L132A1	58
Shell 155MM Illuminating DM106A2 Fuzed L132A1	34
Shell 155MM Practice Inert L17A3 with PRF	102
Fuze Nose Percussion Direct Action and Graze L106A4	907
Primer Percussion DM191A2	337
Primer Percussion M82	907
MLRS Reduced Range Practice Rocket L1A2	86

Total Cost   £26,618,743

Note: During the Financial Year 2009-2010 £19,611,296 was spent on artillery training ammunition.

UNMANNED AIR VEHICLES

Watchkeeper TUAS

(Possibly 54 on order); Take off weight 450 kg; Wingspan 10.51 m; Fuselage length 6.10 m; Max speed 175 kph; Operational ceiling 5,000 m plus; Endurance – more than 20 hours; Payload 150 kg.

In July 2005 a £800 million contract was awarded to Thales to provide the Royal Artillery with a Tactical Unmanned Air System (TUAS) named Watchkeeper designed for all weather, Intelligence, Surveillance, Target Acquisition and Reconnaissance (ISTAR) use.

The Watchkeeper UAV capability is part of the UK's plans for a Network Enabled Capability that will provide UK commanders with accurate, timely and high quality information, including imagery. Watchkeeper will be fully integrated into the wider command and control digitised network, passing data quickly to those who need it via a satellite datalink to a network of ground control stations, where the imagery will be analysed and disseminated.

Watchkeeper will be operated and deployed by 32 and 47 Regiments Royal Artillery to meet the information requirements of HQ Land Manoeuvre Commanders with first aircraft in service during 2011.

Watchkeeper is based on the Elbit Hermes 450 UAV design and each aircraft is believed to cost about £15 million.

Watchkeeper appears to have completely replaced the older Phoenix UAV system in UK Army service.

Desert Hawk

Desert Hawk is a small and portable UAV surveillance system which provides aerial video reconnaissance. It has a flight time of approximately one hour, and can fly almost anywhere within a 10 km radius of its ground control station. Desert Hawk weighs 3.2 kg, has a length of 0.86 m and a wingspan of 1.32 m. The system can be used for a variety of tasks, such as force protection for convoys and patrols, route clearance, base security, reconnaissance or target tracking. It has both day and night time (thermal imaging) capability.

Total acquisition costs of the Desert Hawk UAVs are believed to be about £36 million.and there are 176 Desert Hawk III airframes in service. Another 100 airframes are on order.

Desert Hawk has an extremely good record over the last two years supporting UK forces in Afghanistan.

UAV OPERATED BY THE ROYAL AIR FORCE

MQ-9 Reaper

5 Aircraft available: Operated by one pilot and one sensor operator; Length 11m; Wingspan 20m; Weight 1,676kg(empty); 4,760kg (max); Operational Altitude 25,00ft; Endurance 16-28hrs; Range 3,682 miles; Payload 4,200lb; Max Speed 400km/h/250mph; Cruise Speed 160km/h/100mph; Engines 670 kW Honeywell TP331-10 turboprop; Armament 6 x hardpoints under the wings, can carry a payload mix of 1,500 lb (680 kg) on each of its two inboard weapons stations, 500–600 lb (230–270 kg) on the two middle stations and 150–200 lb (68–91 kg) on the outboard stations. Up to 14 x AGM-114 Hellfire air to ground missiles can be carried or four Hellfire missiles and two 500 lb (230 kg) GBU-12 Paveway II laser-guided bombs. The ability to carry the JDAM in the future is also possible, as well is the AIM 9X, Air to Air missile.

Unmanned air vehicles are growing in importance and the RAF formed 39 Sqn at Creech Air Force Base in Nevada in Jan 2007 to operate US-owned Predator/Reaper aircraft. The UK has purchased a number of Reaper aircraft in support of UK ground forces in operational theatres. Reaper provides real-time video imagery to ground commanders, and has the capability to attack ground targets if required.

On operations Reaper is launched from an airfield in Afghanistan by RAF personnel and as soon as the aircraft is airborne it comes under the operation control of the 39 Squadron mission group in Nevada via their secure communications link.. At the conclusion of the mission control is handed back to the ground crew in Afghanistan who land the aircraft and prepare it for the next mission.

Between October 2007 and October 2010 Reaper had flown 1,344 operational sorties in Afghanistan during which time 84 Hellfire missiles and 36 laser guided bombs had been expended.

During May 2011 the MoD announced the formation of a second Reaper Squadron and an intention for Reaper to be controlled from within the UK. XIII Squadron will be formed in 2012 and based at RAF Waddington and the RAF Reaper strength increased to 10 aircraft. £135 million has been allocated for the purchase of five aircraft and four ground stations.

Project Taranis

The RAF has also taken the first step towards developing its own pilotless combat aircraft. Project "Taranis" was announced in 2010 and a demonstrator is due to fly at Woomera, Australia during late 2011 to evaluate how UCAS (Unmanned Combat Air Systems) will contribute to the RAF's future mix of aircraft.

The demonstrator is believed to be the size of a BAe Hawk, weigh about 8 tons and will be configured for reconnaissance and attack missions. Some analysts believe that a system developed from Project Taranis could be operational by 2018-2020.

Taranis will be one of the world's largest UAV demonstrators and will integrate stealth technology around an intelligent, autonomous system.

CHAPTER 9 – ARMY AVIATION

AVIATION SUPPORT

Battlefield helicopters have played a major role in UK military operations since the 1960s. The Army Air Corps battlefield helicopter fleet has accumulated a vast amount of operational experience in recent years, and is arguably a more capable force than that possessed by any other European nation.

The flexibility of battlefield helicopters was demonstrated in 2003 during Operation TELIC in Iraq. Here 3 Regiment, Army Air Corps, with two Pumas from the Support Helicopter Force attached, was deployed forward as a combined-arms battle group, initially within 16 Air Assault Brigade and later in conjunction with 7 Armoured Brigade. The battle group had responsibility for an area that extended over 6,000 square kilometres, and provided a versatile combat arm during the warfighting phase. In the immediate aftermath of hostilities, helicopters proved to be the most efficient means of covering the vast operational area allocated to British forces, and also in distributing humanitarian aid to isolated villages. Helicopters remain one of the most important military assets available in the current campaign in Afghanistan and AAC helicopters were in action in Libya during 2011.

FORCE STRUCTURE

The Army obtains its aviation support from Army Air Corps (AAC), which is an organisation with eight separate regiments and a number of independent squadrons and flights.

AAC manpower is believed to number some 2,100 personnel of all ranks, including about 500 officers. Unlike the all-officer Navy and Air Force helicopter pilot establishments, almost two-thirds of AAC aircrew are non-commissioned officers. The AAC is supported by REME and RLC personnel numbering some 2,600 all ranks. Total AAC-related manpower is believed to be around 4,600 personnel of all ranks.

With certain exceptions, during peace, all battlefield helicopters come under the authority of the Joint Helicopter Command (JHC).

The introduction into AAC service of the WAH-64D Apache Longbow attack helicopter is transforming AAC doctrine, organisation, and order of battle. The British Army designation of the type is Apache AH Mk1 and approximately 48 aircraft are concentrated in two Attack Regiments. These are 3 and 4 Regts at Wattisham in Suffolk.

Each attack regiment is believed to have 3 x attack squadrons equipped with 8 x Apache AH Mk1.

Current (2011) AAC Regimental and Squadron locations are shown below.

Army Air Corps force structure and helicopters during early 2007

Regiment	Squadron	Location	Helicopter/ aircraft	Fleet (estimate)
1 Regiment	652, 661	Germany	Lynx	16
2 (Trg) Regiment	676, 668	Middle Wallop and support	Ground training	–
3 Attack Regiment	653, 662 & 663	Wattisham	Apache	24
4 Attack Regiment	654, 664 & 656	Wattisham	Apache	24
5 Regiment	651, 665	Aldergrove	Gazelle	8
6 Regiment (V)	655, 677	Bury St Edmunds	Support	n/a
7 (Training) Regiment	670, 671, 673	Middle Wallop	Squirrel, Gazelle, Lynx, Bell 212, Apache	20
9 Regiment	672, 659, 669	Dishforth	Lynx	24
Independent units				
Joint Special Forces Aviation Wing	657	Odiham	Lynx	12
Development & Trials	667	Middle Wallop	All types	Variable

Flights include 3 (TA) Flight (Leuchars), 6 (TA) Flight (Shawbury), 7 Flight (Brunei), 8 Flight (Hereford), 12 Flight (Germany), 25 Flight (UK Trg Support), 29 BATUS Flight – Canada

The AAC Centre at Middle Wallop in Hampshire acts as a focal point for all Army Aviation, and it is here that the majority of corps training is carried out. Although the AAC operates some fixed-wing aircraft for training and liaison flying, the main effort goes into providing helicopter support for the land forces. About 300 AAC helicopters are believed to be in operational service in late 2011.

Employment of Army Aviation

Following significant development during World War II, Army Aviation formally joined the Army order of battle in the early 1950s. Since then its place on the battlefield has developed rapidly as an integral element of the Army's manoeuvre forces. The introduction of attack helicopters clearly identifies the shift of emphasis from combat support towards the combat role, particularly within air manoeuvre operations, and establishes the AAC as the sixth combat arm of the British Army. However, despite this changing emphasis, the Army also has a continuing essential requirement for army aviation to provide both combat support and combat service support roles.

THE AVIATION MISSION

Combat Aviation: To find, fix and strike, either independently, or as the lead element, or as a constituent of combined arms groupings, throughout the depth of the battlefield and the 24 hour battle, and throughout the full spectrum of operations.

Combat Support Aviation: To provide enabling capabilities for combined arms operations, throughout the depth of the battlefield and the 24 hour battle, and throughout the full spectrum of operations.

ROLES OF ARMY AVIATION

In a Combat Role: To conduct air manoeuvre using direct fire and manoeuvre, as part of the land battle component.

In a Combat Support Role: To provide ISTAR (intelligence, surveillance, target acquisition and reconnaissance) as a collection asset in its own right or potentially as a platform for other sensors, including ECM (electronic countermeasures): NBC (nuclear, chemical and biological) reconnaissance: ESM (electronic support measures): radar and other electronic systems.

Other tasks may include:

- To provide direction of fire support (ground/air/maritime/special forces).
- To provide mobility for combat forces.
- To assist in command and control, including acting as airborne command posts.
- To provide a limited extraction capability.

In a Combat Service Support Role: To provide movement for personnel and materiel including casualty evacuation (CASEVAC).

JOINT HELICOPTER COMMAND (JHC)

The majority of AAC helicopters are assigned to the Joint Helicopter Command. The primary role of the JHC is to deliver and sustain effective Battlefield Helicopter and Air Assault assets, operationally capable under all environmental conditions, in order to support the UK's defence missions and tasks. Major formations under JHC command are as follows:

- All Army Aviation Units
- RAF Support Helicopter Force
- Commando Helicopter Force
- Joint Helicopter Force (Northern Ireland)

- 16 Air Assault Brigade
- Combat Support Units
- Combat Service Support Units
- Joint Helicopter Command and Standards Wing

There is more detail regarding the JHC in Chapter 13 – Joint Forces

AAC ORGANISATION

We would expect an AAC Regiment to be organised on the lines shown in the diagrams below.

Army Air Corps – Attack Regiment

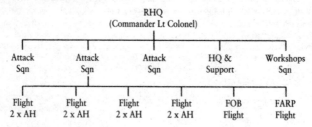

Total: 24 x AH (Attack Helicopters)

Note: FOB – Forward Operating Base: FARP- Forward Arming and Refuelling Point.

Army Air Corps – Divisional Aviation Regiment

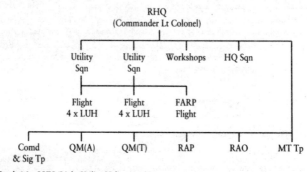

Total: 16 x LUH (Light Utility Helicopters)

Future Helicopter Fleet Requirements

A recent MoD report identified the future helicopter fleet requirements for Army mission tasks under three contingency levels, as shown in the table.

all-scale _contingency_	_Medium-scale_ _contingency_	_Large-scale_ _Contingency_
34	36	48
44	65	110
78	101	158

ARMY AVIATION TRAINING

The School of Army Aviation at Middle Wallop in Hampshire trains Army pilots using the Army's front line aircraft, the Gazelle, the Lynx and the Apache AH Mk 1. It also trains soldiers to support these aircraft on the ground, to protect their operating bases, to provide communications between the ground and aircraft, and to arm and refuel them. The training activity is divided into ground training and flying training.

Ground training is conducted by 2 Regiment AAC and consists of:

> Phase 2 training to provide special to arm training for recruits on completion of their basic training at the Army Training Regiment, and,

> Phase 3 training to provide career progress courses for trained soldiers.

Flying training is conducted by 7 Regiment and consists of:

> Army Flying Grading

> Operational Training Phase of the Army Pilots Course

> Conversion to the Army Air Corps operational aircraft

The AAC Centre at Middle Wallop is under the ownership of the Army Training and Recruitment Agency (ATRA). There is also a detachment of 132 Aviation Support Squadron, Royal Logistics Corps, which comes under the Joint Helicopter Command, based at the AAC Centre. The Headquarters of the Director of Army Aviation is also based at Middle Wallop. There may be up to 12 Attack Helicopters allocated to the School of Army Aviation for training purposes at any one time.

HQ DAAvn (Director Army Aviation) is responsible for providing advice and support on Army Aviation and AAC training matters. In this regard HQ DAAvn is responsible for the training policy for both aircrew and ground crew. The School of Army Aviation (SAAvn) undertakes AAC Special-to-Arm training. AAC Soldier Basic Training takes place at ATR Pirbright.

The AAC recruits pilots from three main sources:

> Direct Entry (Officers only)

> The ranks of the AAC (Corporals and above)

> Officers and soldiers from other arms and branches of the Service (Corporal and above)

Officers join the Corps after completing the Commissioning course at the Royal Military Academy Sandhurst. Unlike the all-officer Navy and Air Force helicopter pilot establishments, almost two-thirds of AAC aircrew are non-commissioned officers. Within the Army, NCOs, of at least LCpl rank with a recommendation for promotion, from within the AAC and from the remainder of the Army may also apply for pilot training. NCO pilots spend the majority of their service flying and many go on to be commissioned as Officers, normally to fill specialist flying appointments such as flying instructors.

There are three phases to selection for Army pilot training:

Aircrew Selection tests are conducted at RAF College Cranwell. These tests are common to the three Services and last two days. Army candidates require a minimum aircrew aptitude score of 80/180 to progress onto the next phase. RAF/RN require higher scores, but the Army is able to accept a lower score at this point, as Army candidates also have to pass Army Flying Grading which the ~~~~ considers a far more accurate indicator of potential to be an Army pilot.

Army Flying Grading (AFG) is conducted at Middle Wallop. This consists of 13 hours, over a three week period, in a Slingsby Firefly 160. The aim of this course is to test aptitude in a live flying environment and to identify whether students have the capability to become an Army pilot.

Students who have successfully demonstrated the necessary flying potential at AFG will progress onto the final phase at the Pilot Selection Centre. This is run by HQ SAAvn and selection includes aptitude tests, a medical, and finally a selection interview.

FLYING TRAINING

There are several stages in AAC flying training.

Groundschool

The Army Flying Course starts with four weeks of groundschool instruction at RAF College Cranwell. Students learn the basic building blocks of aviation – such as Meteorology, Principles of Flight, Aircraft Operations, Navigation and Technical instruction.

Elementary Flying Training (EFT)

EFT is the first element of Army Flying Training at RAF Barkston Heath. This phase consists of 40 flying hours of elementary fixed- wing flying training over 14 weeks on the Slingsby Firefly (260).

Aeromedical and Survival Training

After EFT, students complete a week of aeromedical and survival training at RNAS Yeovilton, Lee-on-Solent and Plymouth.

Defence Helicopter Flying School

The Defence Helicopter Flying School (DHFS) at RAF Shawbury provides basic single-engine helicopter training for the three Services and some overseas countries. The DHFS also provides advanced twin-engine helicopter training for RAF aircrew and other special courses for the three Services.

At the DHFS, much of the training effort is contracted out to FBS Ltd – a consortium of Flight Refuelling Aviation, Bristow Helicopters Ltd and Serco Defence. All DHFS military and civilian instructors are trained by the Central Flying School (Helicopter) Squadron. The single-engine basic flying course incorporates some 36 flying hours over nine weeks on the Squirrel helicopter with the instructors of No 660 Squadron. Army students complete nine weeks training before they leave to start their Operational Training Phase at Middle Wallop.

Operational Training Phase (OTP)

The penultimate phase is conducted at the School of Army Aviation at Middle Wallop. Training is focused on converting helicopter pilots into Army pilots. It starts with a week of tactics training, preparing students for the military part of the course. The OTP phase involves 82 flying hours in 18 weeks, and is conducted on the Squirrel helicopter.

Conversion to Type (CTT)

The final phase is conducted at the School of Army Aviation at Middle Wallop. Before being posted to a regiment, students have to convert onto an operational helicopter type. The Conversion to Type (CTT) course takes around nine weeks. At Middle Wallop, Apache aircrew and ground crew training is conducted by Aviation Training International Limited (ATIL).

CDS - *General Sir David Richards (Crown Copyright/MoD 2011)*

CGS - *General Sir Peter Wall (Crown Copyright/MoD 2011)*

SACEUR – *Admiral Stavridis (NATO 2010)*

Challenger 2 (Crown Copyright/MoD 2011)

Warrior Infantry Fighting Vehicle (Copyright BAe Systems)

Bulldog FV 430 Mk 3 (Crown Copyright/MoD 2011)

Fuchs NBC Reconnaissance vehicle (Crown Copyright/ MoD 2011)

Spartan coming ashore (Crown Copyright/MoD 2011)

Scimitar (Public domain US Government)

Panther CLV (Copyright BAe Systems)

Jackal (Crown Copyright/MoD 2011)

Mastiff 2 vehicles in convoy (Crown Copyright/MoD 2011)

Husky (GNU free documentation/Mattias Kabel)

Warthog all terrain vehicle (Crown Copyright/MoD 2011)

Foxhound LPPV (Crown Copyright/MoD 2011)

Ulan - Austrian ASCOD (GNU free documentation/Mattias Kabel)

Javelin firing (Copyright Eros Hoagland/The Rifles)

81 mm Mortar firing illuminating rounds (Crown Copyright/MoD 2011)

SA 80 being used on exercise (Crown Copyright/MoD 2011)

GPMG (Copyright Eros Hoagland/The Rifles)

Heavy machine gun mounted on a tripod (Copyright John Pearson)

L115 Long Range Rifle (Copyright John Pearson)

AS 90 (Copyright BAe Systems)

GMLRS firing during acceptance trials (Crown Copyright/MoD 2011)

105 mm Light Gun (Copyright BAe Systems)

Starstreak mounted on Stormer (Copyright Thales UK Ltd)

Rapier firing (Copyright BAE Systems)

Watchkeeper (Copyright Thales UK Ltd)

Reaper of 39 Sqn RAF at Kandahar (Crown Copyright/MoD 2011)

Desert Hawk being launched in Afghanistan (Crown Copyright/MoD 2011)

Taranis during flight (Copyright BAe Systems)

Apache (Copyright Augusta/Westland)

AAC Lynx operating in Afghanistan (Crown Copyright/MoD 2011)

RAF Puma (Crown Copyright/MoD 2011)

Chinook (Copyright Alasdair Taylor)

Merlin (Copyright Alasdair Taylor)

RAF C-130 (Crown Copyright/MoD 2011)

A400M (Copyright Airbus Military 2010)

Terrier with fascines (Copyright BAe Systems)

Trojan minefield breaching system (Copyright BAe Systems)

Shielder on Alvis Stormer (Free License – Davric)

Help for Heroes fundraisers 'doing their bit' at Wembley Stadium in 2010

Children 'doing their bit' for Help for Heroes in South London

A junior London Pearly Queen 'doing her bit'.

Conversion to Role (CTR)

Once a pilot has been converted onto type at Middle Wallop, he or she will proceed to a Regiment. At the Regiment a special CTR course will be held to bring the pilot up to combat ready status.

HELICOPTER CREWS

Although this information is now a little dated it is retained as being a reasonable background source. In mid 2006 the number of actual and required helicopter crew personnel for each regular regiment of the AAC was as follows:

Regiment	Helicopter Crew Established (Required)	Helicopter Crew Held (Actual)
1 Regt AAC	60	54
3 Regt AAC	85	57
4 Regt AAC	85	63
5 Regt AAC	93 (31 from 1 Apr 2007)	64
9 Regt AAC	85	69

These figures include qualified helicopter instructors and regimental headquarters personnel, whose primary role is not as helicopter crew. The figures do not include aviation crewmen, such as air door gunners and winch operators. The established figure for 5 Regiment AAC reduced to 31 on 1 April 2007, as part of the planned reductions in Northern Ireland. The deficits shown in the table in 3, 4 and 9 AAC Regiments are mainly due to the re-roling of these regiments to Apache helicopters. As a consequence of re-roling, some aircrew are posted away for re-training.

AAC AIRCRAFT

Apache (AH Mk1)

(67 ordered and delivered) Gross Mission Weight 7,746 kgs (17,077 lb); Cruise Speed at 500 m 272 kph; Maximum Range (Internal Fuel with 20 minute reserve) 462 kms; General Service Ceiling 3,505 metres (11,500 ft); Crew 2; Carries – 16 x Hellfire II missiles (range 6,000 metres approx); 76 x 2.75" CRV-7 rockets; 1,200 30mm cannon rounds; 4 x Air-to-Air Missiles; Engines 2 x Rolls Royce RTM-332.

The UK MoD ordered 67 Apache based on the US Army AH-64D manufactured by Boeing in 1995. Boeing built the first eight aircraft, and partially assembled the other 59. The UK Westland helicopter company undertook final assembly, flight testing and programme support at their Yeovil factory. Full operating capability for all three Apache Attack Regiments was achieved in mid 2007 and in UK service the aircraft is known as the AH Mk1.

We believe that there are 48 in-service aircraft in two regiments (each of 24 aircraft). The remaining aircraft will be used for trials, training and a war maintenance reserve (WMR). The Apache is flown on operations by 3 and 4 Regiments Army Air Corps, based at Wattisham in Suffolk and these two units have provided a continuous presence in Afghanistan since 2006 on rotation.

The Apache can operate in all weathers, day or night, and can detect, classify and prioritise up to 256 potential targets at a time. Apart from the 'Longbow' mast-mounted fire control radar, the aircraft is equipped with a 127 x magnification TV system, 36 x magnification thermal imaging, and 18 x magnification direct view optics. The missile system incorporates Semi-Active Laser and Radio Frequency versions of the Hellfire missile, whose range is at least 6 kms. Apart from the Rolls-Royce engines, specific British Army requirements include a secure communications suite and a Helicopter Integrated Defensive Aids System (HIDAS). Programme cost is some £3 billion.

It is believed that an air-to-air weapon capability will continue to be investigated and trials of the Shorts Starstreak missile onboard an AH-64 have continued in the US. Any longer term decision to proceed will be based on the results of these US Army trials.

The estimated cost (full funded – includes forward and depth servicing, fuel costs, crew costs, training costs etc)) for an Apache flying hour is £42,000. The marginal cost or direct running cost for one hour (most of which are fuel costs) is £5,000.

In May 2011 the UK MoD announced that UK Apache helicopters had achieved a total of 100,000 flying hours, a third of which have been flown on operations in Afghanistan .

There is no doubt that Apache has emerged as a vital battlefield asset on operations in Afghanistan . As well as pinpoint strikes in support of ground forces, Apache has proved itself invaluable through its ability to escort other helicopters (especially on CASEVAC missions), provide top cover for land convoys and ISTAR (Intelligence, Surveillance, Target Acquisition and Reconnaissance) capabilities.

Currently (mid 2011) AAC Apache helicopters are operating against ground targets in Libya from HMS Ocean on station in the Mediterranean.

Apache provides the British Army with an essential element of the 'punch' necessary for operations during the next decade.

Hellfire Missile

Weight 46 kg; Diameter 17.8 cm; Wingspan 33 cm; Length 1163 cm; Warhead HEAT (High explosive ant-tank); Guidance Semi-active laser homing with millimetre wave radar seeker.

The Hellfire missile has shown itself to be a remarkably successful weapon system for Apache attack helicopter operations, proving to be an accurate and reliable and providing airborne fire support to ground forces.

Hellfire Missiles fired by Apache January 2009 – December 2010

	Number of missiles fired
January 2008 – December 2008	151
January 2009 – December 2009	164
January 2010 – December 2010	128

Note: Includes training and operational expenditure.

Lynx AH – Mark 7/9

(Approximately 77 x AH Mark 7 and 22 AH Mark 9 available) Length Fuselage 12.06 m; Height 3.4 m; Rotor Diameter 12.8 m; Max Speed 330 kph; Cruising Speed 232 kph; Range 885 km; Engines 2 Rolls-Royce Gem 41; Power 2 x 850 bhp; Fuel Capacity 918 litres (internal); Weight (max take off) 4,763 kg; Crew one pilot, one air-gunner/observer; Armament 8 x TOW Anti-Tank Missiles; 2-4 7.62 mm machine guns; Passengers-able to carry 10 PAX; Combat radius approximately 100 kms with 2 hour loiter.

Until the introduction of Apache, Lynx was the helicopter used by the British Army to counter the threat posed by enemy armoured formations. Armed with 8 x TOW missiles the Lynx was the mainstay of the British armed helicopter fleet.

With the introduction into service of the Apache AH Mk 1 Lynx is now only used as a utility helicopter providing fire support using machine guns, troop lifts, casualty evacuation and many more vital support battlefield tasks.

Although the total Lynx inventory is 112 aircraft we believe that there are currently 99 available (77 Lynx Mark 7 and 22 Lynx Mark 9).

Lynx will start to be withdrawn from service in 2015 when it should be replaced by Lynx Wildcat.

Lynx Wildcat

Currently (early 2011) the UK MoD has 62 x Lynx Wildcat helicopters on order from Augusta Westland. Of these, 34 x Lynx Wildcat (Army variant) are due to be delivered incrementally between 2012 and 2016, with the remaining 28 x Lynx Wildcat (Naval variant) being delivered between 2013 and 2017.

Lynx Wildcat will incorporate a range of technological improvements including: configurable cockpit display, networked enabled capability, more powerful engines, better defensive aids and a new tail rotor system. Technology improvements mean that the aircraft will have greater reliability, resulting in significant reductions to support and maintenance costs over life of the aircraft which will stay in service for 30 years.

Lynx Wildcat should be available for deployment to theatre in 2015. The Lynx Wildcat contract is believed to be £1.221 billion.

Gazelle

(Approx 115 available) Fuselage Length 9.53 m; Height 3.18 m; Rotor Diameter 10.5 m; Maximum Speed 265 kph; Cruising Speed 233 kph; Range 670 km; Engine Turbomeca/Rolls-Royce Astazou 111N; Power 592 shp; Fuel Capacity 445 litres; Weight 1,800 kg (max take off); Armament 2 x 7.62 mm machine guns (not a standard fitting).

Gazelle is the general purpose helicopter in use by the AAC, and it is capable of carrying out a variety of battlefield roles. Gazelle is a French design built under licence by Westland Aircraft. It is equipped with a Ferranti AF 532 stabilised, magnifying observation aid. The fleet is now some 30 years old and due to be withdrawn progressively by 2018 – being replaced by the Wildcat Lynx and possibly some leased aircraft.

RAF Support

The second agency that provides aviation support for the Army is the Royal Air Force. In general terms, the RAF provides helicopters that are capable of moving troops and equipment around the battlefield, and fixed-wing fighter ground attack (FGA) aircraft that provide close air support to the troops in the vicinity of the Forward Edge of the Battlefield Area (FEBA). The RAF also provides the heavy air transport aircraft that will move men and material from one theatre of operations to another. In general terms, the RAF support available is as follows:

RAF SUPPORT HELICOPTERS

Squadron	Aircraft	Location
7 Squadron	11 x Chinook	Odiham
18 Squadron	11 x Chinook	Odiham
27 Squadron	10 x Chinook	Odiham
28 Squadron	14 x Merlin	Benson
33 Squadron	15 x Puma HC1	Benson
78 Squadron	14 x Merlin HC3	Benson
230 Squadron	12 x Puma HC1	Aldergrove

All the above aircraft are under the control of the Joint Helicopter Command (JHC).

Puma

(28 being upgraded to HC2 standard) Crew 2 or 3; Fuselage Length 14.06 m; Width 3.50 m; Height 4.38 m; Weight (empty) 3,615 kg; Maximum Take Off Weight 7,400 kgs; Cruising Speed 258 km/ph (192 mph); Service Ceiling 4,800 m; Range 550 kms; 2 x Turbomeca Turmo 111C4 turbines.

Following the retirement of the last Wessex in 2003, the Puma is now the oldest helicopter in RAF service. The 'package deal' between the UK and France on helicopter collaboration dates back to

February 1967. The programme covered the development of three helicopter types – the Puma, Gazelle and Lynx. Production of the aircraft was shared between the two countries, the UK making about 20% by value of the airframe, slightly less for the engine, as well as assembling the aircraft procured for the RAF. Deliveries of the RAF Pumas started in 1971. Capable of many operational roles, Puma can carry 16 fully equipped troops, or 20 at light scales. In the casualty evacuation role (CASEVAC), six stretchers and six sitting cases can be carried. Underslung loads of up to 3,200 kg can be transported over short distances and an infantry battalion can be moved using 34 Puma lifts. 41 x RAF Puma helicopters received an avionics upgrade between 1994 and1998.

A contract was signed with Eurocopter UK in September 2009 for the Puma Life Extension Programme. In addition a contract was placed with Turbomeca for the supply of new Makila engines. This includes the one-off costs associated with developing the required modifications and undertaking the trials activity necessary to certify the aircraft; the provision of initial support and conversion training for aircrew and maintainers; and the cost of modifying each helicopter. The total value of contracts placed in support of the Puma Life Extension Programme is £347 million.

Following the Puma Life Extension Programme the Puma HC2 aircraft should be capable of remaining in service until 2022.

Chinook

(40 available – 34 x HC2 and 6 x HC2A) Crew 3; Fuselage Length 15.54 m; Width 3.78 m; Height 5.68 m; Weight (empty) 10,814 kgs; Internal Payload 8,164 kgs; Rotor Diameter 18.29 m; Cruising Speed 270 km/ph (158 mph); Service Ceiling 4,270 m; Mission Radius (with internal and external load of 20,000 kgs including fuel and crew) 55 kms; Rear Loading Ramp Height 1.98 m; Rear Loading Ramp Width 2.31 m; Engines 2 x Avco Lycoming T55-L11E turboshafts.

The Chinook is a tandem-rotored, twin-engined medium-lift helicopter and the first aircraft entered service with the RAF in 1982. It has a crew of four (pilot, navigator and two crewmen) and is capable of carrying 54 fully equipped troops or a variety of heavy loads up to approximately 10 tons. The triple hook system allows greater flexibility in load carrying and enables some loads to be carried faster and with greater stability. In the ferry configuration with internally mounted fuel tanks, the Chinook's range is over 1,600 km (1,000 miles). In the medical evacuation role the aircraft can carry 24 stretchers.

RAF Chinook aircraft were upgraded to the HC2 standard between 1993 and 1996 for some £145 million. The HC2 upgrade modified the RAF Chinooks to the US CH-47D standard. New equipment included infra-red jammers, missile approach warning indicators, chaff and flare dispensers, a long-range fuel system, and machine gun mountings. In 1995, the UK MoD purchased a further 14 x Chinooks (6 x HC2 and 8 x HC3) for £240 million.

During 2003 the Chinook Night Enhancement Package (NEP) was installed in the HC2 fleet. The NEP was based upon experience gained during operations in Afghanistan in 2001 and allows Chinook aircraft to operate at night and in very low-light conditions, often at the limit of their capabilities.

HC2 aircraft are due to be phased out during 2015 and HC2A aircraft in 2025.

It would appear that the HC3 aircraft never entered operational service.

During early 2011 it was announced that the MoD was in discussion with Boeing in preparation for the main investment decision point for the 12 new and two replacement HC6 Chinooks announced during the 2010 SDSR.

Merlin HC3

(28 available) Crew 4; Capacity up to 24 combat-equipped troops, or 16 stretchers and a medical team, or 4 tonnes of cargo (2.5 tonnes as an underslung load). Length 22.81m; Rotor Diameter 18.59m; Max Speed 309k/ph (192mph); Engine 3 x Rolls Royce/Turbomeca RTM 322 turboshafts.

The EH101 Merlin Mk 3 is the newest RAF helicopter, the RAF having ordered an initial 22 x EH101 (Merlin) support helicopters for £755m in March 1995. Merlin is a direct replacement for the Westland Wessex, and it operates alongside the Puma and Chinook in the medium-lift role. Its ability to carry troops, artillery pieces, light vehicles and bulk loads, means that the aircraft is ideal for use with the UK Army's 16 Air Assault Brigade. Deliveries took place between 2000-2002.

The aircraft can carry a load of 24-28 troops with support weapons. The maximum payload is 4,000 kg and Merlin has a maximum range of 1,000km, which can be extended by external tanks or by air-to-air refuelling. The Merlin Mk 3 has sophisticated defensive aids, and the aircraft is designed to operate in extreme conditions with corrosion-proofing for maritime operations. All weather, day/night precision delivery is possible because of GPS navigation, a forward-looking infra-red sensor and night vision goggle compatibility. In the longer term, the aircraft could be fitted with a nose turret fitted mounting a .50 calibre machine gun.

During March 2007 the UK MoD announced the acquisition of 6 x additional Merlin Mk 3a from Denmark. These aircraft were able to support operations in Afghanistan from 2009.

RAF Merlin aircraft are due to be phased out of service in 2030.

RAF TRANSPORT AIRCRAFT

C-130 Hercules

24 Squadron	9 x Hercules	Lyneham
30 Squadron	9 x Hercules	Lyneham
47 Squadron	9 x Hercules	Lyneham
70 Squadron	8 x Hercules	Lyneham

The LTW (Lyneham Transport Wing) appears to have a total of 35 (11 x K and 24 x J versions) aircraft, none of the aircraft carry squadron markings. The squadron totals are given as a guide to what we believe are the average aircraft figures per squadron at any one time.

Hercules C-130K

Crew 5/6; Capacity 92 troops or 64 paratroops or 74 medical litters; Max freight capacity 43,399lb/19,685kg; Length C1 29.79m C3 34.69m; Span 40.41m; Height 11.66m; Weight Empty 34,287kg; Max All-up Weight 45,093kg; Max speed 374 mph/602 kph; Service Ceiling 13,075m; Engines 4 x Allison T-56A-15 turboprops.

C-130J (differences from the K version) Crew: 2 Pilots and 1 Loadmaster; Engines: Four Allison AE 2100D3 turboprops; Max speed; 355kts Range: 3,700 nautical miles; Max altitude: 32,000ft; Length: 34.34 m; Span: 40.38m.

The C-130 Hercules is the workhorse of the RAF transport fleet. Over the years it has proved to be a versatile and rugged aircraft, primarily intended for tactical operations including troop carrying, parachuting, supply dropping and aeromedical duties. The Hercules can operate from short unprepared airstrips, but also possesses the endurance to mount-long range strategic lifts if required. The aircraft is a derivative of the C-130E used by the United States Air Force, but is fitted with British Avionic equipment, a roller-conveyor system for heavy air-drops and with more powerful engines. The crew of five (K version) includes, pilot, co-pilot, navigator, air engineer and air loadmaster.

As a troop carrier, the Hercules can carry 92 fully armed men, while for airborne operations 64 paratroops can be dispatched in two simultaneous "sticks" through the fuselage side doors. Alternatively, 40 paratroops can jump from the rear loading ramp. As an air ambulance the aircraft can accommodate 74 stretchers. Freight loads that can be parachuted from the aircraft include. 16 x 1 ton containers or 4 x 8,000 pound platforms or 2 x 16,000 pound platforms or 1 x platform of 30,000 pounds plus. Amongst the many combinations of military loads that can be carried in an air-landed operation are. 3 x Ferret scout cars plus 30 passengers or 2 x Land Rovers and 30 passengers or 2 x Gazelle helicopters.

Of the original 66 C1 aircraft, some 31 were given a fuselage stretch producing the Mark C3. The C3 "stretched version" provides an additional 37% more cargo space. Refuelling probes have been fitted above the cockpit of both variants and some have received radar warning pods under the wing tips. This is known as the Hercules K and it would appear that 14 remain in service.

Hercules C-130J C4/C5

The RAF has replaced some of its Hercules K C1/C3 aircraft with second-generation C-130Js (C4/C5)on a one-for-one basis. Twenty-five Hercules C4 and C5 aircraft were ordered in December 94, and the first entered service in 2000. Deliveries were completed by 2003 at a total cost of just over £1bn.The C4 is the same size as the older Hercules C3 which features a fuselage lengthened by 4.57 m (15ft 0 in) than the original C1. The Hercules C5 is the new equivalent of the shorter model. With a flight deck crew of two plus one loadmaster, the C-130J can carry up to 128 infantry, 92 paratroops, 8 pallets or 24 CDS bundles. The Hercules C4/C5s have new Allison turboprop engines, R391 6-bladed composite propellers and a Full Authority Digital Engine Control (FADEC). This propulsion system increases take-off thrust by 29% and is 15% more efficient. Consequently, there is no longer a requirement for the external tanks to be fitted. An entirely revised 'glass' flight deck with head-up displays (HUD) and 4 multi-function displays (MFD) replacing many of the dials of the original aircraft. These displays are compatible with night-vision goggles (NVG). MoD figures suggest that there are 24 Hercules J in service.

VC-10

(11 in service) Crew 4; Carries 150 passengers or 78 medical litters; Height 12.04 m; Span 44.55 m ; Length 48.36 m; Max Speed (425 mph); Range 7596 kms; All Up Operational Weight 146,513 kgs; Engines 4 x Rolls Royce Conway turbofans.

The VC-10 is a fast transport aircraft which is the backbone of Strike Command's long-range capability, providing flexibility and speed of deployment for British Forces. This multi-purpose aircraft can be operated in the troop transport, freight and aeromedical roles in addition to maintaining scheduled air services.

The VC10 is due to be replaced in RAF service by the Airbus A400M and the Future Strategic Tanker Aircraft. The RAF ordered its first VC-10 in 1961 and the last VC-10 should be withdrawn from RAF service in 2014.

C-17 Globemaster

99 Squadron	7 x C-17A	Brize Norton

Crew of 2 pilots and 1 loadmaster. Capacity Maximum of 154 troops. Normal load of 102 fully-equipped troops, up to 172,200lb (78,108 kg) on up to 18 standard freight pallets or 48 litters in the medevac role; Wingspan 50.29m; Length overall 53.04m; Height overall 16.8 m; Loadable width 5.5m; Cruising speed 648 kph (403 mph); Range (max payload) 4,444 km (2,400 miles); Engines 4 x Pratt and Whitney F117 turbofans.

The C-17 meets an RAF requirement for a interim strategic airlift capability pending the introduction of Future Transport Aircraft (A400). The decision to lease four C-17 aircraft for some £771m from Boeing was taken in 2001, and the aircraft entered service in 2001. The lease was for a period of seven years, with the option to buy or extend at the end of that period. The option to buy the leased aircraft was exercised in August 2006 together with a contract to procure a fifth new C-17 aircraft which was delivered in April 2008. A sixth C-17 was ordered as a result of a £130 million contract signed in December 2007 and was delivered in July 2008. The seventh C-17 was delivered during early 2011.

The C-17 fleet is capable of the deployment of 1,400 tonnes of freight over 3,200 miles in a seven day period. The aircraft is able to carry one Challenger 2 MBT, or a range of smaller armoured vehicles, or up to three WAH-64 Apache aircraft at one time. Over 150 troops can be carried. Inflight refuelling increases the aircraft range.

No 99 Sqn has some 158 flight crew and ground staff.

A400M

The MoD has committed to 22 x Airbus A400M to meet the Future Transport Aircraft (FTA) requirement for an airlift capability to replace the remaining Hercules C-130K and C130J fleet. The A400 is a collaborative programme involving eight European nations (Germany, France, Turkey, Spain, Portugal, Belgium, Luxembourg and United Kingdom), procuring a total of 174 aircraft. The expected UK cost is some £2.4 billion for 22 aircraft.

The A400M should provide tactical and strategic mobility to all three Services. The capabilities required of the A400M include. the ability to operate from well established airfields and semi-prepared rough landing areas in extreme climates and all weather by day and night; to carry a variety of vehicles and other equipment, freight, and troops over extended ranges; to be capable of air dropping paratroops and equipment; and to be capable of being unloaded with the minimum of ground handling equipment. The A400M should also meet a requirement for an airlift capability to move large single items such as attack helicopters and some Royal Engineers' equipment.

Airbus Military SL of Madrid, a subsidiary of Airbus Industrie, is responsible for management of the whole of the A400M programme. Companies involved in the programme are. BAE Systems (UK), EADS (Germany, France and Spain), Flabel (Belgium) and Tusas Aerospace Industries (Turkey). Final assembly will almost certainly take place in Spain. In May 2003, the European consortium engine TP400-D6 was selected for the A400M military transport aircraft over the rival Pratt & Whitney proposal.

The most commonly quoted argument in favour of the A400M over the C-130J is that this aircraft could carry a 25 ton payload over a distance of 4,000 km. Thus, it is argued that a fleet of 40 x A400M could carry a UK Brigade to the Gulf within 11.5 days, as opposed to the 28.5 days required to make a similar deployment with 40 x C-130s. To operate a fleet of 40 x A400M would of course require aircraft from elsewhere in Europe. In any event, we believe that the RAF will probably retain its C-17s, and will operate a mixed transport fleet comprising the C-130J, A-400 and C-17.

The first aircraft was completed in June 2008 and deliveries commenced in 2009 with the in-service date (after delivery of the seventh aircraft) in 2011.

Air-to-Air Refuelling Aircraft

The RAF Air-to-Air Refuelling fleet mainly comprises 15 x VC10 K3 and K4 aircraft flown by No 101 Squadron based at RAF Brize Norton. These are supported by 8 x Tristar K1/KC1/C2/C2A (216 Sqn, Brize Norton) aircraft used for both transport and AAR. The RAF AAR capability is the most specialised in NATO, and has been extensively deployed in recent allied coalition operations in Afghanistan, and Iraq.

Funded Helicopter Hours 2008-2011 (Training and Operations)

Aircraft type	*Financial year*		
	2008-09	2009-10	2010-11
Apache	14,400	16,500	18,500
Lynx Mk 3/8	11,200	10,440	9,260
Lynx Mk 7/9	18,599	15,500	15,500
Gazelle	10,935	5,988	4,450
Chinook Mk 2	15,912	16,500	18,503
Puma	12,000	9,756	7,250
Merlin Mk 1 (RN)	9,380	9,380	9,380
Merlin Mk 3 (RAF)	7,550	7,000	8,400
Sea King Mk 3/3a	9,180	9,721	9,720
Sea King Mk 4/6	11,186	12,502	12,504
Sea King Mk 5	4,122	4,135	4,399
Sea King Mk 7	3,601	3,770	3,686

Note: The reduction in flying hours for the Puma is as a consequence of fewer airframes being available due to the Puma upgrade programme. Gazelle hours are reducing as this aircraft is being withdrawn from service.

CHAPTER 10 – ENGINEERS

OVERVIEW

The engineer support for the Army is provided by the Corps of Royal Engineers (RE). Known as Sappers, the Royal Engineers are one of the Army's three Combat Support Arms, and are trained as fighting soldiers, combat engineers and artisan tradesmen as well as holding specialist qualifications within EOD, Search and Diving. The Corps of Royal Engineers performs highly specialised combat and non-combat tasks, and is active all over the world in conflict and during peace. The Corps has no battle honours, its motto *'ubique'* (everywhere), signifies that it has taken part in every battle fought by the British Army in all parts of the world.

Force structure

As of 2011, the RE had a Regular Army establishment of some 9,528 personnel and a strength of 9,640 personnel. These figures are for UK trained regular army (including Full Time Reserve Service Personnel) and exclude Gurkhas, and mobilised reservists.

This large corps comprises 17 Regular Regiments and 5 TA regiments – presently organised as follows:

Royal Engineers: Regular Army units and locations during 2011

Unit	Location	Country	Notes
1 Royal School of Military Engineering Regiment	Chatham	UK	
3 Royal School of Military Engineering Regiment	Minley	UK	
21 Engineer Regiment	Ripon	UK	3 (UK) Division
22 Engineer Regiment	Perham Down	UK	3 (UK) Division
23 Engineer Regiment (Air Assault)	Woodbridge	UK	16 Air Assault Brigade
24 Commando Engineer Regiment	Barnstaple	UK	3 Commando Brigade
25 Engineer Regiment	Waterbeach	UK	Air Support
26 Engineer Regiment	Perham Down	UK	3 (UK) Division
28 Engineer Regiment	Hameln	Germany	1 (UK) Armoured Division
32 Engineer Regiment	Hohne	Germany	1 (UK) Armoured Division
33 Engineer Regiment (EOD)	Wimbish	UK	
35 Engineer Regiment	Paderborn	Germany	1 (UK) Armoured Division
36 Engineer Regiment (Search)	Maidstone	UK	
38 Engineer Regiment	Aldergrove	UK	3 (UK) Division
39 Engineer Regiment	Waterbeach	UK	Air Support
42 Engineer Regiment (Geo)	Hermitage	UK	Geographic Survey
101 Engineer Regiment (EOD)	Wimbish	UK	

Queen's Gurkha Engineers (QGE) are held within 36 Engineer Regiment (Search), within 69 Gurkha Field Squadron (Search) and 70 Gurkha Field Squadron (Search). The listing of Regiments by role is as follows:

	Germany	UK
Close Support Regiment	2	4
Air Assault Regiment		1
Commando Regiment		1
Air Support Regiment		2
Force Support Regiment	1	
EOD and Search Regiment		3

Geographic Regiment	1
Training Regiments	2
TA Engineer Regiments	5

There are also a number of specialist headquarters in the UK, as shown in the next table:

Royal Engineers: Specialist Headquarters and locations during 2011

Unit	Location	Country	Notes
12 (Air Support) Engineer Group	Waterbeach	UK	
29 EOD and Search Group	Aldershot	UK	
170 (Infrastructure Support) Engineer Group	Nottingham	UK	
Works Group RE (Airfields)	Waterbeach	UK	
Royal School of Military Engineering	Chatham	UK	Also in Minley, Surrey
Joint Aeronautical and Geospatial Organisation	Hermitage	UK	Geographic survey
Regimental Headquarters Royal Engineers	Chatham	UK	Including Corps Band

Territorial Army Royal Engineer Regiments and independent units are shown below:

Royal Engineers: Territorial Army units and locations in 2011

Unit	Location
71 Engineer Regiment (V)	Leuchars
72 Engineer Regiment (V)	Newcastle
73 Engineer Regiment (V)	Nottingham
75 Engineer Regiment (V)	Warrington
Royal Monmouthshire RE (Militia)	Monmouth
131 Independent Commando Squadron (V)	London
135 Independent Geographic Squadron (V)	Ewell
591 Independent Field Squadron (Volunteers)	Bangor (N Ireland)
65 Works Group (V)	Chilwell

Contingents of Royal Engineers (including Volunteer Reservists) are likely to be deployed in all combat zones, including most recently Afghanistan, Iraq, Balkans, Democratic Republic of Congo, Georgia, Liberia and Sierra Leone.

COMBAT ENGINEERING ROLES

Combat engineer support to military operations may be summarised under the following headings:

- Mobility
- Counter-mobility
- Protection

Mobility

The capability to deliver firepower, troops and supplies to any part of the battlefield is crucial to success. Combat engineers use their skills to overcome physical obstacles both natural and man-made, ensuring that armoured and mechanised troops can reach their targets and fight effectively.

Combat Engineers employ a wide variety of equipment, including tank-mounted, amphibious and girder bridges, to cross physical barriers. This equipment can be rapidly deployed to any part of the battlefield to ensure minimum interruption to progress.

Combat engineers are trained and equipped to clear enemy minefields which block or hinder movement. All combat engineers are trained to clear minefields by hand with the minimum risk. They also employ a number of explosive and mechanical devices to clear paths through minefields.

Combat engineers are also trained to detect and to destroy booby traps.

Improving the mobility of own and friendly forces may include the following tasks:

- ♦ Route clearance and maintenance
- ♦ Construction and maintenance of diversionary routes
- ♦ Routes to and from hides
- ♦ Bridging, rafting and assisting amphibious vehicles at water obstacles
- ♦ Detection and clearance of mines and booby traps
- ♦ Assisting the movement of heavy artillery and communications units
- ♦ Preparation of landing sites for helicopters

Counter-mobility

Counter-mobility is the term used to describe efforts to hinder enemy movement. Combat engineers aim to ensure that hostile forces cannot have freedom of mobility. Combat engineers are trained in the use of explosive charges to create obstacles, crater roads and destroy bridges. In this role, the combat engineer may be required to delay detonation until the last possible moment to allow the withdrawal of friendly forces in the face of an advancing enemy.

Combat engineers are also responsible for laying anti-tank mines, either by hand or mechanically, to damage vehicles and disrupt enemy forces. Combat engineers are trained to handle these devices safely and deploy them to maximum effect. Combat engineers are also trained for setting booby traps.

Earthwork defences, ditches and obstacles – one of the earliest forms of battlefield engineering – are also used to prevent the advance of enemy vehicles. Hindering enemy movement may include the following tasks:

- ♦ Construction of minefields
- ♦ Improvement of natural obstacles by demolitions, cratering, and barricades
- ♦ Nuisance mining and booby traps
- ♦ Route denial
- ♦ Construction of obstacles to armoured vehicle movement, such as tank ditches

Protection

Construction of field defences is a core task for combat engineers. The capability to protect troops, equipment and weapons is critical. Combat engineers provide advice and assistance to the other parts of the Land Forces and the other services on the best methods of concealment and camouflage, and use mechanised plant to construct defensive positions and blast-proof screens.

Protection for troops in defensive positions may include field defences, minefields, wire, and other obstacles. Because of their commitment to other primary roles, there may be little engineer assistance available for the construction of defensive positions. What assistance can be given would normally be in the form of earth-moving plant to assist in digging, and advice on the design and methods of construction of field defences and obstacles.

Combat Engineers Military Works units have design and management teams that can provide military infrastructure support to all armed services and other government departments. Secondary protection roles include:

- ♦ Water and power supply in forward areas
- ♦ Technical advice on counter-surveillance with particular reference to camouflage and deception
- ♦ Destruction of equipment
- ♦ Intelligence

A major Engineer commitment in the forward area is the construction, maintenance and repair, of dispersed airfields for aircraft and landing sites for helicopters.

Non-Combat Engineering

Combat engineers also perform non-combat tasks during national peacetime contingencies and multilateral peace support operations in foreign countries, including:

- General support engineering, including airfield damage repair and repair of ancillary installations for fuel and power, construction of temporary buildings, power and water supplies, repair and construction of POL pipelines and storage facilities, and construction and routine maintenance of airstrips and helicopter landing sites
- Survey – including maps and aeronautical charts
- Explosive Ordnance Disposal – including terrorist and insurgent bombs
- Traffic Movement Lights for mobilisation and exercises

Recent coalition and peace support operations have highlighted the importance of combat engineers in all spheres of military activity. During the period 1993 – 2011, the multitude of tasks for which engineer support has been requested has stretched the resources of the Corps to its limit. Engineers are almost always among the first priorities in any call for support: tracks must be improved, roads built, accommodation constructed for soldiers and refugees, clean water provided and mined areas cleared. For example during 2003, 22 Engineer Regiment (operating in Iraq) was tasked to supply a quick fix to problem areas along the diesel pipeline for the Oil Security Force (OSF), and to ensure regular supplies of water for the Iraqi population in Basra and the surrounding urban areas.

Engineer Regiments

Close Support. The in barracks organisation for a Close Support Engineer Regiment is as follows:

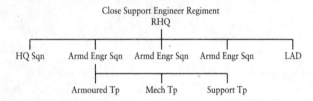

Strength: Approx 650-750 All Ranks

This whole organisation is highly mobile and built around the AFV 43, CVR(T) and PANTHER series of vehicles with TITAN, TROJAN and TERRIER armoured vehicles. In addition to the Regimental REME LAD, each squadron has its own REME section of some 12-15 men. The smallest engineer unit is the Troop which is usually commanded by a Lieutenant and consists of approximately 30 men. Following Future Army Structure changes, each Close Support Engineer Regiment is almost identical in structure irrespective of whether it supports a Mechanised or Armoured Brigade. Each Armoured Sqadron will have at least one affiliated Battlegroup to which it offers Engineer Support by default, although the Regiment will flex engineer effort to where it is most required.

Force Support: Engineer Force Support is provided by 28 Engineer Regiment which consists of 1 Sp Sqn, 1 Fd Sqn, 1 Fd Sp Sqn, and 1 Amphibious Engineer Squadron with 1 TA Amphibious Engineer Troop.

EOD and Search: 101 and 33 Engineer Regiment provide EOD and Search through 5 Regular and 3 TA EOD Sqns, assisted by a Support Squadron. In addition 36 Engineer Regiment provide Advanced Search through 5 Search Squadrons (of which 2 are QGE). 36 Engineer Regiment retains the ability to re-role to provide Force Support as required.

Close Support: 16 Air Assault Brigade and 3 Commando Brigade support is provided by 23 and 24 Engineer Regiments respectively. They have no heavy armour and are made up of Field Squadrons, each containing 3 Field Troops.

COMBAT ENGINEER TRAINING

All RE officers undergo officer training at RMA Sandhurst (44 weeks) before taking the Royal Engineers Troop Commanders Course (RETCC) with 1 and 3 RSME Regiments. The RETCC is 27 weeks long. All RE officers are expected to have or to obtain university degree-level engineering qualifications, and many qualify for higher degrees in the course of their career.

Recruit training for other ranks involves three phases:

♦ Soldier training (12 to 32 weeks)
♦ Combat engineer training (10 weeks)
♦ Trade training (10 – 49 weeks)

For both officers and other ranks, specialist engineer training is mainly conducted by 1 and 3 Royal School of Military Engineer (RSME) Regiments based at Chatham and Blackwater. 1 RSME Regiment is the support regiment for training. During a year, some 4,000 students may pass through 1 RSME Regiment, many of whom have recently joined the army and who have arrived at Chatham for a long engineering course lasting, in some cases, up to 44 weeks. 1 RSME Regiment incorporates the Construction Engineer School at Chatham, where civil and mechanical engineering skills are taught.

3 RSME Regiment is responsible for combat engineer training. The Combat Engineer School is located at Minley. 55 and 57 Training Squadrons are responsible for Combat Engineer and Assault Pioneer training, Driver Training Troop, 63 Training Support Squadron, is responsible for ABLE and RE Module Driver training.

COMBAT ENGINEERING VEHICLES AND EQUIPMENT

Terrier

Terrier is an armoured, highly mobile, general support engineer vehicle optimised for battlefield support by providing mobility support (obstacle and route clearance), counter-mobility (digging of anti-tank ditches and creating other earthworks/obstacles) and survivability (digging of trenches and Armoured Fighting Vehicle slots).

Terrier will be operated by a crew of two and has a remote control capability in particularly hazardous environments. The vehicle is able to tow the AVRE trailer carrying midi fascines, Cl 70 trackway or general stores. It is also capable of towing and firing the Python minefield beaching system. The vehicle can also be fitted with an array of ancillaries including the Surface Clearance Device for the clearance of scatterable mines, earth orger, rippers and hammers. Terrier will also be able to launch single midi fascines in order to breach shot gaps and therefore establish routes while keeping pace with other armoured vehicles such as the Challenger 2 MBT, Warrior ICV and its sister Combat Engineer Vehicles Titan and Trojan. Terrier will be fitted with day and night vision systems and will be air-portable in An-124, C17 or A400M transport aircraft. 60 vehicles have been ordered in a contract that over the life of the Terrier programme is believed to be worth some £700 million.

Trojan and Titan

Trojan and Titan are Armoured Engineer Vehicles based on an improved Challenger 2 MBT chassis. These replacements of the Chieftain AVRE and AVLB systems means that the British Army has a common heavy armour fleet based on the Challenger 2 chassis. These vehicles represent the first armoured engineer vehicles specifically designed (rather than adapted from battle tank chassis) for their role and incorporate the very latest mobility and survivability features. Improved visibility is achieved by incorporating direct and indirect vision devices with low light, image intensifying and thermal imaging capabilities. The interior, and to some extent the exterior, of the vehicles have been designed around the crew station positions.

A contract worth £250 million was awarded during early 2001 for the supply of 66 vehicles – 33 x Trojan and 33 x Titan. Deliveries to the RE commenced in late 2006 and will be complete, including final upgrade in late 2012.

Trojan Armoured Vehicle Royal Engineers (AVRE)

Trojan is designed as a breaching vehicle to open routes through complex battlefield obstacles and clear a path through minefields. Standard equipment includes a breaching-arm with opposing thumb that allows items such as trees and beams can be gripped and moved. A Full Width Mine Plough can be mounted as well as a Bulldozer blade to the vehicle as can a marking system. The breaching arm is also used to launch the midi-fascine, carried on the rear of the vehicle, into ditches enabling a short gap crossing capability. Trojan also tows the trailer-mounted Python mine-clearing system or AVRE trailer. Trojan has the flexibility to support a wide range of operations, including humanitarian missions, and is currently deployed on Operation HERRICK in Afghanistan.

Titan Armoured Vehicle Launcher Bridge (AVLB)

Titan is designed to provide a gap crossing capability of 45m, or less, using the in service Close Support Bridge (CSB) system (No 10,11 and 12 CSB) in combination or singly. It has a .8m step up and down capability in order to provide ground manoeuvre formations with improved capability over a greater range of terrain conditions. Titan can also be fitted with a dozer blade to prepare its own bank seats or Track Width Mine Plough.

BR90 Bridges

The RE BR-90 family of bridges are built from a range of seven modular panels of advanced aluminium alloy fabrication. These form two interconnecting trackways with a 4 m overall bridge width and a 1 m girder depth. BR90 is deployed with Royal Engineer units in both Germany and the UK with the bridges entering service in 1999 and comprising the following elements:

- General Support Bridge
- Close Support Bridge
- Two Span Bridge
- Long Span Bridge

Close Support Bridge – This consists of three tank-launched bridges capable of being carried on a tank bridgelayer and a Tank Bridge Transporter truck.

There are three basic Tank Launched Bridges (also known as Close Support or Assault Bridges): the No 10, No 11 and No 12.

General Support Bridge – This system utilises the Automated Bridge Launching Equipment (ABLE) that is capable of launching bridges up to 44 m in length. The ABLE vehicle is positioned with its rear pointing to the gap to be crossed and a lightweight launch rail extended across the gap. The bridge is then assembled and winched across the gap supported by the rail, with sections added until the gap is crossed. Once the bridge has crossed the gap the ABLE launch rail is recovered. A standard ABLE system set consists of an ABLE vehicle and 2 x TBT carrying a 32 m bridge set. A 32 m bridge can be built by 10 men in about 25 minutes

Spanning Systems – There are two basic spanning systems. The long span system allows for lengthening a 32 m span to 44 m using ABLE and the two span system allows 2 x 32 m bridge sets to be constructed by ABLE and secured in the middle by piers or floating pontoons, crossing a gap of up to 60 m.

BR-90 carrier – The Unipower 8x8 TBT is an improved mobility transporter for the BR 90 bridging system. It can carry one No 10 bridge or two No 12 bridges. The TBT can self load from, and off-load to, the ground. The TBT task is to re-supply the Chieftain and Titan AVLB with replacement bridges.

Medium Girder Bridge (MGB)

The MGB is a simple system of lightweight components that can be easily manhandled to construct a bridge capable of taking the heaviest AFVs. The MGB has been largely replaced by the BR90 system, although some MGB have been retained for certain operational requirements. Two types of MGBs are fielded: Single span bridge – 30 m long which can be built by about 25 men in 45 minutes; Multi span bridge – a combination of 26.5 m spans: a two span bridge will cross a 51 m gap and a three span bridge a 76 m gap. If necessary, MGB pontoons can be also be joined together to form a ferry. MGB is deployed in support of operations in Afghanistan.

Class 16 Airportable Bridge

In service since 1974 and a much lighter bridge than the MGB, the Class 16 can be carried assembled under a Chinook helicopter or in 3 x 3/4 ton vehicles with trailers. A 15 m bridge can be constructed by 15 men in 20 minutes. The Class 16 can also be made into a ferry which is capable of carrying the heaviest AFVs. In the near future, the British Army will replace the Class 16 bridge with the Future Light Bridge (FLB) systems. This bridge will also be capable of being used as a ferry.

M3 Ferry

Weight 24,500 kg; Length 12.74 m; Height 3.93 m; Width 3.35 m; Max Road Speed 80 kph; Water Speed 14 kph; Road Range 725 kms; 3 Man crew.

The M3 can be driven into a river and used as a ferry or, when a number are joined together from bank to bank, as a bridge, capable of taking vehicles as heavy as the Challenger MBT. The M3 has a number of improvements over the M2 which it has replaced (the M2 was in service for over 25 years). The M3 can deploy pontoons on the move, in or out of water; it needs no on-site preparation to enter the water; it can be controlled from inside the cab when swimming and its control functions have been automated allowing the crew to be reduced from four to three.

A single two-bay M3 can carry a Class 70 tracked vehicle, where two M2s would have been required for this task with additional buoyancy bags. Eight M3 units and 24 soldiers can build a 100 m bridge in 30 minutes compared with 12 M2s, 48 soldiers and a construction time of 45 minutes. The M3 is only 1.4 m longer and 3,300 kg heavier than the M2. It is still faster and more manoeuvrable on land and in water. A four-wheel steering facility gives a turning diameter of 24 m.

Mine Clearance

Python

Python is a minefield breaching system that replaces the Giant Viper in RE service. The Python has the ability to clear a much longer 'safe lane' than its predecessor. It is also faster into action and far more accurate. It can clear a path 230 m long and 7 m wide through which vehicles are safe to pass.

The system works by firing a single rocket from a newly designed launcher trailer which has been towed to the edge of a mined area. Attached to the rocket is a coiled 230 m long hose packed with one and a half tons of powerful explosive. After the hose lands on the ground it detonates and destroys or clears any mines along its entire length. It is claimed that in a cleared lane, over 90% of anti-tank mines will have been destroyed. Python is deployed in support of operations in Afghanistan.

Mine Warfare

Anti-tank minefields laid by the Royal Engineers will usually contain Barmines (anti-tank) or Mk.7 (anti-tank) mines and anti-disturbance devices may be fitted to some Barmines. Minefields will always be recorded and marked; they should also be covered by artillery and mortar fire to delay enemy mine clearance operations and maximise the attrition of armour. ATGWs are often sited in positions covering the minefield that will give them flank shoots onto enemy armour; particularly the ploughs or rollers that might spearhead a minefield breaching operation. The future of UK mine warfare capability is currently under review.

Shielder

Shielder provides the facility to create anti-tank barriers quickly and effectively. The system consists of modular dispensers of anti-tank mines that can be fired to either side or to the rear, mounted on a flatbed version of the Stormer Armoured Personnel Carrier. The anti-tank mines have a programmable life, at the end of which they self-destruct.

Ordered in 1995, Shielder is derived from the US Alliant Techsystems M163 Volcano system. It is believed that the total value of the order was approximately £110 million for 29 x Volcano systems, anti-tank mines, training, spares and the Stormer flatbed carrier. The first vehicles entered service in 1999.

Claymore Mine (Anti-Personnel)

The Claymore Mine has a curved oblong plastic casing mounted on a pair of bipod legs. The mine is positioned facing the enemy and fired electrically from distances up to 300 m away. On initiation, the mine scatters about 700 ball-bearings out to a range of 50 m across a 60 degree arc. First purchased from the US in 1963, the Claymore is an effective anti-infantry weapon that is likely to remain in service for many years to come.

CHAPTER 11 – COMMUNICATIONS

OVERVIEW

Royal Signals is the Combat Command Support Arm (CCS) that provides the Communications and Information Systems (CIS – the bearer network) and Information Communication Services (ICS – infrastructure and applications) used throughout the command structure of the Army, as well as supporting the other armed services and coalition partners. Traditionally this has been concentrated at Brigade level and above, but with the increasing demand for information at the tactical level, this now stretches down to battle group level and below in direct support of the combat arms.

In addition to these tasks the Royal Signals also provide Electronic Warfare (EW) and Signals Intelligence (SIGINT). Life support and force protection duties also fall to Royal Signals units supporting certain formations.

Information is the lifeblood of any military formation in battle and it is the responsibility of the Royal Signals to ensure the speedy and accurate passage of information that enables commanders to make informed and timely decisions, and to ensure that those decisions are passed to the fighting troops in contact with the enemy. The rapid, accurate and secure employment of command, control and communications systems maximises the effect of the military force available and consequently the Royal Signals act as an extremely significant 'Force Multiplier'. The Corps motto is 'Certa Cito' (Swift and Sure) and its soldiers are usually some of the first in and last out during any operation. The Corps possesses a large Special Forces element as well as air assault, air support and special communications units.

Royal Signals is currently (2011) on a campaign footing and has temporarily restructured in order to better support current operational commitments. Key to this is the formation of Campaign Signal Regiments (CSRs). There are 5 CSRs (1, 2, 3, 16 and 21 Sig Regts) under 11 Sig Bde who rotate through 6 month deployments to Afghanistan providing a wide range of communications and force protection support to UK military operations.

Several battle groups now deploy with a Royal Signals Regimental Signals Officer (RSO) and a highly trained multi-discipline Royal Signals Infantry Support Team (RSIST) in order to deliver the increasingly sophisticated and complex communications requirements at battle group level and below.

Royal Signals Mission

To deliver elements of deployable integrated Combat Command Support, Electronic Warfare and Force Protection in order to enable decisive command.

Force structure

Royal Signals provides about 9% of the Army's manpower with eleven regular regiments, one training regiment, and 5 Territorial Army regiments, each generally consisting of between three and six squadrons with between 400 and 600 personnel. There are also independent troops and detachments supporting various units around the world.

Royal Signals personnel are found wherever the Army is deployed including every UK and NATO headquarters in the world. The Headquarters and "Home" of the Corps is at Blandford Camp in Dorset.

Royal Signals units based in the United Kingdom provide command and control communications for forces that have operational roles. There are a number of Royal Signals units, or elements of, permanently based in Germany, Holland and Belgium from where they provide the necessary command support and Electronic Warfare (EW) support for both the British Army and other NATO forces based in Europe. Royal Signals personnel are also based in several other locations including Cyprus, the Falkland Islands, Kenya, Canada, and Gibraltar.

During early 2011 the personnel strength of the Royal Corps of Signals was 7,600.

Regular Army Royal Signals units are shown in the following table:

Royal Signals: Regular Army units during 2011

Unit	Location	Notes
HQ 1 Sig Bde	Gloucester	Corps Combat Command Support for the Allied Rapid Reaction Corps (ARRC) and Combat Command Support for the Joint Rapid Reaction Force (JRRF).
HQ 2 Sig Bde	Corsham	Mainly TA. Provide contingency national communications and specialist functions.
HQ 11 Sig Bde	Donnington	Delivery of Op ENTIRETY to the execution of the COIN campaign in Afghanistan. Force Generation elements and individuals for current ops, primarily Afghanistan. Campaign Signal Brigade.
1(UK) Armd Div HQ and Sig Regt	Germany	Communications for 1 (UK) Armd Div HQ and Bdes and Campaign Signal Regiment.
3 (UK) Div HQ & Sig Regt	Bulford	Communications for 3 (UK) Div HQ and Bdes and Campaign Signal Regiment.
2 Sig Regt	York	Campaign Signal Regiment.
7 Sig Regt	Germany	Supports Allied Rapid Reaction Corps (ARRC).
10 Sig Regt	Corsham	Information Communications Services, Information Management and ECM (FP).
11 (RSS) Sig Regt	Blandford	Royal School of Signals Training Regt, responsible for officer and soldier training.
14 Sig Regt (EW)	Brawdy	Electronic Warfare.
16 Sig Regt	Germany	Campaign Signal Regiment.
18 (UKSF) Sig Regt	Hereford	Communications for DSF Group.
21 Sig Regt (AS)	Colerne	Communications for the Joint Helicopter Force and AAC Apache and Campaign Signal Regiment.
22 Sig Regt	Stafford	Supports Allied Rapid Reaction Corps (ARRC). Lead for the introduction of Falcon .
30 Sig Regt	Bramcote	Communications for JRRF, including very high readiness support to the Joint Force HQ.
JSSU Cyprus	Cyprus	Joint Service Signal Unit.
Queens Gurkha Signals	Various	Supports 2 x Gurkha Inf Bns, 2, 22 and 30 Sig Regts and others in UK, Nepal and Brunei.
USSO	Blandford	Unified System Support Organisation.
200 Signal Sqn	Germany	Independent squadron, supporting 20 Armd Brigade HQ.
204 Signal Sqn	Catterick	Independent squadron, supporting 4 Mech Brigade HQ.
207 Signal Sqn	Germany	Independent squadron, supporting 7 Armd Brigade HQ.
209 Sig Sqn	Northern Ireland	Independent squadron, supporting 19 Light Brigade HQ.
215 Sig Sqn	Tidworth	Independent squadron, supporting 1 Mech Brigade HQ.

216 (Para) Sig Sqn	Colchester	Independent squadron, supporting 16 Air Assault Bde HQ.
228 Sig Sqn	Bulford	Independent squadron, supporting 12 Mech Bde HQ.
299 Sig Sqn (SC)	Bletchley	Independent squadron, supporting special communications.
HQ 38 (Irish) Bde Sig Tp	Northern Ireland	Independent Tp, supports 38 (Irish) Bde HQ.
628 (GBR DCM D) Sig Tp	Germany	UK Independent Tp within 1st NATO Signal Battalion.
660 Sig Tp	Didcot	Independent Tp within 11 EOD Regt RLC.
661 Sig Tp	Aldershot	Independent Tp, supports 101 Log Bde HQ.
662 Sig Tp	Germany	Independent Tp, supports 102 Log Bde HQ.
JCU (FI)	Falklands	Joint Communications Unit (Falkland Islands).

The Royal Signals TA units are shown in the next table.

Royal Signals : Territorial Army units during 2011

Unit	Location
32 Sig Regt (V)	Scotland, North of England and Northern Ireland
37 Sig Regt (V)	Wales, West Midlands and East Anglia
38 Sig Regt (V)	Yorkshire, Nottinghamshire, Buckinghamshire and Highlands
39 Sig Regt (V)	Somerset, Gloucestershire and the Home Counties
71 Sig Regt (V)	London and Essex
HQ Specialist Group Royal Signals	Corsham
Central Volunteer HQ R SIGNALS	Corsham
81 Sig Sqn (V)	Corsham
Land Information Assurance Group (V)	Corsham
Land Information Communications Systems Group (V)	Corsham

Notes: (1) Within 2 Sig Brigade, a total of five signal regiments provide national communications in support of the Home Defence role, plus other bespoke support. (2) 43 Sig Sqn (V) will continue to support the Joint Helicopter Command as part of 21 Sig Regt (AS). (3) 63 (SAS) Sig Sqn (R) will continue to support the DSF Group as part of 18 (UKSF) Sig Regt. (4) In addition, Royal Signals TA will provide individual augmentees to regular regiments, including on operations.

ROLES OF MILITARY COMMUNICATIONS

Communications have enabling capabilities that support all military operations in war and peace. These roles may be summarised under the following headings:

Command and Control: Communications enable commanders at all levels to exercise command and control over their own forces. Communications enable commanders to receive information, convey orders and move men and materiel, and select and position their attacking and defensive forces to maximum effect in order to take advantage of their own strengths and enemy weaknesses.

The capacity to deliver firepower, troops and supplies to any part of the battlefield is crucial to success. From the earliest days of messengers, flags, bugles and hand signals, this has been vital to successful command. Modern electronic communications systems have vastly added to this capacity, increasing the distances over which Command and Control can be exercised – from line of sight or hearing to any geographical area where forces are deployed. The amount and type of information delivered for this purpose has also expanded massively.

Computerised Command Information: Communications enables commanders to receive information from the battlefield to build up a picture of the state and disposition of their own forces as well as enemy forces. Commanders have always sought to have the fullest possible information of both their own and enemy forces – but were typically limited by constraints of time, space and information carrying capacity.

Computer hardware and software – allied to the geographical spread, bandwidths and data-carrying capacity of modern military networks – have removed many of these constraints. Computer processing power enables information received from all sources to be sorted into meaningful patterns of use to commanders.

Such sources include:

♦ Voice and data reports from troops in the field
♦ Intelligence reports
♦ Mapping
♦ Battlefield sensors
♦ Multi-spectral imaging from ground reconnaissance units
♦ Reconnaissance and surveillance satellites, aircraft, helicopters and unmanned aerial vehicles
♦ Electronic Warfare systems on ground, air and sea platforms

In modern war, to capture the full scope of computer information systems, this communications effect is typically described as Command, Control, Communications, Computers, Intelligence, Surveillance and Reconnaissance (C4ISR).

Electronic Warfare: Secure communications that deny the enemy knowledge of own and friendly force activities, capabilities and intelligence (Communications Security). Communications that enable the penetration, compromise and destruction of enemy communication systems (Electronic Warfare).

ROYAL SIGNALS OPERATIONAL MISSIONS

Royal Signals units have three principal operational missions:

Communications Engineering

Communications units design, build and dismantle the tactical communications networks used on operations.

Communications Operations

Communications units operate the tactical communications networks at division and brigade levels. Some communications are delivered by Royal Signals at battle group and even company or platoon level on many operations.

Communications Management

Communications units are responsible for the management of the whole communications nexus at division and brigade level, or across a designated area of operations.

These missions will need to be performed in all phases of battle:

Offensive: In the offensive: setting up command posts, setting up area communications networks and setting up networks to connect battalions to brigades and elsewhere as far as possible. Specialist units can set up air portable communications systems shortly after a foothold is secured on an air base or other point of entry.

Advance: In the advance: continuing to keep forward and area communications running and providing logistics and maintenance needs for company and brigade forces as appropriate. Running networked services forwards as far as possible with the advance. Setting up alternate HQs. Relocating and maintaining relay and retransmission points and ensuring communications to rear and flanks remain open.

Defensive: In the defence: re-enforcing command posts and relay points. Increasing the complexity and robustness of networks. Providing alternate and redundant communications for all users.

Withdrawal: In the withdrawal: Preventing communications assets falling into enemy hands, setting up alternate command posts on the line of withdrawal, running networks backwards to rear. Keeping nodes open and supplying logistics and maintenance support as required.

Non-Combat missions: Communications perform non-combat roles during peacetime, including national peacetime contingencies and multilateral peace support operations in foreign countries.

FUNCTIONS OF MILITARY COMMUNICATIONS

Military communications roles undertaken by the Royal Signals may be divided into three separate functions:

Strategic communications: Communications between the political leadership, military high command, and military administrative and field commands at the divisional level. In terms of capability as opposed to function, modern communications systems increasingly blur the distinction between strategic and tactical systems as a consequence of technological advance.

Tactical communications: Communications between field formations from corps to division through brigade down to battalion level.

Electronic Warfare: The security of own forces and friendly forces communications, and the penetration, compromise and degradation of hostile communications.

TRAINING

All Royal Signals officers undergo officer training at RMA Sandhurst (44 weeks) before taking the Royal Signals Troop Commanders Course at 11th (Royal School of Signals) Signal Regiment, Blandford Camp. Many Royal Signals officers have on entry, or obtain through the course of their careers, university degree-level engineering qualifications.

Recruit training for other ranks involves two phases:

- Phase 1 – Soldier training (14 to 23 weeks)
- Phase 2 – Trade training (7 to 50 weeks)

All Royal Signals soldiers, whether arriving from the Army Training Regiments at Pirbright, Winchester or Harrogate also complete trade, leadership, ethos and additional military training at 11th (Royal School of Signals) Signal Regiment. The length of the course depends on the trade chosen, varying from 7 weeks up to 50. Electronic Warfare operators also attend additional modules at the Defence Intelligence and Security Centre, Chicksands.

Soldiers will return to the Regiment for periods throughout their careers to complete Phase 3 trade upgrading courses and specialist operational pre-deployment or pre-employment training. The Regiment is also responsible for Royal Signals special-to-arm command, leadership and management training to qualify for junior and senior non-commissioned officer and warrant officer promotion. Soldier training provides modern apprenticeship and national vocational qualifications.

Supervisor training is also undertaken in Blandford Camp after a rigorous selection process. Supervisors are known as Yeoman, Foreman, Yeoman (EW) or Foreman (IS) of Signals depending on their specialism. On successful completion of training they receive degree level accreditation for their skills. Officers similarly return to complete additional career and specialised training up to masters degree level.

Approximately 130 different types of courses are delivered by 11th (Royal School of Signals) Signal Regiment, including to students from other Arms and Services and foreign and Commonwealth forces, in addition to those of the Corps itself. Over 700 courses are run per year. There are in excess of 7,000 students completing courses throughout the year with about 1,000 students on courses at any one time. These figures equate to approximately some 250,000 man training days a year.

Organisation

Campaign Signal Regiments are currently structured to support Op HERRICK in Afghanistan.

Equipment

Royal Signals units are currently operating the following types of major equipment:

- Static strategic communications
- Mobile strategic satellite communications
- Fixed and mobile electronic warfare (EW) systems
- Tactical Area Communications – corps to brigade down to battalion HQ
- VHF Combat Net Radios – battalion and sub-units
- Tactical HF and UHF radios – battalion and sub-units
- Teleprinters, Fax, CCTV and ADP Equipment
- Computer Information Systems

Local area networks (LAN) and wide area networks (WAN) for computers

Tactical Area Communications

The principal tactical role of the Royal Signals is to provide corps to brigade level communications that link higher commands to battalion HQs. The area communications systems used by the Royal Signals include:

FALCON

FALCON is Royal Signals' replacement for Ptarmigan, the mobile, secure wide area battlefield CIS which was in service between 1986 and 2009. It also replaces the Royal Air Force's (RAF's) Tactical Trunk Communications System (RTTS) and the Deployed Local Area Network (DLAN) network. FALCON incorporates large elements of Commercial Off The Shelf (COTS) technologies and equipments including Internet Protocol (IP). Reflecting the growing importance of data over voice communications (although both are provided), FALCON has been designed to be the communications bearer and switching network for various command and control information infrastructures. FALCON may use its own line of sight radios as the bearer, with the range being extended by the use of satellite ground stations (including Reacher) or other bearers of opportunity (including landlines).

FALCON is provided in vehicle-mounted containers, dismounted containers and palletised boxes. The principal communications bearer detachments providing the wide area network are known as Wide Area Switching Points (WASPs). Headquarters and other command nodes are served by Command Post Support (CPS) detachments which provide the Local Area System (LAS). FALCON is being delivered by BAE Systems and is expected to enter service sometime in 2012.

Cormorant

Cormorant delivers CIS capabilities to both Royal Signals and the RAF. Cormorant is comprised of 3 primary equipments: a local access component, based on an Asynchronous Transfer Mode (ATM) switch, which provides digital voice subscriber facilities; a high speed data local area network (LAN) for headquarters; and a wide area component which provides the interconnection of these headquarters on a 'backbone' communications network across a large geographical area. The wide area component also provides the means to interconnect with single service and multinational systems.

Designed to link all components of a Joint Force, the system enables the force to deploy and operate its CIS Wide Area Network (WAN) across the spectrum of conflict (peacekeeping, military stabilisation or warfighting). The system is fully containerised and can be operated in either a (vehicle) mounted or dismounted mode.

A Cormorant network may consist of the following vehicle-mounted (or dismounted) installations:

- Local Area Support module
- Core Element
- Bearer Module
- Long-Range Bearer Module (Tropospheric)
- Management Information Systems
- Interoperable Gateways
- Tactical Fibre Optic cabling
- Short-Range Radio.

Promina

Promina networks deliver pulse code modulation (PCM) and compressed digital analogue voice, video conferencing, Internet Protocol (IP) frame relay, Asynchronous Transfer Mode (ATM) and legacy Synchronous and Asynchronous data services over satellite, microwave radio and leased line services. It is used to multiplex CIS infrastructure in use within in the Land Environment.

Bowman

Bowman is the main radio system used by the Army and other ground forces. It is primarily a powerful combat network radio system sending secure digital voice and data around the battlefield. By enabling transmission of large quantities of electronic data Bowman can also provide information on the position of UK forces.

It also forms the underlying network to carry the CIP (Combat Infrastructure Programme). CIP is an automated battlefield command and control system. It is key to the concept of 'Network Enabled Capability'; joining up military communications and electronic systems in a 'network of networks'. The ability to see the position of UK forces, on screens in vehicles and headquarters, should amongst other benefits, help to reduce the frequency of 'friendly fire' incidents. An extremely capable system, regular updates continue to add extra utilities allowing better communications and more efficient command and control.

Satellite Communications (SATCOM)

Paradigm Services Limited (PSL)), a wholly owned subsidiary of EADS, signed the Skynet 5 Private Finance Initiative (PFI) contract worth £3.6 billion with the MoD in October 2003, making it the world's first commercial provider of military satellite services. Paradigm took over the operation, maintenance and ownership of the existing Skynet 4 system (3 satellites) which are expected to continue providing satellite services to the UK MoD and NATO beyond their original run out date of 2012.

PSL was responsible for upgrading Skynet by launching the '5' series. Skynet 5A and Skynet 5B entered service in April 2007 and January 2008 respectively. Skynet 5C was launched in June 2008. Skynet 5D is expected to be launched in 2013.

The Land, Air and maritime environments utilise different equipment for their principal terminal capabilities. The Land and Air environments primarily use Reacher. The maritime environment uses the Satellite Communications Terminal (SCOT).

Reacher Satellite Ground Terminal

Reacher replaced the VSC 501 and is the main satellite ground terminal (SGT) used by the Army. It is delivered in 3 variants:

Reacher Medium is a land terminal specifically designed for X-Band military satellite communications. Designed to operate with a Forward Operating Headquarters unit, it is mounted on a Bucher Duro 6 x 6 vehicle and has a detachable Intermediate Group cabin and associated trailer.

Reacher Large is mounted on the same vehicle as the Reacher Medium. The equipment has a larger antenna for greater bandwidth capacity.

Reacher All Terrain is mounted on 2 x BV206 vehicles with associated trailers. It is used by the Royal Marines (RM) and is sometimes referred to as Reacher (RM).

All Reacher terminals are transportable using Chinook helicopters, C130 Aircraft, sea and rail.

Other SGTs used by the Army include Tacsat 117F, SWE-DISH and V-Sat.

Communications Information Systems (CIS)

JOCS: The formation of the Joint Rapid Reaction Force led to a requirement for a joint computer system. The Joint Operational Command System (JOCS) was brought into service during 1999. This system provides a sophisticated operational picture, along with staff tools for controlling joint operations. It is scheduled to be withdrawn from service in 2012.

Overtask: British Forces operating in Afghanistan largely use Overtask in order to share mission specific information with ISAF coalition partners.

DII: The Defence Information Infrastructure (DII) is the replacement for the numerous networks currently connected via the Restricted LAN Interface (RLI) and is currently being rolled out in phases across the armed forces and on operations. There is also a version that can connect to the Secret LAN Interface (SLI).

J1/J4 IOS: This is an Interim Operating System (IOS) to provide secure personnel (J1) and logistical (J4) information services on operations or in remote locations via the Restricted LAN Interface (RLI). A Bantam satellite terminal is used to connect each node to the RLI but a bearer of opportunity can also be used. J1/J4 IOS will eventually be superseded by a deployable variant of DII.

Electronic Warfare Systems

SEER: SEER is a lightweight man-portable EW system able to prosecute a wide range of electronic communications targets whilst static, on a vehicle or within a dismounted patrol. It comprises of both an Electronic Surveillance sensor and an Electronic Attack system (capable of undertaking simple jamming missions). The Electronic Surveillance sensors can be networked in order to allow the establishment of a fully interconnected and automated sensor baseline that is capable of providing an effective position fix for any intercepted electronic target. It is supported by a system laptop which has a sophisticated software suite that can provide technical analysis and geographic representation of target.

LANDSEEKER: LANDSEEKER will provide a family of (modular) EW capabilities able to conduct Electronic Surveillance for the full range of electronic target sets (both communications and non-communications) and undertake complex Electronic Attack tasks. It will provide an interface with other government departments in order to allow a fully integrated approach to the prosecution of EW missions under the framework of the Single SIGINT Battlespace. It will replace all existing EW equipment including SEER, the medium-weight Odette Electronic Surveillance communications system and the Ince non-communications Electronic Surveillance system. The system will provide modules that are optimised for light (dismounted), medium and heavy forces and will be introduced into the Service from 2018.

ECM Force Protection Suite: A range of devices are used in order to protect forces from the threat caused by radio-controlled explosive devices.

CHAPTER 12 – COMBAT SERVICE SUPPORT

LOGISTIC OVERVIEW

In the British Army logistic support is based upon the twin pillars of service support (the supply chain) and equipment support (the maintenance of equipment).

Combat Service Support within the British Army is provided by the Royal Logistic Corps (RLC), the Royal Electrical and Mechanical Engineers (REME) and the Royal Army Medical Corps (RAMC).

Within any fighting formation units from these Corps typically represent about 30% of the manpower total of a division, and with the exception of certain members of the RAMC all are fully trained fighting soldiers.

The task of the logistic units on operations is to maintain the combat units in the field which entails:

- ◆ Supply and Distribution – of ammunition, fuel, lubricants, rations and spare parts
- ◆ Recovery and Repair – of battle damaged and unserviceable equipment.
- ◆ Treatment and Evacuation – of casualties.

In an operational division the commanders of the logistic units all operate from a separate, self contained headquarters under the command of a Colonel who holds the appointment of the Division's Deputy Chief of Staff (DCOS). This headquarters, usually known as the Divisional Headquarters (Rear), co-ordinates the whole of the logistic support of the Division in battle.

Supplies, reinforcements and returning casualties pass through an area located to the rear of the division where some of the less mobile logistic units are located. This area is known as the Divisional Admin Area (DAA) and the staff are responsible for co-ordinating the flow of all materiel and personnel into and out of the Divisional Area.

THE ROYAL LOGISTIC CORPS

The Royal Logistic Corps (RLC) is the youngest Corps in the Army and was formed in April 1993 as a result of the recommendations of the Logistic Support Review. The RLC is formed from an amalgamation of the Royal Corps of Transport, the Royal Army Ordnance Corps, the Army Catering Corps, the Royal Pioneer Corps and the postal and courier element of the Royal Engineers. As at June 2011, the RLC makes up almost 15 per cent of the Regular Army, comprising of 15,265 personnel, serving across 972 different units. About 59 per cent of officers and soldiers serve within RLC units, with the remaining 41 per cent serving throughout the Ministry of Defence. The RLC TA component makes up 17 per cent of the total TA strength, with TA personnel serving in one of the 16 major units, or, as with the regular component, elsewhere within the Ministry of Defence.

The primary roles of the RLC are supply, distribution and specialist logistic functions. Within these functions, soldiers are employed within trade groups, known as Main Trades For Pay. These RLC functions and the list of soldier trades are as follows.

Roles and Functions of the RLC

Role	Function	Trade
Supply	Materiel	Logistic Specialist (supply)
	Combat Supplies	Petroleum Operator
	Medical Stores	Vehicle support specialist
	Vehicles	
Distribution	Road	Driver
	Rail	Driver Tank Transporter
	Air Despatch	Driver Air Despatch
	Maritime – littoral	Driver Communications Specialist

Specialist	Explosive Ordnance Disposa	Ammunition Technician
	Postal and Courier	Postal and Courier Operator
	Movement Control	Movement Controller
	Port and Maritime	Marine Engineer
	Catering	Mariner
	Pioneer	Port Operator
	Photography	Chef
	Labour Support	Pioneer
	Systems Analysis	Photographer
	Contract Management	Systems Analyst

The RLC is formed of 18 major regular units, and 16 major units within the TA component, of which 10 are regional and 6 are national. The next table shows the regular and TA regiments and their worldwide locations, with notes on the roles of each unit.

REGIMENTS OF THE RLC

Regiment	*Location*	*Remarks*
	Regular RLC Regiments	
1 Logistic Support Regiment	Gütersloh	LSR
2 Logistic Support Regiment	Gütersloh	LSR
3 Logistic Support Regiment	Abingdon	LSR
4 Logistic Support Regiment	Abingdon	LSR
5 Training Regiment	Grantham	Phase 1 and 2 training regiment for TA
6 Regiment	Gütersloh	Theatre Logistic Regiment
7 Regiment	Bielefeld	Theatre Logistic Regiment
9 Regiment	Chippenham	Theatre Logistic Regiment
10 The Queen's Own Gurkha Logistic Regiment	Aldershot	Theatre Logistic Regiment
11 Explosive Ordnance Disposal	Didcot	Squadrons dispersed through UK and Germany.
12 Logistic Support Regiment	Abingdon	1 Squadron in Germany.
13 Air Assault Support Regiment	Colchester	Support 16 Air Assault Brigade.
17 Port and Maritime Regiment	Southampton	Port and Maritime capability
23 Pioneer Regiment	Bicester	Commands 47 (Air Despatch) Squadron
25 Training Regiment	Deepcut	Training regiment for RLC
27 Regiment	Aldershot	Theatre Logistic Regiment.
29 Regiment	Cirencester	Postal and Courier and Movements Regiment.
Commando Logistic Regiment	Barnstaple	Support to 3 Commando Brigade.
	Territorial Army Regiments and Units	
Catering Support Regiment	Grantham	
88 Regiment (V)	Grantham	Postal and Courier and Movements Regiment.
89 Regiment (V)	Ruislip, London	Postal and Courier and Movements Regiment.
150 (Yorkshire) Transport Regiment (V)	Hull	Transport function
151 (London) Transport Regiment (V)	London	Transport function
152 (Ulster) Transport Regiment (V)	Ulster	Transport function
155 Transport Regiment (V)	Plymouth	Transport function
156 (North West) Transport Regiment (V)	Liverpool	Transport function
158 (Royal Anglian) Transport Regiment (V)	Peterborough	Transport function

159 Supply Regiment (V)	West Bromwich	Supply function
160 Transport Regiment (V)	Grantham	Transport function
165 Port Regiment (V)	Grantham	Port and Maritime function
166 Supply Regiment (V)	Grantham	Supply function
168 Pioneer Regiment (V)	Grantham	Pioneer function
Scottish Transport Regiment (V)	Dunfermline	Transport function
Welsh Transport Regiment (V)	Cardiff	Transport function

Logistic Support Regiments

Every Logistic Support Regiment (LSR) is affiliated to a deployable Brigade within the Army. An LSR is comprised of a General Support Squadron which looks after the supply function and 2 x Close Support Squadrons which execute distribution. On operations each LSR also deploys up to 6 Logistic Support Detachments (LSDs) who work with the formation Battlegroups and form the logistic link back to the LSR. 13 Air Assault Support Regiment and the Commando Logistic Regiment perform the same role as the LSRs for their specialist Brigades, 16 Air Assault Brigade and 3 Commando Brigade respectively.

Theatre Logistic Regiments

Theatre Logistic Regiments undertake more specialist roles, such as the control and distribution of supplies and materiel moving in and out of the theatre of conflict and specialist transport and distribution requirements, for example movement of heavy equipment over land. On operations they retain responsibility for these areas and may also encompass contractor management, the management of logistic support at unit level and the deployment and command of Logistic Support Teams, working with forward based sub-units from Battlegroups in the Brigade. The specialist Medical Supply Squadron is also within the Theatre Logistic Regiment group and permanently has personnel deployed undertaking this specialist provisioning role. Theatre Logistic Regiments fall under the command of 101 and 102 Logistic Brigades.

Enablers

The final group of major units within the RLC are the 'enablers'. The enablers consist of 11 Explosive Ordnance Disposal (EOD) Regiment, 17 Port and Maritime Regiment, 23 Pioneer Regiment and 29 Regiment. The majority of these units come under the command of 104 Logistic Support Brigade, with the exception of 11 EOD Regiment. These regiments provide specialist support from the home base and elements are routinely deployed to the theatre of operations. Some niche capabilities have personnel deployed on operations continuously, such as the Ammunition Technical officers and soldiers from 11 EOD Regiment, Movement Controllers and Postal and Courier operators from 29 Regiment, and a number of personnel from 23 Pioneer Regiment who are trained in Specialist Search skills.

Due to the ever changing nature of conflict, the RLC doctrine undergoes constant review and remains flexible to suit the requirement of the fighting force. Supplies are held both within supply areas across the theatre of operations, and on wheels, ready for rapid deployment forwards to the battle. This is facilitated by intelligent, computerised provisioning and forecasting, allowing movement of materiel and combat supplies as needed, removing the requirement for vast stores of equipment and supplies at the forward edge of the battle. Where urgent supplies are identified, or a short notice replenishment is to be undertaken, the RLC has the ability to move stocks forward to the fighting troops through combat logistic patrols on the ground or by air, using the air despatch capability.

The Army do not just use the RLC for movement of supplies and materiel for our own force – the protected distribution capability has also been used for infrastructure re-building for nations such as Iraq and Afghanistan. For example, the movement of the Kajaki Dam equipment in Afghanistan was completed by an RLC combat logistic patrol.

Due to the specialist nature of many aspects of the RLC and the importance of logistics within an armed force, the RLC have also become involved in the training and mentoring of a number of foreign armies, including the Afghan National Army. This has included training in the provisioning and accounting of stores, distribution through logistic patrols and specialist functions such as counter-Improvised Explosive Device (c-IED) work with 11 EOD Regiment.

With the threat from improvised explosive devices prevalent in operational theatres the RLC are developing vehicles and equipment to combat the threat.. Protected mobility platforms are driven by the RLC for the command and control of convoys using platforms such as PANTHER and RIDGEBACK, with convoy protection being delivered by RLC soldiers from the standard armoured infantry wheeled vehicle such as MASTIFF. For distribution, the RLC use the MAN Support Vehicle EPLS (Enhanced Palletised Load System) which has replaced the previous DROPS load carrying vehicle. The MAN Support Vehicle also comes in a standard 15 ton variant with loads greater than the capacity of the MAN SV carried on the Heavy Equipment Transporter (HET). For liquid loads, such as water and fuel, the Close Support Tanker provides protection and mobility to allow replenishment forward to the fighting troops.

Logistics within the Army is becoming increasingly complex due to the multi-dimensional threat faced in conflict. Close combat is often needed to achieve the logistic mission and a flexible, highly responsive logistic support network is needed to maintain the momentum for the fighting troops. Defence does not exclusively use army logistics for the replenishment of our own troops and manoeuvrability to enable our sustainment role to work for others, such as local government and security forces, is becoming increasingly important. The use of the logistic capability to reinforce and assist with local infrastructure issues can be just as vital to winning the battle as the troops closing with the enemy in a more traditional role.

Vehicles

Although many of the vehicles operated by the RLC are common to all arms, RLC units are in the main the majority users.

During 2011 the British Army vehicle fleet was based around the following vehicles:

Logistics vehicle in service (2011)

Vehicle type	Number in service
Bulk Fuel	1,189
Cargo	12,446
Container Handler	23
Crane	92
Equipment Transporter	732
Forklift	649
Medical	915
Recovery	466
Bulk Water	57
Airfield Support	631
Fire Vehicles	162

Daily Messing Rates

The allowances per day for catering purposes are based on a ration scale costed at current prices and known as the daily messing rate (DMR). The ration scale is the same for all three services and contrary to popular army belief the RAF are not supplied with wine etc at public expense. The rate per day is the amount that the catering organisation has to feed each individual serviceman or servicewoman.

The scale is costed to the supply source of the food items. When the source of supply is more expensive due to local conditions the DMR is set higher to take account of local costs. A general overseas ration scale exists for overseas bases and attachments. This scale has a higher calorific value to take into account the conditions of heat, cold or humidity that can be encountered.

RLC Catering Units feed the Army generally using detachments of cooks attached to units.

During mid 2011 the daily messing rate (DMR) was approximately £2.44 per day per soldier in the UK. With this amount RLC cooks, in barracks have to provide three meals per day. The DMR for personnel serving in Afghanistan is £4.03 per day. These figures are adjusted on a monthly basis.

Ration scales vary according to location. The home ration scale in the UK is designed to provide 2,900 kilo-calories nett – that is, after loss through preparation and cooking. The general overseas ration scale used in overseas bases, includes an arduous duty allowance, to allow for climate and provides 3,400 kilo-calories nett. In field conditions, where personnel are fed from operational ration packs, 3,800 kilo-calories are provided.

Army cooks are trained at the The Defence Food Services School – Army (DFSS (A)) which was established in April 2004 as part of an organisation to serve the Army, Royal Navy and Royal Air Force. Before this, it was known as The Army School of Catering, founded in 1943, as part of the Army Catering Corps. DFSS (A) is located at Aldershot.

Postal

The Central Army Post Office (APO) is located in London and there are individual British Forces Post Offices (BFPO) wherever British Forces are stationed, plus Postal and Courier Squadrons with 29 Regiment (UK) .

THE ROYAL ELECTRICAL & MECHANICAL ENGINEERS – REME

Equipment Support remains separate from the other logistic pillar of Service Support and consequently the REME has retained not only its own identity but expanded its responsibilities. Equipment Support encompasses equipment management, engineering support, supply management, provisioning for vehicle and technical spares and financial management responsibilities for in-service equipment.

The aim of the REME is "To keep operationally fit equipment in the hands of the troops" and in the current financial environment it is important that this is carried out at the minimum possible cost. The equipment that REME is responsible for ranges from small arms and trucks to helicopters and main battle tanks. All field force units have some integral REME support (first line support) which will vary, depending on the size of the unit and the equipment held, from a few attached tradesmen up to a large Regimental Workshop of over 200 men. In war, REME is responsible for the recovery and repair of battle damaged and unserviceable equipment.

The development of highly technical weapon systems and other equipment has meant that REME has had to balance engineering and tactical considerations. On the one hand the increased scope for forward repair of equipment reduces the time out of action, but on the other hand engineering stability is required for the repair of complex systems.

Seven REME Equipment Support Battalions have been established. Six of these battalions provide second line support for the British contribution to the ACE Rapid Reaction Corps (ARRC) and formations in the UK and Germany. An Equipment Support Aviation Battalion in the UK supports the Army Air Corps units assigned to the Joint Helicopter Command.

During early 2011 the REME had a total of 10,010 personnel.

REME Equipment Support Battalion (Outline)

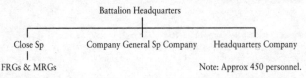

Battalion Headquarters

Close Sp Company   General Sp Company   Headquarters Company

FRGs & MRGs   Note: Approx 450 personnel.

The Close Support Company will normally deploy a number of FRG's (Forward Repair Groups) and MRGs (Medium Repair Groups) in support of brigades. The company is mobile with armoured repair and recovery vehicles able to operate in the forward areas, carrying out forward repair of key nominated equipment often by the exchange of major assemblies. It is also capable of carrying out field repairs on priority equipment including telecommunications equipment, and the repair of damage sustained by critical battle winning equipments.

The role of the General Support Company is to support the Close Support Companies and Divisional Troops. Tasks include the regeneration of fit power packs for use in forward repair and the repair of equipment back loaded from Close Support Companies. The General Support Company will normally be located to the rear of the divisional area in order to maximise productivity and minimise vulnerability.

Expect an Equipment Support Battalion to have approximately 450 personnel.

REME LAD (Light Aid Detachment)

Major divisional units have their own REME support organisation generally called the LAD which can vary in size from about 60 to 120 personnel. Usually commanded by a Captain, LADs are capable of quick repairs at the point of failure.

In manpower terms the REME LAD support available to the units of a division might resemble the following:

Armoured Regiment	120
Formation Reconnaissance Regiment	90
Armoured Infantry Battalion	90
Close Support Engineer Regiment	85
General Support Engineer Regiment	110
Field Regiment Royal Artillery	115
Air Defence Regiment Royal Artillery	160
Army Air Corps Regiment	130
Signals Regiment	60
RLC Logistic Support Regiment	75

ARMY MEDICAL SERVICES (AMS)

Medical support to members of the British Army is provided by the Army Medical Services which consists of the following Corps:

Royal Army Medical Corps

Queen Alexandra's Royal Army Nursing Corps

Royal Army Dental Corps

Royal Army Veterinary Corps

The Army Medical Services is the army single service element of the Defence Medical Services (DMS) . There is more information regarding the Defence Medical Services in Chapter 13 – Joint Service Units.

It is probable that without the superb support provided by the Defence Medical Services in both Iraq and Afghanistan, a large number of service personnel who would have been unlikely to have survived their wounds in earlier conflicts are still alive today.

The Royal Army Medical Corps (RAMC)

In peace, the personnel of the RAMC are based at the various medical installations throughout the world or in field force units and they are responsible for the health of the Army.

On operations, the RAMC is responsible for the care of the sick and wounded, with the subsequent evacuation of the wounded to hospitals in the rear areas. This is achieved by the provision of Close Support Medical Regiments (to treat front line casualties) and General Support Medical Regiments where more major procedures can be carried out some distance behind the front line, before evacuation to a Field Hospital where a full range of medical facilities is available.

Each Brigade has a medical squadron (usually from a Close Support Medical Regiment) allocated which is generally a regular unit (in some cases this may be a TA unit) that operates in direct support of the battle groups. These units are either armoured, airmobile or parachute trained. There are generally extra medical squadrons that provide support at the divisional level; once again these squadrons can be either regular or TA. These divisional squadrons provide medical support for the divisional troops and can act as manoeuvre units for the forward brigades when required.

All medical squadrons have medical sections that consist of a Medical Officer and eight Combat Medical Technicians. These sub-units are located with the battle group or units being supported and they provide the necessary first line medical support. In addition, the field hospital provides a dressing station where casualties are treated and may be resuscitated or stabilised before transfer to a field hospital. These units have the necessary integral ambulance support both armoured and wheeled, to transfer casualties from the first to second line medical units.

Field hospitals may be Regular or TA and all are 200 bed facilities with a maximum of eight surgical teams capable of carrying out life saving operations on some of the most difficult surgical cases. Since 1990 regular medical units have been deployed on operations either in the Persian Gulf, the Former Yugoslavia, Sierra Leone, Afghanistan and Iraq.

Casualty Evacuation (CASEVAC) is by ambulance, either armoured or wheeled and driven by RLC personnel, or by helicopter when such aircraft are available. A Chinook helicopter is capable of carrying 24 stretcher cases and a Puma can carry six stretcher cases and six sitting cases.

In early 2011 there were 5 x Regular Medical Regiments and three Field Hospitals. The TA provides 10 x independent field hospitals, 2 x General Support Medical Regiments and 1 x Casualty Evacuation Regiment. The early 2011 personnel figure for the Regular RAMC was 3,010 against a liability of 3,270.

The Queen Alexandra's Royal Army Nursing Corps (QARANC)

The QARANC is an all-nursing and totally professionally qualified Corps. Its male and female, officer and other rank personnel, provide the necessary qualified nursing support at all levels and cover a wide variety of nursing specialities. QARANC personnel can be found anywhere in the world where Army Medical Services are required.

During early 2011 the QARANC personnel total was approximately 900.

Royal Army Dental Corps (RADC)

The RADC is a professional corps that fulfils the essential role of maintaining the dental health of the Army in peace and war, both at home and overseas. Qualified dentists and oral surgeons, hygienists, technicians and support ancillaries work in a wide variety of military units – from static and mobile dental clinics to field medical units, military hospitals and dental laboratories.

During early 2011 the RADC personnel total was approximately 370.

The Royal Army Veterinary Corps (RAVC)

The RAVC look after the many animals that the Army has on strength. Veterinary tasks in today's army are mainly directed towards guard or search dogs, and horses for ceremonial duties. Personnel total in early 2011 was 350.

THE ADJUTANT GENERAL'S CORPS (AGC)

The Adjutant General's Corps formed on 1 April 1992 and its sole task is the management of the Army's most precious resource, its soldiers. The Corps absorbed the functions of six existing smaller corps; the Royal Military Police, the Royal Army Pay Corps, the Royal Army Educational Corps, the Royal Army Chaplains Department, the Army Legal Corps and the Military Provost Staff Corps.

The Corps is organised into four branches with early 2011 personnel figures as follows:

Staff and Personnel Support (SPS)	3,750
Provost	1,810
Educational and Training Services	340
Army Legal Services	120

The Role of SPS Branch

The role of SPS Branch is to ensure the efficient and smooth delivery of Personnel Administration to the Army. This includes support to individual officers and soldiers in units by processing pay and Service documentation, first line provision of financial, welfare, education and resettlement guidance to individuals and the provision of clerical skills and information management to ensure the smooth day to day running of the unit or department.

AGC (SPS) officers are employed throughout the Army, in direct support of units as Regimental Administrative Officers or AGC Detachment Commanders. They hold Commander AGC (SPS) and SO2 AGC (SPS) posts in district/Divisional and Brigade HQs and fill posts at the Adjutant General's Information Centre (AGIC) and general staff appointment throughout the Army headquarters locations.

AGC (SPS) soldiers are employed as Military Clerks in direct support of units within the AGC Field Detachments, in fixed centre pay offices, in headquarters to provide staff support and in miscellaneous posts such as embassy clerks, as management accountants or in AGIC as programmer analysts.

The principal functional tasks of AGC (SPS) personnel on operations are:

a. The maintenance of Field Records, including the soldiers 'Record of Service', casualty reporting and disciplinary documentation.

b. Clerical and staff support to Battlegroup HQs and independent Sub Units such as Engineer and Logistic Squadrons.

c. The issue of pay and allowances to personnel.

d. The maintenance of Imprest Accounts (the MoD Public Accounts) which involve paying local suppliers for services, receiving cash from non-Army agencies such as NAAFI and Forces Post Office receipts.

e. The deployment of a Field Records Cell which co-ordinates all personnel administration in the field.

f. AGC (SPS) personnel play a full part in operational duties by undertaking such tasks as local defence, guard and command post duties. In addition, Commanding Officers can employ any soldier in their unit as they see fit and may require AGC (SPS) personnel to undertake appropriate additional training to allow them to be used in some specialist roles specific to the unit, or as radio operators or drivers.

Currently, about 70% of AGC (SPS) soldiers are based in UK, 20% in Germany and 10% elsewhere. The majority, currently 70% are serving with field force units, with the remaining 30% in base and training units or HQs, such as MoD.

Members of AGC (SPS) are first trained as soldiers and then specialise as Military Clerks. AGC (SPS) officers complete the same military training as their counterparts in other Arms and Services, starting as the Royal Military Academy, Sandhurst. They are required to attend all promotion courses such as the Junior Command and Staff Course, and to pass the standard career exams prior to promotion to the rank of Major.

The Role of the Provost Branch

Provost comprises the Royal Military Police (RMP), the Military Provost Staff (MPS) and the Military Provost Guard Service (MPGS). The main role of the RMP is to 'Police the Force', and 'provide Police Support to the Force'. The MPS provide advice and support to Commanders on all custody and detention issues. The MPGS is the Army's professional armed guarding service, established to release general service personnel from armed guarding duties.

Provost Mission: To provide the necessary military police, custodial and guarding service to the Army in order to ensure military effectiveness.

The Royal Military Police (RMP)

The RMP is regulatory body with unique investigative and policing skills and competencies which also undertakes military tasks complementary to its specialist role.

The RMP has three specialist areas:

Investigations: Supporting the Military Criminal Justice System is the highest priority for the RMP, who alone have the unique capability to deliver the full range of policing functions throughout the spectrum of conflict at home, in overseas garrisons and on operations. This police support is both proactive and visible, contributing to success on operations by enforcing the law, deterring crime and thus underpinning the Military Criminal Justice System.

Special Investigations: The Special Investigations Branch (SIB) of the RMP is responsible for all special and sensitive investigations. In high intensity conflict they continue to police, investigating a range of offences ranging from murder to fratricide; the investigative procedure is the same, only the operational context changes.

Close Protection (CP): RMP provide CP personnel and training for others on CP duties, both for at risk military personnel and those of other government departments. The RMP provides a core of trained manpower at high readiness to cover contingencies and can also generate Short Term Training Teams.

In addition, the RMP also provide:

♦ The provision of a specialist Crime Reduction service to reduce the opportunities for crime, to shape attitudes and to maintain morale.
♦ The regulation of movement and manoeuvre, such as route reconnaissance, route selection, signing and manning of routes, and the establishment of Military Police Stations and Posts.
♦ The training and mentoring of Indigenous Civilian and Police Forces through the provision of basic police training in the form of an investigative capability with crime scene management, interviewing skills, file preparation and possibly forensics.
♦ Special to arm advice directly to the operational commanders on: arrest and detention, searches of people, property or vehicles, incident control, and crime scene management. They will also provide surety to correct handling of evidence in support of pre-planned operations.

The Military Provost Staff (MPS)

The principal function of the Military Corrective Training Centre (MCTC) at Colchester, Essex, is to detain personnel, both male and female, of the three Services and civilians subject to the Services Disciplinary Acts, in accordance with the provisions of the Imprisonment and Detention (Army) Rules 1979. The MCTC is an establishment that provides corrective training for those servicemen and women sentenced to periods of detention; it is not a prison. The MCTC takes servicemen and women who have been sentenced to periods of detention from 14 days to two years. Up to 316 detainees can be held at the MCTC. The MCTC has extensive Military Training facilities and an Education Wing that includes trade training. The MPS has approximately 110 personnel.

The Military Provost Guard Services (MPGS)

The Military Provost Guard Service (MPGS) was established in 1997 as the Army's professional armed guarding service to relieve the Ministry of Defence Police and general service personnel from armed guarding duties at nominated Tri-Service locations.

The MPGS comprises regular soldiers employed on a Military Local Service Engagement that is restricted to the United Kingdom. All MPGS soldiers have had previous service experience and service may be up to the age of 55. The MPGS has approximately 1,745 personnel.

The Role of the ETS Branch

The AGC (ETS) Branch has the responsibility of improving the efficiency, effectiveness and morale of the Army by providing support to operations and the developmental education, training, support and resettlement services that the Army requires to carry out its task. ETS personnel provide assistance at almost all levels of command but their most visible task is the manning of Army Education Centres wherever the Army is stationed. At these centres officers and soldiers receive the educational support necessary for them to achieve both civilian and military qualifications.

The Role of the ALS Branch

The AGC (ALS) Branch advises on all aspects of service and civilian law that may affect every level of the Army from General to Private soldiers. Members of the branch are usually qualified as solicitors or barristers.

Smaller Corps

THE INTELLIGENCE CORPS (Int Corps) – The Int Corps deals with operational intelligence, counter intelligence and security. During early 2011 the personnel strength of the Intelligence Corps was 1,530.

THE ARMY PHYSICAL TRAINING CORPS (APTC) – Consists mainly of SNCOs who are responsible for unit fitness. The majority of major units have a representative from this corps on their strength. Early 2011 personnel total was in the region of 480.

ROYAL ARMY CHAPLAIN'S DEPARTMENT (RAChD) – Provides officers and soldiers with religious and welfare support/advice. The RAChD has approximately 130 chaplains who represent all of the mainstream religions.

THE GENERAL SERVICE CORPS (GSC) – A holding unit for specialists. Personnel from this corps are generally members of the reserve army.

SMALL ARMS SCHOOL CORPS (SASC) – A small corps with the responsibility of training instructors in all aspects of weapon handling. Early 2011 personnel total was in the region of 160.

CHAPTER 13 – JOINT SERVICE UNITS

The Leven Report published in June 2011 proposed the creation of a 4 star-led Joint Forces Command, to strengthen the focus on joint operations and joint warfare development.

SPECIAL FORCES

Although the exact detail is highly classified, the UK Special Forces Group (UKSF) is under the command of the Director Special Forces (DSF). Units known to be part of the UK Special Forces Group include:

22nd Special Air Service Regiment (Army)	22 SAS
Special Boat Service (Royal Marines)	SBS
Special Forces Support Group	SFSG
Special Reconnaissance Regiment	SRR
18 (UKSF) Signal Regiment	18 SIG REGT
Reserve Components	

Special Forces Support Group

Based around a core group from the 1st Battalion The Parachute Regiment, The Special Forces Support Group (SFSG) is a unit within the UK Special Forces that was established in April 2006. SFSG directly supports Special Forces operations worldwide and also provides an additional counter-terrorist capability. Personnel for the SGSG also come from the Royal Marines, and the Royal Air Force Regiment. Members of the Special Forces Support Group (SFSG) retain the cap badges of their parent units but also wear the SFSG insignia.

All SFSG personnel have passed either the Royal Marines Commando course, the Airborne Forces Selection course run by the Parachute Regiment or the RAF Pre-Parachute Selection course. Quaified personnel are then equipped and provided with additional training to fit their specific specialist role on joining the SFSG.

The UK MoD has described the main role of the SFSG as "Providing direct support to UK Special Forces intervention operations around the world. They will be prepared to operate in war-fighting, counter-insurgency and counter-terrorism operations at short notice. Their roles may include provision of supporting or diversionary attacks, cordons, fire support, force protection and supporting training tasks. Prior to the creation of the SFSG, these tasks have been carried out by other units on an ad hoc basis".

SFSG consists of four strike companies and a support company with specialist units such as a CBRN detection troop and tactical air control parties. The group is believed to be equipped with Jackal vehicles.

Special Reconnaissance Regiment

The Special Reconnaissance Regiment (SRR) was formed in April 2005 to meet a growing worldwide demand a for special reconnaissance capability. The term 'special reconnaissance' covers a wide range of highly classified specialist skills and activities related to covert surveillance.

The SRR draws its personnel from existing units and can recruit new volunteers from serving members of the Armed Forces where necessary.

Other sub-units provide combat and service support.

18 (UKSF) Signal Regiment

This regiment provides communications and electronic warfare support to the whole of the UK Special Forces Group. Squadrons under command include:

> 264 (SAS) Signals Squadron
>
> SBS Signals Squadron
>
> 267 (SRR) Signals Squadron
>
> 268 (SFSG) Signals Squadron

Special Forces Reserve (SF-R)

The two reserve SAS Regiments (21 and 23 SAS) together with 63 SAS Signal Squadron and the SBS Reserve have evolved into the Reserve Component of the UKSF Group.

JOINT HELICOPTER COMMAND (JHC)

The majority of UK service helicopters are assigned to the Joint Helicopter Command which is under the command of Commander Land Forces. The primary role of the JHC is to deliver and sustain effective Battlefield Helicopter and Air Assault assets, operationally capable under all environmental conditions, in order to support the UK's defence missions and tasks. Major formations under JHC command are as follows:

- All Army Aviation Units
- RAF Support Helicopter Force
- Commando Helicopter Force
- 16 Air Assault Brigade
- Combat Support Units
- Combat Service Support Units
- Joint Helicopter Command and Standards Wing

Our estimate for the JHC service personnel total is approximately 13,000 from all three services.

Our figures suggest that the JHC appears to have about 350 aircraft (forward fleet) available as follows.

Possible UK Helicopter types available during 2011 (The Forward Fleet)

Royal Navy	Merlin HM1	23
	Lynx Mk 3	21
	Lynx Mk 8	20
	Sea King Mk 2/7	9
	Sea King Mk 5	11
	Sea King Mk 4 and 6c	29
		113
Army Air Corps	Apache	50
	A109	4
	Gazelle	42
	Lynx Mk 7 and 9	59
		155
Royal Air Force	Chinook	29
	Merlin Mk 3	17
	Puma	23
	Sea King Mk 3/3a (Search and Rescue)	17
		86

Note: These figures suggest numbers of aircraft available for operations and not the total inventory which includes aircraft being used for training or being upgraded etc.

In a normal non-operational environment (with the exception of Lynx), each individual aircraft is resourced to fly approximately 400 hours per year. The Lynx fleet is generally resourced for 23,900 hours, which averages about 405 hours per aircraft.

Helicopters not under the command of the JHC include the Royal Navy's fleet helicopters (in support of ships at sea), and the Royal Air Force and Royal Navy's search and rescue aircraft.

JOINT CHEMICAL, BIOLOGICAL, RADIOLOGICAL AND NUCLEAR REGIMENT (JT CBRN REGT)

The Jt CBRN Regt was created in 1999 and is based at RAF Honington, Suffolk. The Regiment is composed of two squadrons from 1 RTR and 27 Sqn RAF Regiment plus supporting staff from other army units. The Jt CBRN Regt fields specialist CBRN defence equipment, specifically the Fuchs nuclear and chemical reconnaissance and survey vehicle, the Integrated Biological Detection System (IBDS) and the Multi-Purpose Decontamination System (MPDS). The Regiment is an essential element for any joint force operation where there is an CBRN threat, enhancing the integral CBRN defence capabilities of the remainder of the force. Not only does the Regiment support Army formations but also other vital assets such as air bases, logistic areas and key lines of communication.

Joint CBRN Regiment

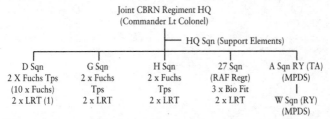

Note:
(1) The Light Role Team (LRT) consists of specialist personnel with dedicated vehicles and communications equipment plus the required detection systems.
(2) Where appropriate the Direct Application Decontamination System (DADS) is available.

In peace the Army may be asked to provide Military Assistance to the Civil Authorities. In these circumstances, the Joint CBRN Regiment may be called on to deal with radiological, biological or chemical hazards.

The regiment has made a major contribution to almost every UK military operation during the past decade.

Note: 27 Squadron RAF Regiment recently re-roled as a Field Defence Squadron for service in Afghanistan. The Squadron has now returned to the Joint CBRN Regiment. During late 2011 the MoD announced a future change in the role of !RTR. From late 2012 we expect to see the RAF Regiment providing the bulk of the personnel assigned to the JT CBRN Regiment.

DEFENCE MEDICAL SERVICES (DMS)

The Defence Medical Services include the whole of the medical, dental, nursing, health professional, paramedical, veterinary and support personnel (about 7,000 uniformed personnel) including civilian staff, employed by the three Armed Services. These elements are responsible for providing healthcare to service personnel serving in the UK and overseas and on operations. In addition and where appropriate the families of service personnel and entitled civilians (possibly about 260,000 people). DMS also provides some aspects of healthcare to other countries' personnel overseas, in both permanent military bases and in areas of conflict and war zones.

The range of services provided by the Defence Medical Services includes:

- Primary healthcare
- Dental care
- Hospital care
- Rehabilitation
- Occupational medicine
- Community mental healthcare
- Specialist medical care

Defence Medical Services also provide healthcare in a range of facilities, including medical and dental centres, regional rehabilitation units and in field hospitals. The Surgeon General is the professional head of the Defence Medical Services and responsible for the healthcare and medical operational capability. His responsibilities include defining the standard and quality of healthcare needed in both operational and non-operational environments and assuring its delivery. He is also responsible for setting the strategy and the associated (non-clinical) policies for the Defence Medical Services.

The Deputy Chief of Defence Staff – Health (DCDS(H) is accountable for the overall outputs of the Defence Medical Services.

These two senior officers oversee the work of three separate organisations:

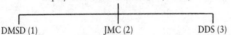

HQ DMS
Surgeon General
(Litchfield)

Deputy Chief of the Defence Staff (Health)

DMSD (1) JMC (2) DDS (3)

Notes:

(1) The Defence Medical Services Department (DMSD) is the headquarters for the Defence Medical Services providing strategic direction to ensure delivery of defence medical outputs. The DMSD operates through the following four directorates: Medical Operations; Medical Policy; Healthcare; Finance and Secretariat.

(2) Joint Medical Command (JMC) – This is a joint service agency providing secondary care personnel to meet requirements for operational deployments. It also supports the front line units by educating and training medical personnel through the Defence Medical and Training Agency (DEMTA). DMETA runs about 2,000 clinical courses (providing about 300,000 training days) to all three services. JMC has responsibility for the following:

- MDHUs (Ministry of Defence Hospital Units)
- RCDM (The Royal Centre for Defence Medicine)
- DMRC (The Defence Medical Rehabilitation Centre at Headley Court
- DMSTC (The Defence Medical Services Training Centre in Aldershot
- The Defence Medical Postgraduate Deanery

The JMC provides a single headquarters responsible for healthcare delivery.

(3) Defence Dental Services (DDS) – this is a joint service organisation employing both Armed Forces and civilian personnel that provides dental services in the UK at service establishments and to personnel on operations overseas. The DDS came under the 'umbrella' of the JMC from mid 2009.

Figures in early 2010 suggest the following personnel totals for the DMS:

Regular Personnel – Defence Medical Services

	Trained Personnel
Medical officers	476
Nurses	1,500
Medical support services	3,882
Dental officers and allied dental healthcare professionals	764
Total	6,622

Single Service Medical Care

The three armed services are responsible for delivering primary healthcare to their respective services and for providing the required medical support on operations.

Royal Naval Medical Service (RNMS)

Army Medical Services (AMS)

Royal Air Forces Medical Services (RAF MS)

Late 2008 personnel figures for these agencies were as follows:

	Trained Personnel	Personnel in initial training	Personnel total
Royal Navy	1378	271	1649

Army	3783	561	4344
Royal Air Force	1574	63	1637
Tri-service Totals	6735	895	7630

Although the above table is about two years older than the previous table showing trained strength for the complete DMS, the total trained strength figure in each table is very much the same..

Defence Nursing Staff

On operations, nursing staff from all three services deliver primary and emergency care at the front line and secondary and critical care in field hospitals. Aeromed evacuation of casualties is supported by defence nurses who deliver intensive care nursing during patient transfers both in theatre and on return to the UK working within the Critical Care Air Support Teams.

When not deployed on operations, defence nurses work within Ministry of Defence Hospital Units within NHS Trusts across the UK to maintain their clinical skills and care for the general public. In particular, Defence Nurses working at the Royal Centre for Defence Medicine in Birmingham and at the Defence Medical Rehabilitation Centre at Headley Court contribute directly to the health care provision of military personnel.

Hospital Care

In the UK hospital care is provided at Ministry of Defence Hospital Units (MDHU).

The Defence Medical Services Department (DMSD) has contracts with the NHS for provision of care in MDHUs, which are run as military units embedded within selected NHS hospitals. There are MDHUs at Derriford (Plymouth), Frimley Park (Aldershot), Northallerton (near Catterick), Peterborough and Portsmouth.

In addition, the Defence Medical Services runs a number of other units which include the Royal Centre for Defence Medicine (Birmingham), Defence Services Medical Rehabilitation Centre (Headley Court) and the Duchess of Kent's Psychiatric Unit (Catterick). There are also about 245 DMS medical and dental primary care facilities mostly located in the UK. Outside of the UK primary healthcare, and some secondary healthcare, is provided on board Royal Navy ships and in overseas bases and theatres of military operations.

The Military Ward at the new Queen Elizabeth Hospital in Birmingham started taking patients in 2010 and service personnel are cared for in single rooms or four-bedded bays that have additional features for the exclusive use of military patients. The ward has more staff than a normal NHS ward, a quiet room for relatives as well as a communal space for military patients to gather. A dedicated physiotherapy area has also been provided close to the ward for service patients.

On operations in Afghanistan and other overseas locations Field Hospitals provide medical support that includes primary surgery, an intensive care unit, medium and low dependency nursing care beds and diagnostic support, as well as emergency medical care. These Field Hospital may be staffed by medical personnel from all three services.

Service personnel serving in Germany who require hospital care are treated in one of the five German Provider Hospitals.

Royal Centre for Defence Medicine (RCDM)

The RCDM in Birmingham provides a centre for military personnel requiring specialised care, and incorporates a facility for the treatment of service personnel who have been evacuated from an overseas deployment area after becoming ill or wounded/injured. RCDM also acts as a centre for the training of Defence Medical Service personnel.

In operation since 2001 the RCDM operates on a contract between the DMSD and the University Hospitals Birmingham (UHB) NHS Trust.

The RCDM is a Joint Service establishment with medical personnel from all three of the armed services wearing their respective Naval, Army, or Air Force uniforms.

Midlands Medical Accommodation Project

From 2010 Whittington Barracks in Lichfield has become the home of military medicine The Midlands Medical Accommodation project (MMA) will ensure that the area becomes the central focus for military medical expertise and assets. About 2,000 military and civilian staff will eventually work at the barracks when the MMA project completes in 2014.

The first phase – MMA Increment 1 – has already delivered a modern headquarters office building for the DMS at Whittington Barracks that incorporates both the Surgeon General's strategic Headquarters and those of the Joint Medical Command, both of which are fully operational.

The second phase – MMA Increment 2 – will see the DMS elements relocate from Keogh Barracks near Aldershot to a new modern training centre at Whittington Barracks. The new complex will include training facilities, a learning centre; llecture theatre, messes for Officers, Warrant Officers and Senior Non Commissioned Officers, living accommodation for permanent staff and a new Junior Ranks' dining and leisure facility.

Work began on site at the beginning of summer 2011, with the relocation planned to begin at the end of 2013.

MMA1 and 2 will see around £200 million invested in the redevelopment of Whittington Barracks.

MINISTRY OF DEFENCE POLICE AND GUARDING AGENCY

This agency has two major elements, The Ministry of Defence Police and the Ministry of Defence Guarding Agency:

Ministry of Defence Police (MDP)

The MDP has its headquarters at Wethersfield, in Essex, and is deployed across the British Isles at over 100 MoD sites from Culdrose in Cornwall to the Clyde in Scotland. Organised into five divisional commands, with headquarters at York, Aldershot, Aldermaston, Foxhill and the Clyde Naval Base, the personnel total is approximately 3,400.

The majority of MDP tasks are security orientated and include the security of military bases, protecting against the sabotage of assets and the threat of terrorist incursion. At the same time the MDP has a role as a civilian police force creating a safe crime free environment. The MDP is supported by a number of specialist units that include the largest fraud squad in the UK, marine units that are equipped with a large number of amphibious craft, over 400 police dogs, a special escort group and a multi-capability operational support unit.

During early 2011 it was announced that the MDP had established a Defence Crime Board, to provide strategic direction to the defence-wide effort to reduce the harm done to the defence budget, safety, security and military operational capability by crime and fraud.

All MDP officers are trained in the use of firearms and at any one time about 70 per cent of MDP officers on duty will be armed.

Ministry of Defence Guard Service

The Ministry of Defence Guard Service (MGS) is the uniformed, unarmed element forming part of the larger Ministry of Defence Police and Guarding Agency. The Ministry of Defence Guard Service was formed into a corporate structure as part of the Ministry of Defence Police and Guarding Agency in April 2004. The MGS has a personnel total of around 3,900 personnel who are based at over 200 locations across the UK. There are six regional headquarters locations at Aldershot, Bath, Clyde Naval Base, London, Shrewsbury and York.

The Training Centre is at Weathersfield in Essex.

The forecast cost of the MGS for FY2010-2011 was £112 million.

Military Corrective Training Centre (MCTC)

The MCTC takes servicemen and women who have been sentenced to periods of detention from 14 days to two years. The vast majority are serving periods of detention to which they have been sentenced by court martial or after summary hearing by their commanding officers. Most detainees have offended against Armed Forces law rather than criminal law, and few are committed for offences that would have resulted in custody had they been in civilian life.

All detainees are held in accordance with rules determining committal to custody within the Armed Forces Act 2006.

Staff at the MCTC are drawn mainly from the Military Provost Staff Corps (MPSC) with representatives from the other services.

CHAPTER 14 - RECRUITING, SELECTION, TRAINING

OVERVIEW

Recruiting is carried out to attract sufficient men and women of the right quality to meet the Army's personnel requirements. Selection is the process that is carried out to ensure that those who are accepted into the Army have the potential to be good soldiers and are capable of being trained to carry out their chosen trade. Training is the process of preparing those men and women for their careers in the Army. Training is progressive and continues all the way through a soldier and an officers' career.

The Army Recruitment and Training Division is responsible for the delivery of army recruiting and training.

ARMY RECRUITMENT AND TRAINING DIVISION

The Army Recruitment and Training Division (ARTD) is responsible for each stage of a potential recruit's progress from the recruiting office, through a Recruit Selection Centre, into recruit training, through specialist courses before they are finally posted to their regiment in the Field Army. The ARTD is headed by the Director General Army Recruitment and Training (DG ART), a Major General who is responsible for ensuring that sufficient men and women of the right quality are recruited and trained to meet the needs of the service.

The ARTD Headquarters is based at Upavon in Wiltshire, close to many of the training units. Recruiting is carried out from over 100 locations in towns and cities throughout the country, and individual training is conducted at some 40 schools. With a permanent staff of about 12,000 across the whole of the recruiting and training organisation, the Division is responsible for Ministry of Defence land, buildings and field assets valued at more than one and a quarter billion pounds.

The ARTD is required to enlist about 12,000 recruits each year and to train a total of about 100,000 officers and soldiers. ARTD conducts almost 1,500 different types of courses, with over 6,000 actual courses run each year. There are over 10,000 officers and soldiers under training at any time. Across all training phases, the average annual unit cost of training a soldier or officer is believed to be in excess of £19,000.

ARTD operations are divided into four inter-related functions: Recruiting, Recruit training (Phase 1), Specialist training (Phase 2), and Career training (Phase 3).

ARTD was formerly named Army Training and Recruitment Agency. It was renamed on 1 July 2006.

RECRUITING

An MoD committee called the Standing Committee Army Manpower Forecasts (SCAMF) calculates the numbers that need to be enlisted to maintain the Army's personnel at the correct level. The Committee needs to take account of changing unit establishments, wastage caused by servicemen and women leaving the service at the end of their engagements, and those who might choose to leave before their engagements come to an end (PVR – Premature Voluntary Release). The number required in each trade in the Army is assessed and figures are published at six monthly intervals so that adjustments may be made during the year.

Within ARTD, the Recruiting Group runs all Army Recruiting from the headquarters in Upavon. Recruiting activities take place all over the country, using the network of over 100 Careers Offices, about 60 Schools Advisers, over 20 Army Youth Teams and Regimental Recruiting Teams. The Commander Recruiting Group, a Brigadier serving in ARTD and his staff, located throughout the United Kingdom are responsible for the recruiting and selection to meet the personnel targets.

Potential recruits are attracted into the Army in a number of ways including advertisements on the television, on the internet and in the press. Permanently established recruiting teams from many Regiments and Corps tour the country and staff from the Armed Forces Careers Offices (AFCO) and Army Careers Information Offices (ACIO) visit schools, youth clubs and job centres. There is a network of AFCOs and ACIOs located throughout the UK and Army Careers Advisers who access schools and universities throughout the country. Young, recently trained soldiers are also sent back to their home towns and schools to talk to their friends about life in the Army and are regularly interviewed by the local press.

The overall national marketing (advertising) spend for FY2009-2010 was £29.5 million (for both Regular and TA). These activities included television and press advertising, the production of DVDs, leaflets, pamphlets and brochures as well as the overarching production and design costs.

Annual Army recruiting figures (intake to untrained strength) during the recent past are as follows:

	2007/2008	*2008/2009*	*2009/2010*
Officers	1,060	890	800
Soldiers	13,480	13,620	13,390

Outflow figures (untrained personnel leaving the army) in the recent past are:

	2007/2008	*2008/2009*	*2009/2010*
Officers	330	160	140
Soldiers	4,530	3,620	4,120

Outflow figures (trained personnel leaving the army) in the recent past are:

	2007/2008	*2008/2009*	*2009/2010*
Officers	1,160	1,100	840
Soldiers	9,310	8,240	6,730

SOLDIER SELECTION

Potential recruits are normally aged between 16 years and nine months and 32 years, except when they are applying for a vacancy as a junior soldier when the age limits are from 16 years to 18 years and six months. As a trained soldier the minimum length of service will be four years from the age of 18, or from the start of training, if over 18.

Under the selection system, a potential recruit will have a two day assessment at the Army Development and Selection Centre (ADSC). There are ADSC at (Pirbright, Lichfield, Penicuik (near Edinburgh) and Ballymena in Northern Ireland.

At the ADSC he or she will take the Army Entrance Test which is designed to assess ability to assimilate the training required for the candidate's chosen trade. The staff at the ADSC will then conduct a number of interviews to decide on overall suitability for the Army. A medical examination will also be carried out that checks on weight, eyesight and hearing. The potential recruit will also see at first hand the type of training that they will undergo, and the sort of life that they will lead in barracks if successful in getting into the Army. Physical fitness is assessed based on a 'best effort' 1.5 mile timed run and some gymnasium exercises. After further interviews the candidate is informed if he or she is successful and if so is offered a vacancy in a particular trade and Regiment or Corps.

PHASE 1 BASIC TRAINING FOR RECRUITS

Basic Recruit or Phase 1 training comprises the Combat Infantryman's Course (CIC) for infantry and the Common Military Syllabus Recruit (CMSR) for all other British Army regiments and corps.

As part of ARDT, the Initial Training Group (ITG) is responsible for Phase 1 (Basic) Training of the majority of soldier recruits, which is undertaken primarily at the Army Training Centres; Bassingbourn in Cambridgeshire, and Pirbright in Surrey. Exceptions to this are the adult Infantry recruits who go direct to the School of Infantry at Catterick in Yorkshire.

There is an Army Technical Foundation College at Winchester in Hampshire and the Army Foundation College at Harrogate in Yorkshire.

ARTD has its own Staff Leadership School (ASLS), at Alexander Barracks, Pirbright. ASLS has the task of training the Army's trainers, from corporal section commanders and trade instructors to Commanding Officers, as well as administrative and support staff. In all, up to 2,400 military and civilian training, supervisory and support staff are trained each year. ASLS opened in 2007.

School of Infantry, Catterick

Catterick is the home of all Infantry Training at Phase 1 and Phase 2, except Junior soldiers destined for the Infantry who continue to receive Phase 1 training at the Army Foundation College. Catterick comprises the Headquarters School of Infantry and the Infantry Training Centre, Catterick. Also under its Command are the Infantry Battle School at Brecon and the Infantry Training Centre at Warminster, which both provide Phase 3 training for Infantry officers and soldiers.

Combat Infantryman's Course

The Combat Infantryman's Course (CIC) is the framework upon which all regular infantry recruit training is based. The course equips recruits with infantry special to arms skills needed for a rifle platoon ready to deploy on an operational tour after minimal further appropriate pre-operational training in the Field Army.   Successful completion of the CIC marks the end of initial army training.

The majority of recruits joining the infantry choose line infantry regiments; they undertake the standard CIC which lasts for 24 weeks. Recruits joining the Foot Guards, Parachute Regiment and the Gurkhas, carry out additional training to meet the particular needs of these regiments.   Similarly, recruits from the Army Foundation College at Harrogate undertake a specially adapted, but shorter CIC.

Royal Irish Regiment recruits also undertake the CIC at Catterick.

The Combat Infantryman's Course (Single) is structured around three phases as follows:

> Weeks 1-6 Individual skills, drill, weapons training, fitness and fieldcraft.

> Weeks 7-21 Team skills, endurance training including long runs, patrolling skills.

> Weeks 22 – 24 Live firing and battle camp at Sennybridge in Wales.

The unit costs of recruiting and training infantry are substantial, as shown in the next table.

Costs of infantry recruiting and training (Phase 1 and Phase 2)

Infantry Group	Length of course (weeks)	Cost per trainee for financial year 2003–04 (£)
Line	24	£22,000
Guards	26	£26,000
Para	28	£37,000

Other figures published in 2010 suggest that the average cost of training an infantry soldier from recruitment to graduation from the ITC had risen to £31,000.

Gurkhas

Recruits from Nepal joining the Royal Gurkha Rifles, Queen's Gurkha Engineers, Queen's Gurkha Signals and the Queen's Own Gurkha Transport Regiment are trained at the ITC on a 38 week CIC (G).This combines the normal Common Military Syllabus Recruits (CMS(R)) course taught at the Army Training Regiments with the CIC course and it includes a special English language and British culture package.

As many as 30,000 potential Gurkha recruits apply to join the British Army each year and between 150 and 200 are selected.

Army Training Centres

Phase 1 training for all regiments and corps except infantry comprises Common Military Syllabus Recruit (CMSR). This includes training in the basic military skills required of all soldiers and incorporates weapon handling and shooting, drill, physical fitness, field tactics, map reading, survival in nuclear chemical and biological warfare and general military knowledge. It is an intensive course and requires the recruit to show considerable determination and courage to succeed.

Phase 1 training for regiments and corps excluding infantry is undertaken by Army Training Centres as shown below:

ATC Pirbright – Royal Regiment of Artillery; Royal Corps of Signals; Army Air Corps; Royal Logistic Corps; Adjutant General's Corps (including the Royal Military Police); Intelligence Corps; Royal Army Medical Corps; all female adult entry soldiers.

ATC Bassingbourne – Royal Armoured Corps; Royal Engineers; Royal Electrical and Mechanical Engineers.

Army Foundation College – Harrogate

The Army Foundation College (AFC) at Harrogate delivers Phase 1 (initial military) training to Junior Entry recruits destined for the Royal Armoured Corps, Royal Artillery and Infantry. Recruits make their final capbadge selection after week 21. The aim of the course is to develop the qualities of leadership, character, and team spirit required of a soldier to achieve a full career in the Army. The 42-week course is a progressive and integrated package divided into three 14-week terms. It combines the Common Military Syllabus (Recruits) with Vocational Education and Leadership and Initiative Training. Recruits achieve a Foundation Modern Apprenticeship and up to Key Skills Level 3.

Entrants to the college are aged between 16 and 17 years. At the College, they undertake a course that provides a supportive environment allowing students to develop a broad range of skills and qualifications that are equally valuable, in both Army and civilian life. There are three main elements to the course:

There are 23 weeks of military training, which include basic or advanced soldiering, progressive physical training, infantry weapons, grenades, military leadership, marksmanship, parade ground drill. There is also a two week final exercise in the field.

There are five weeks of leadership and initiative training which takes in hill walking, hiking, caving, rock climbing, abseiling, and all kind of leadership and command tasks.

Lastly, there are 14 weeks of vocational education which can result in an NVQ or SVQ in Information Technology.

Army Technical Foundation College – Winchester

The Army Technical Foundation College Winchester was opened in 2010 and provides basic training to Junior Entry recruits wishing to join the Technical Corps. Recruits are found from the following: Royal Engineers;   Royal Signals; Army Air Corps; Royal Logistics Corps; Army Medical Services; Royal Electrical and Mechanical Engineers; Adjutant General's Corps.

This is a 23-week course, designed to develop the Junior Soldiers' individual and team skills in a progressive manner, preparing them for Phase 2 training, where they will lean the specific skills for their chosen Army trade. Course modules include: Fieldcraft;   Skill at Arms;   Fitness Training; Qualities of a Soldier; Military Knowledge; Battlefield Casualty Drills; Individual Health;   Education.

PHASE 2 SPECIAL TO ARM RECRUIT TRAINING

Phase 2 training is the 'Special to Arm' training that is required to prepare soldiers who have recently completed their basic Phase 1 training, to enable them to take their place in field force units of their Regiment or Corps. This phase of training has no fixed period and courses vary considerably in length.

From 2005 Phase 2 training for the major Arms and Services of the British Army has been carried out as follows:

Infantry – Infantry recruits do all of their recruit training (Phase 1 and Phase 2) at the Infantry Training Centre at Catterick.

The Royal Armoured Corps – Training takes place at the Armour Centre at Bovington Camp and Lulworth. Recruits into the Household Cavalry Regiment also undergo equitation training.

The Royal Artillery – Training takes place at the Royal School of Artillery at Larkhill in Wiltshire.

The Royal Engineers – Training takes place at the Combat Engineering School at Minley, the Construction Engineer School in Chatham and Blackwater and the Defence Explosive Ordnance Disposal School.

Royal Signals – Training takes place at 11th (Royal School of Signals) Regiment at Blandford Camp in Dorset. Since April 2004, the Defence College of CIS (DCCIS), also based at Blandford Camp, assumed the responsibility for Royal Signals training as well as that for the Royal Navy and Royal Air Force Signals communications specialists.

Army Air Corps – Training takes place at the School of Army Aviation in Middle Wallop

The Royal Logistic Corps – Training takes place at the RLC Training Regiment and Depot at Deepcut and the School of Logistics at Marchwood – previously under the joint Defence Logistic Support Training Group (DLSTG) and since April 2004 under Defence College of Logistics (DCL), also based at Deepcut. Under these new arrangements, ARTD is also responsible for Royal Navy and Royal Air Force Logistics training. The Army School of Catering, Aldershot, the Army School of Ammunition at Kineton and the School of Petroleum, West Moors are also ARTD logistics training facilities, as is the Defence School of Transport at Leconfield.

Royal Electrical and Mechanical Engineers – Vehicle Mechanics are trained at Bordon and other trades at Arborfield. Since April 2004, the Electro Mechanical elements of the ARTD REME Training Group transferred to the new Defence College of Electro Mechanical Engineering under the command of the Naval Recruiting and Training Agency (NRTA). The Aeronautical elements of the REME Training Group transferred to the Defence College of Aeronautical Engineering under the command of the RAF Training Group Defence Agency (TGDA). The ARTD REME Training Group ceased to exist in name at the end of 2003.

The Adjutant General's Corps – Pay and Clerks are trained at the AGC Depot at Worthy Down near Winchester; Defence School of Languages at Beaconsfield and the Defence Animal Centre at Melton Mowbray. From April 2002, the School of Finance and Management, previously part of the Group and located at Worthy Down, became part of the Defence Academy, although it will remain at Worthy Down for the present. From April 2004, the Royal Military Police (RMP) training school transferred to the Defence College of Policing and Guarding (DCPG) at Southwick Park, Portsmouth.

Intelligence Corps – Have trained since 1997 at the Defence Intelligence and Security Centre (DISC) in Chicksands in Bedfordshire. The DISC is responsible for training all personnel in intelligence, security and information support. In June 2003, command of the Defence School of Languages transferred to DISC, although the school remained at Beaconsfield.

Army Medical Services (AMS) – Made up of the Royal Army Medical Corps (RAMC), Royal Army Dental Corps (RADC), Queen Alexandra's Royal Army Nursing Corps (QARANC), and the Royal Army Veterinary Corps (RAVC). Training is conducted by the joint service Defence Medical Training Organisation at Aldershot and Birmingham, the Defence Dental Agency in Birmingham and the RAVC training centre at Melton Mowbray respectively.

Recruit Physical Training Assessments – During Recruit Training personnel are assessed at different stages of training as follows:

Test	Introduction	Interim	Final
Heaves	2	4 6	
Sit Up Test	1 Min (20 reps)	2 min (42 reps)	3 min (65 reps)
1.5 Mile Run	11 min 30 sec	11 mins	10 min 30 sec

CONDITIONS OF SERVICE – SOLDIERS AND OFFICERS

Length of Service

As a general rule, all recruits enlist on an Open Engagement. This allows a recruit to serve for 22 years from their 18th birthday or date of attestation, whichever is the later, and so qualify for a pension.

A soldier enlisted on this engagement has a statutory right to leave after four years reckoned from the 18th birthday or from three months after attestation, whichever is the later, subject to giving 12 months notice of intention to leave and providing the soldier is not restricted from leaving in any way. Certain employments, particularly those involving a lengthy training, carry a time bar which requires a longer period before soldiers have the statutory right to leave.

For the initial period after joining the Army individuals are able to be "Discharged As Of Right" (DAOR). There is no obligation to stay during this time. The length of the period of DAOR is six months for under 18s and three months for over 18s after turning up at the Army Training Regiment. Individuals after this time are committed to serve for a minimum engagement of four years. There are of course allowances made for medical and exceptional compassionate circumstances.

Officer Commissions

There are five main types of commission in the Army. These are:

The Short Service Commission (SSC) – the SSC is the normal first commission for those who become an officer in the Army. It is a commission for those who do not wish to commit to a long career but would like to benefit from the high quality training and exceptional experience available to young officers. The SSC is also a first step to a mid-length or full career in the Army. SSCs are awarded for a minimum of three years (six years for the Army Air Corps on account of the length of pilot training) but can be extended to eight.

Candidates for commissions should be over 17 years and nine months and under 29 years old when they begin officer training.

The Intermediate Regular Commission (IRC) – The IRC offers a mid length career for a maximum of 18 years and can be applied for after two years SSC, subject to being recommended. On completion of 18 years after the age of 40 the officer will be entitled to a lump sum and regular monthly payments, which will convert at 65 to a further lump sum and pension.

The Regular Commission (Reg C) – The Reg C offers a full career of 35 years or to age 60 whichever is first. It can be applied for after two years IRC, subject to recommendation. Those completing a full career will receive an immediate lump sum and pension from age 55.

Undergraduate Army Placement (UGAP) – UGAP is a Commission for highly motivated undergraduates studying at UK universities requiring a placement as part of their degree. Up to 10 places are available each year. In all other respects the commission is identical to the GYC.

Late Entry Commissions – A number of vacancies exist for senior Non Commissioned Officers and Warrant Officers to be granted commissions known as Late Entry Commissions. They attend the Late Officer Entry Course (LEOC) at Sandhurst before commencing their officer careers. Because of their age they generally do not rise above the rank of Lieutenant Colonel.

Educational Requirements

All except LE officers require an indicative level of 35 ALIS points (34 for Scottish Standards) gained from the best seven subjects at GCSE, or equivalent, which must include English language, mathematics and either a science subject or a foreign language.

In addition a score of 180 UCAS Tariff points must be acquired in separate subjects at AS and A level, or equivalent. These must include a minimum of two passes at A level, or equivalent, at grades A-E. Note that the General Studies paper does not qualify for UCAS Tariff points.

The attainment of a degree will normally override the requirement for UCAS Tariff points.

Officer Selection and Sandhurst (RMAS)

Officer candidates are normally advised by an Army Careers Adviser of the options open to them and they will also arrange for interviews and familiarisation visits to an appropriate Regiment or Corps. If the Regiment or Corps is prepared to sponsor a candidate they then guide him or her through the rest of the selection procedure. All candidates, except those seeking an Army Sixth Form Scholarship or entry to Welbeck – The Defence Sixth Form College, are required to attend a briefing at the Army Officer Selection Board (AOSB) at Westbury, Wiltshire for psychometric tests and a two day briefing (AOSB Briefing). So long as they meet the minimum standards they will be invited back for another three and a half day assessment also at AOSB (AOSB Main Board). Here they will also undergo a medical examination.

AOSB Main Board consists of a series of interviews and tests that assess the personality and the leadership potential in applicants. Candidates need to be themselves, be prepared to discuss the issues of the day and be physically fit. In 2008/09, AOSB Main Board filtered over 1,482 candidates down to 816 passes.

All potential officers accepted for training attend the RMAS (Royal Military Academy Sandhurst) Commissioning Course which lasts for 44 weeks with three entries a year in January, May and September. After successfully completing the Sandhurst course a young officer then completes a further specialist course with his or her chosen Regiment or Corps. Females cannot be accepted in the Household Cavalry, The Royal Armoured Corps or the Infantry.

In 2009-2010, the RMAS commissioned 645 Direct Entry Regular Officers into the British Army and 157 Territorial Army Officers.

Welbeck – The Defence Sixth Form College/Army Sixth Form Scholarship

Welbeck DSFC offers a two year residential A level course to motivated young people who would like, in the future, a commission in one of the more technical branches of the three Services, as well as the MoD Civil Service. Of those destined for the Army, most Welbexians will be commissioned into the Royal Engineers, the Royal Signals, the Royal Logistic Corps or the Royal Electrical and Mechanical Engineers. Both potential Welbexians and those seeking an Army Sixth Form Scholarship attend a similar 24 hour selection board at AOSB.

PHASE 3 IN-SERVICE TRAINING

An officer or soldier will spend as much as one third of their career attending training courses. Following basic Phase 1 and Phase 2 training soldiers are posted to their units and progressive training is carried out on a continual basis. Training is geared to individual, sub-unit or formation level and units regularly train outside of the UK and Germany. As would be expected there are specialist unit training packages for specific operational commitments such as Afghanistan.

For example the training package for personnel warned off for deployment to Afghanistan includes a special-to-mission package. The training is carried out by specialist training advisory teams at in the UK and in Germany.

Phase 3 training facilities are the same as those listed under Phase 2, and also include the Defence Academy located mainly at Shrivenham. Defence Academy training and education facilities incorporate the Joint Services Command and Staff College at Shrivenham; the Defence Academy College of Management and Technology (previously known as the Royal Military College of Science, Shrivenham); the Royal College of Defence Studies;the Defence Leadership Centre, and the Defence School of Finance and Management. The Joint Doctrine and Concepts Centre is collocated at Shrivenham. A Joint Services Warrant Officer's School is part of the Joint Services Command and Staff College at Shrivenham.

Overseas Students

During any one year, about 4,000 students from over 90 different countries take part in training in the United Kingdom. The charges for training depend on the length of the course, its syllabus and the number taking part. Receipts from overseas governments for this training are believed to be in the region of £50 million annually.

Training areas outside the UK and Europe

The British Army's main training areas outside of the Europe are:

Canada – Suffield

British Army Training Unit Suffield (BATUS) has the responsibility to train battlegroups in the planning and execution of armoured operations through the medium of live firing and tactical test exercise. There are 6 x 'Medicine Man' battlegroup exercises each year in a training season that lasts from March to November.

Canada – Wainwright

The British Army Training Support Unit at Wainwright (BATSU(W)) provides the logistic and administrative support for Infantry units at the Canadian Forces training base in Western Canada.

Kenya

British Army Training and Liaison Staff Kenya (BATLSK) is responsible for supporting Infantry battalion group exercises and approximately 3,000 British troops train in Kenya each year in a harsh unforgiving terrain ranging in altitude from 8,000 feet down to 2,300 feet. BATLSK has been based at its present site in Kahawa Barracks since Kenya's independence in 1963.

Belize

The British Army Training Support unit Belize (BATSUB) was formed on 1 October 1994. Its role is to give training and logistic support to Land Command units training in a tropical jungle environment. In general terms BATSUB costs about £3 million per year. BATSUB was placed in 'suspended animation' during mid 2011 while a review was conducted regarding its future.

Jungle Warfare School

The Jungle Warfare Wing (JWW) is located at Brunei on the island of Borneo close to the border with Sarawak (Malaysia) and is supported by the British Army's Brunei Garrison. JWW exists to provide a jungle training facility to meet the requirement to train jungle warfare instructors for the Field Army of the United Kingdom's Land Forces.

FITNESS REQUIREMENTS

All recruits and soldiers of all ranks and ages are required to take a basic fitness test. At the Recruiting Selection Centres, potential recruits undergo a series of tests known as Physical Standards Selection for

Recruits (PSSR). These are 'best effort' tests that take place in the gymnasium. Recruits are required to complete the 1.5 mile (2.4 km) run.

Adult Entry candidates have to complete the run within 14 minutes or less. All Junior Entrants – Army Foundation College, Army Technical Foundation College or the School Leavers Scheme – are required to complete the run in 14 minutes 30 seconds or less. Officer candidates at the AOSB have to undertake a multi stage fitness test (known as the Beep Test) and aim to achieve a personal standard of 10.2 for males and 8.1 for females, as well as a number of sit-ups and press-ups.

In-service fitness requirements seek to maintain these standards. Tests typically require a 2.4 km run on level ground and in training shoes, in 10.5 minutes for those under 30. There are gradually rising time limits for older personnel. For women the requirement for the 2.4 km run is 13 minutes.

Standard fitness tests currently applied for infantry personnel include:

BPFA Basic Personal Fitness Assessment. Sit-ups, press-ups, and a 1.5 mile (2.4km) run, all carried out against the clock. This tests individual fitness generally. The minimum fitness goals are: 54 continuous sit ups (with feet supported) and a 2.4 km (1.5 mile) run in 11 minutes 45 seconds.

ICFT Infantry Combat Fitness Test. A distance of three miles as a squad carrying 56 pounds of kit each, including personal weapon. Timed to be completed in one hour, individuals must stay with the squad, or be failed.

Most TA volunteers commit to a minimum of some 40 days training a year, comprising one drill night in a week, one weekend in a month and 14 days annual training. Some reservists exceed these minimum commitments.

The Reserve Forces Act 1996 provided for other categories of reservists, such as:

- ♦ Full Time Reserve Service (FTRS) – reservists who wish to serve full time with regulars for a predetermined period in a specific posting.
- ♦ Additional Duties Commitment – part-time service for a specified period in a particular post.

The Act also provided a category of service:

- ♦ Sponsored Reserves, are contractor staff who have agreed to join the Reserves and have a liability to be called up when required to continue their civilian work on operations alongside the Service personnel who depend upon them. Some 3,000 sponsored reservists have served in Iraq and Afghanistan.

Territorial Army units are widely dispersed across the country – much more so than the Regular Forces, and in many areas they are the visible face of the Armed Forces. They help to keep society informed about the Armed Forces, and of the importance of defence to the nation, and have an active role supporting the Cadet organisations. They provide a means by which the community as a whole can contribute to the security of the United Kingdom.

CHAPTER 15 - RESERVE FORCES

OVERVIEW

There have been reserve land forces in Britain since medieval times. Over the years, the titles and structures of these reserve forces have changed, but until World War Two essentially comprised four separate elements: Volunteers, Militia, and Yeomanry provided the part-time, voluntary territorial forces; while retired Regular Army personnel made up the Army Regular Reserve on a compulsory basis, subject to diminishing obligations with age. Today the Army Reserve is formed from the same components – both Regular and Volunteers, with the difference that the erstwhile Volunteers, Militia, and Yeomanry are now incorporated into a single volunteer force as the Territorial Army (TA).

The Territorial Army is the reserve element at the highest state of readiness:

Volunteer Reserves – Personnel Strength as of 1 April 2011

	Officers	Other Ranks	Total
Territorial Army	4,150	21,660	25,810
Non-Regular Permanent Staff	500	550	1,050
Officer Training Corps		4120	4,120
Total Volunteer Reserves			30,980

Some 40 per cent of regular Army recruits are said to come from the TA and Army Cadet Force. According to some sources the annual budget for the TA is in the area of £500 million for 2010-2011 but an accurate figure has yet to be disclosed.

A MoD Report published in 2009 suggested that the average annual cost of a TA Volunteer was in the region of £10,678. When related to the TA personnel strength of 25,810 this would result in an annual expenditure of around £275.5 million on personnel alone.

At the end of May 2011 approximately 3 per cent of UK armed forces personnel (about 285) deployed on overseas operations in Afghanistan were members of the Territorial Army. The exact figure varies from day to day.

The UK has a far lower proportion of reservist to regular soldiers than major allies – presently around 15 to every 85 full-timer compared with a 50:50 split in the United States and 40:60 in Australia.

Territorial Army Order of Battle, as identified in Mid 2011

Arm or Corps	Number of regiments or battalions
Infantry	14
Armour	4
Royal Artillery	7
Royal Engineers	5
Special Air Service	2
Royal Signals	5
Equipment Support	2
Logistics	16
Intelligence Corps	2
Aviation	1
Medical	13 (1)
Total	71

(1) Total includes Medical Regiments and Field Hospitals.

The Territorial Army consists mainly of people who have joined directly from the civilian community. These personnel form the main part of the active, ready reserve for the British Army, train regularly, and are paid at the same rates as the regular forces on a pro-rata basis.

TERRITORIAL ARMY (TA) COMMAND STRUCTURE AND ORGANISATION

The basic command structure and organisation of TA units is the same as for Regular units, by way of Regimental or Battalion, Brigade, Divisional and District Headquarters. In addition, the Directors of the various Arms and Services have the same responsibilities for the TA as their Regular units. At the Headquarters of Regional Forces, the Commander is also Inspector General of the TA.

Types of TA Units

The most familiar type of unit is the 'Independent'. This will be found at the local Territorial Army Centre (formerly called Drill Hall). One or more Army units will be accommodated at the centre, varying in size from a platoon or troop (about 30 Volunteers) to a Battalion or Regiment (about 600 Volunteers). These units will have their place in the Order of Battle, and as with Regular Army units, are equipped for their role. Most of the personnel will be part-time. Volunteers parade one evening each week and perhaps one weekend each month in addition to the annual two-week unit training period.

Some staff at each TA Centre will be regular soldiers. Many units have regular Commanding Officers, Regimental Sergeant Majors, Training Majors, Adjutants and Instructors. The Permanent Staff Instructors (PSI) who are regular Senior Non-Commissioned Officers, are key personnel who help organise the training and administration of the Volunteers.

In the main, TA Infantry Units have a General Purpose structure which will give them flexibility of employment across the spectrum of military operations. All Infantry Battalions, including Parachute Battalions, have a common establishment of three Rifle Companies and a Headquarters Company. Each rifle company sometimes has a support platoon with mortar, anti-tank, reconnaissance, Medium Machine Gun (MMG) and assault pioneer sections under command.

The other type of unit is the 'Specialist'. These are located centrally, usually at the Headquarters or Training Centre of the Arm or Corps. Their members, spread across the country, are mainly civilians who already have the necessary skills or specialities, and require a minimum of military training.

An example of these can be found in the Army Medical Services Specialist Units whose doctors, surgeons, nurses and technicians from all over the country meet at regular intervals on a training area at home or abroad. They are on the lowest commitment for training, which is the equivalent of just two weekends and a two week camp each year, or it can be even less for some medical categories.

RECRUITING AND TRAINING

Recruits need to be at least 17 years old in order to join the TA. The upper age limit depends on what an individual has to offer, but it is normally 30 for those joining as an officer and 32 as a soldier. There are exceptions to the upper age limit for those with certain specialist skills or previous military experience.

Unless recruits have previous military experience, when they join the TA they will have to undergo basic recruit training. This consists of a number of training weekends, midweek drill nights and finally a two-week recruit's course at one of the Army recruit training centres.

During this stage, recruits will learn basic soldiering skills according to the TA Common Military Syllabus. This covers areas as diverse as how to wear uniform, physical fitness, weapon handling, first aid, fieldcraft, map reading and military terminology.

Officer recruiting and training may take one of two forms. Officers can be recruited from the ranks, and appointed officer cadets by their unit commander, before taking the TA Commissioning Course at the Royal Military Academy, Sandhurst. Alternatively, the new direct entry officer training scheme allows potential officers to enter officer training right from the very start of their time in the TA. Initial Officer Training is designed to produce officers with the generic qualities to lead soldiers both on and off operations and includes three weeks spent on the TA Commissioning Course at the Royal Military Academy, Sandhurst.

MOBILISATION AND CALL OUT

Before reservists can be mobilised and sent on operations, a Call Out Order has to be signed by the Defence Secretary. He has the power to authorise the use of reserves in situations of war or on humanitarian and peacekeeping operations.

Before they are sent to their postings, reservists must undergo a period of induction where they are issued with equipment, given medical examinations and receive any specialist training relevant to their operations. For the TA and the RMR (Royal Marines Reserve), this takes place at the new Reserves Training and Mobilisation Centre.

Under the Reserve Forces Act 1996, principal call out powers would be brought into effect in a crisis by the issue of a call out order. Members of the Reserve Forces are then liable for service anywhere in the world, unless the terms of service applicable in individual cases restrict liability to service within the UK.

Call out powers are vested in and authorised by Her Majesty the Queen who may make an order authorising call out:

♦ If it appears to her that national danger is imminent
♦ Or that a great emergency has arisen
♦ Or in the event of an actual or apprehended attack on the United Kingdom.

The Secretary of State for Defence may make an order authorising call out:

♦ If it appears to him that warlike preparations are in preparation or progress
♦ Or it appears to him that it is necessary or desirable to use armed forces on operations outside the UK for the protection of life or property
♦ And for operations anywhere in the world for the alleviation of distress or the preservation of life or property in time of disaster or apprehended disaster

Under normal circumstances, the maximum continuous periods of permanent service which individuals can serve under the above powers are respectively three years, 12 months and nine months. In exceptional circumstances the three years may be increased to five and the 12 months to two years but under the third power, no extensions can be ordered beyond the maximum of nine months. Under each power, provisions also limit the maximum aggregated time a reservist can spend in permanent service over given lengths of time.

Reservists and employers may apply for deferral of, or exemption from call out. It is recognised that those called out may not find the outcomes of their initial applications to their satisfaction. Therefore a system of arbitration has been set up.

Reimbursement

The Reserve Forces Act (RFA) 1996 enables reimbursement to be made to Employers and Reservists for some of the additional costs of employees being called out. Some reservists will have financial commitments commensurate with their civilian salary and so provisions are in place to minimise financial hardship.

The MoD is also able to offset the indirect costs of employees being called out incurred by an employer, for example, the need to recruit and train temporary replacements. If employers or reservists are dissatisfied with the financial assistance awarded they may appeal to tribunals set up for this.

Full and Part Time Service

One provision of the RFA 96 is that reservists can now undertake periods of full or part time employment with the Armed Forces. This is not a call out but a voluntary arrangement to make it possible for the Services to make more flexible use of their manpower assets. There are no fixed time limits. If a task needs doing, there is sufficient budget and a suitable volunteer is available for the job, then it can be done.

Call Out Procedure

TA soldiers are called out using the same procedures as for Individual Reservist (IR), they are sent a Call Out Notice specifying the time, date and place to which they are to report. If TA Units or Sub-Units are called out, they form up with their vehicles and equipment at their TA Centres or other designated locations. They would then be deployed by land, sea and air to their operational locations in the UK or overseas. However, if TA personnel are called out as individuals, they would report to a Temporary Mobilisation Centre where they would be processed before posting to reinforce a unit or HQ.

IR are required to keep at home an Instruction Booklet (AB 592A), their ID card and a personalised Booklet (AB 592B). The AB 592A provides IR with general instructions on what they have to do if mobilised. It contains a travel warrant and a special cash order. The AB 592A is computer produced and updated quarterly as required to take account of such changes as address, medical category and age. It explains where the reservist is to report on mobilisation and arrangements for pay and allotments, next-of-kin, clothing held etc.

Under present legislation IR may only be mobilised if called out by Queen's Order. Mobilisation may involve only a few individuals/units or any number up to general mobilisation when all are called out. If mobilisation is authorised Notices of Call Out are despatched to those IR concerned by Recorded Delivery as the legal notification. Announcements of call out are also made by the press, radio and television.

Under the Reserve Forces Act 1996, IR are liable to call out under the same new provisions as described above for the TA. In addition, the Act brings the conditions relating to all three Services in line and includes officers and pensioners who were previously covered by separate legislation/Royal Warrants.

Pay

TA personnel are paid for every hour of training. They also receive an annual bonus, known as a bounty, subject to achieving a minimum time commitment. Travel costs for training are refunded. As of 2011, daily rates of pay are the same for TA personnel and their Regular Army equivalents. The latest 2011 rates are just over £45 (starting rate following completion of training) for a Private to £140 for a Major (mid rate). The exact rate also varies according to particular trade and type of commitment.

Hourly income is taxable, but the Annual Training Bounty is a tax-free lump sum. The value of the bounty depends on the specific unit and individual training requirement but, on a higher commitment, TA soldiers and officers start by receiving £405 in their first year. After five years satisfactory service, this rises to £1,674.

The annual training commitment to qualify for bounty is:

♦ Independent/Regional Units: 27 days including 15 days continuous at camp
♦ Specialis/National Units: 19 days including 15 days continuous at camp.

In each case, individuals may attend one or more courses aggregated to at least eight days duration in lieu of camp, with the balance of seven days being carried out in extra out-of-camp training.

Management

Two structures have been set up within the Territorial Army in order to improve management of reserves:

♦ Reserves Manning and Career Management Division
♦ Reserves Training and Mobilisation Centre (RTMC)

The role of the first is to centralise the coordination of all personnel management for the TA, bringing it more into line with the regular Army and also providing a single focus for identifying and notifying individuals for mobilisation, while the second is in charge of administrative preparation, individual training and provision of human resources requirements of individual reservists. The RTMC at Chilwell, which was inaugurated in April 1999, managed a first group of reservists in May 1999 for the British forces stationed in Bosnia and Kosovo.

There have been major efforts to improve TA recruiting but in spite of these efforts, there appears to have been a constant decline in the number of reservists during the last decade. The drop-out rate among volunteers can be as high as 30% in the first three years of their engagement and unless figures like these can be turned around it will be difficult to make any meaningful increase in the numbers available.

Territorial Army and Volunteer Reserve Associations (TAVRA)

At local level, administration and support of the major elements of the Reserve Forces are carried out through the TAVRAs, working within the context described in the 1996 Reserve Forces Act. This is a tri-Service role which has been carried out by the TAVRAs and their predecessor organisations for many years. It is an unusual arrangement, but has been found to be a successful one. The TAVRA system ensures that people from the local communities in which the Reserve Forces and cadets are based are involved in the running of Reserve and cadet units. It also provides Reserve Forces and cadets representatives with the right of direct access to Ministers, so that they can make representation about Reserves issues. This provides an important balance and ensures that the case for the Reserves is clearly articulated at a high level.

TAVRAs have a second role as administrators and suppliers of services to the Reserve and cadet forces organisations. To reflect the increasing operational integration of Army Reserve and Regular forces, there have been certain changes in the way in which TAVRAs are organised since 1998. It is important that regional commanders take on full responsibility for the operational standards of Army Reserve units in their area; as a result, TAVRA boundaries were altered and brought more in line with the Army's Regular command structure. The new arrangement also took account of the needs of the other Services' Reserve Forces and all the cadet organisations.

SaBRE (Supporting Britain's Reservists and Employees)

Formerly the National Employers' Liaison Committee (NELC)

SaBRE has grown out of the the National Employers' Liaison Committee (NELC) which was formed in 1986 with a brief to provide independent advice to Ministers on the measures needed to win and maintain the support of employers, in both the public and private sectors, for those of their employees who are in the Volunteer Reserve Forces (VRF). The committee is made up of prominent businessmen and is supported by the secretariat. SaBRE provides advice on:

♦ The ways of educating employers on the role of the Reserve Forces in national defence, the vital role employers have to play in giving their support, and the benefits to employers and their employees of Reserve Forces training and experience.
♦ The current problems and attitudes of employers in relation to service by their employees in the Reserve Forces.
♦ Methods and inducements needed to encourage and retain the support of employers.

♦ Appropriate means of recognising and publicising support given by employers to the Reserve Forces.

TERRITORIAL ARMY UNITS DURING 2011

Royal Armoured Corps: Territorial Army units during 2011

Unit	Location
Royal Yeomanry	London
Queen's Own Yeomanry	Newcastle
Royal Wessex Yeomanry	Bovington
Royal Mercian and Lancastrian Yeomanry	Telford

Infantry: Territorial Army units during 2011

Unit	Location
The London Regiment	Battersea, London
6th Bn The Royal Regiment of Scotland	Walcheren Bks, Glasgow
7th Bn The Royal Regiment of Scotland	Queen's Bks, Perth
3rd Bn The Princess of Wales Royal Regiment	Leros TA Centre, Canterbury
5th Bn The Royal Regiment of Fusiliers	Gilesgate Armoury, Durham
3rd Bn The Royal Anglian Regiment	Blenheim Camp, Bury St Edmonds
4th Bn The Duke of Lancaster's Regiment	Kimberley Bks, Preston
4th Bn The Yorkshire Regiment	Worsley Bks, York
4th Bn The Mercian Regiment	Wolseley House, Wolverhampton
3rd Bn The Royal Welsh Regiment	Maindy Bks, Cardiff
6th Bn The Rifles	Wyvern Bks, Exeter
7th Bn The Rifles	Brock Bks, Reading
2nd Bn The Royal Irish Regiment	Portadown, Northern Ireland
4th Bn The Parachute Regiment	Thornbury Bks, Pudsey

Royal Artillery: Territorial Army units during 2011

Unit	Location
Honourable Artillery Company	Finsbury Barracks, London
100th (Yeomanry) Regiment Royal Artillery (V)	RHQ TA Centre, Luton
101st (Northumbrian) Regiment Royal Artillery (V)	RHQ, Napier Armoury, Gateshead
103rd (Lancashire) Regiment Royal Artillery (V)	RHQ, Jubilee Barracks, St Helens
104th Regiment Royal Artillery (V)	Raglan Barracks, South Wales
105th Regiment Royal Artillery (V)	RHQ, Artillery House, Edinburgh
106th (Yeomanry) Regiment Royal Artillery (V)	Napier House, Grove Park, London
Central Volunteers Headquarters Royal Artillery	Royal Artillery Barracks, Woolwich

Royal Engineers: Territorial Army units during 2011

Unit	Location
71 Engineer Regiment (V)	Leuchars
72 Engineer Regiment (V)	Newcastle
73 Engineer Regiment (V)	Nottingham
75 Engineer Regiment (V)	Warrington
Royal Monmouthshire RE (Militia)	Monmouth
131 Independent Commando Squadron (V)	London
135 Independent Geographic Squadron (V)	Ewell
591 Independent Field Squadron (Volunteers) (N Ireland)	Bangor
65 Works Group (V)	Chilwell

Army Air Corps : Territorial Army units during 2011

Unit	*Location*
6 Regiment (V)	Bury St Edmunds

Royal Signals : Territorial Army units during 2011

Unit	*Location*
32 Sig Regt (V)	Scotland, North of England and Northern Ireland
37 Sig Regt (V)	Wales, West Midlands and East Anglia
38 Sig Regt (V)	Yorkshire, Nottinghamshire, Buckinghamshire and Highlands
39 Sig Regt (V)	Somerset, Gloucestershire and the Home Counties
71 Sig Regt (V)	London and Essex
HQ Specialist Group Royal Signals	Corsham
Central Volunteer HQ R SIGNALS	Corsham
81 Sig Sqn (V)	Corsham
Land Information Assurance Group (V)	Corsham
Land Information Communications Systems Group (V)	Corsham

Royal Logistic Corps: Territorial Army units during 2011

Unit	*Location*	*Role*
Catering Support Regiment	Grantham	
88 Regiment (V)	Grantham	Postal and Courier and Movements Regiment
89 Regiment (V)	London	Postal and Courier and Movements Regiment
150 (Yorkshire) Transport Regiment (V)	Hull	Transport function
151 (London) Transport Regiment (V)	London	Transport function
152 (Ulster) Transport Regiment (V)	Ulster	Transport function
155 Transport Regiment (V)	Plymouth	Transport function
156 (North West) Transport Regiment (V)	Liverpool	Transport function
158 (Royal Anglian) Transport Regiment (V))	Peterborough	Transport function
159 Supply Regiment (V)	West Bromwich	Supply function
160 Transport Regiment (V)	Grantham	Transport function
165 Port Regiment (V)	Grantham	Port and Maritime function
166 Supply Regiment (V)	Grantham	Supply function
168 Pioneer Regiment (V)	Grantham	Pioneer function
Scottish Transport Regiment (V)	Dunfermline	Transport function
Welsh Transport Regiment (V)	Cardiff	Transport function

Royal Electrical & Mechanical Engineers: Territorial Army units during 2011

Unit	*Location*
101 Force Support Battalion REME (V)	Wrexham
102 Battalion REME (V)	Newton Aycliffe
103 Battalion REME (V)	Crawley
104 Force Support Battalion REME (V)	Bordon

Army Medical Services: Territorial Army units during 2011

Unit	*Location*
201 Field Hospital (V)	Newcastle
202 Field Hospital (V)	Birmingham

203 Field Hospital (V)	Cardiff
204 Field Hospital (V)	Belfast
205 Field Hospital (V)	Glasgow
207 Field Hospital (V)	Manchester
208 Field Hospital (V)	Liverpool
212 Field Hospital (V)	Sheffield
243 Field Hospital (V)	Bath
256 Field Hospital (V)	London
225 Divisional General Support Medical Regiment (V)	Dundee
254 Divisional General Support Medical Regiment (V)	Cherry Hinton
144 Parachute Medical Squadron	London/Hornsey

Adjutant General's Corps: Territorial Army units during 2011

Unit	*Location*
116 Provost Company Royal Military Police (V)	Manchester
243 Provost Company Royal Military Police (V)	Edinburgh
252 Provost Company Royal Military Police (V)	Stockton
253 Provost Company Royal Military Police (V)	Tulse Hill, London

Intelligence Corps: Territorial Army units during 2011

Unit
3 Military Intelligence Bn (V)
5 Military Intelligence Bn (V)

Special Air Service: Territorial Army Units during 2011

Unit
21 Regiment SAS
23 Regiment SAS

THE REGULAR ARMY RESERVE

Types of Reservist

We estimate the strength of the Regular Army Reserve during mid 2011 as follows:

Component	*Category*	*Total*
Regular Reserve (Retired)	Regular Army Reserve (our estimate)	50,000
Long Term Reserve	Individuals liable to recall (our estimate)	100,000

Regular Reserve (Retired)

The Regular Reserve is comprised of people who have a mobilisation obligation by virtue of their former service in the regular army. For the most part, these reservists constitute a standby rather than ready reserve, and are rarely mobilised except in times of national emergency or incipient war. Some 420 retired regular reservists were called-up for Iraq operations in 2003.

The Regular Reserve consists of Individual Reservists (IR), some of whom may have varying obligations in respect of training and mobilisation, depending on factors such as length of regular service, age and sex.

Many ex-regulars join the Volunteer Reserve Forces after leaving regular service – giving them a dual Reserve status.

Long Term Reserve

In general terms consists of individuals who have left the service and have a statutory liability for service until their 45th birthday (for those who enlisted before 1997 and the age of 55 for those who enlisted after 1997).

ARMY CADETS

Consists of two separate organisations, The Combined Cadet Forces and the Army Cadet Force:

The Role of the CCF

The Combined Cadet Force (CCF) is a tri-Service military cadet organisation based in schools and colleges throughout the UK. Although it is administered and funded by the Services it is a part of the national youth movement.

The CCF receives assistance and support for its training programme from the Regular and Reserve Forces, but the bulk of adult support is provided by members of school staffs who are responsible to head teachers for the conduct of cadet activities. CCF officers wear uniform but they are not part of the Armed Forces and carry no liability for service or compulsory training.

There are some 240 CCF contingents with 40,000 cadets, of whom about 25,000 are Army Cadets. The role of the CCF is to help boys and girls to develop powers of leadership through training which promotes qualities of responsibility, self-reliance, resourcefulness, endurance, perseverance and a sense of service to the community. Military training is also designed to demonstrate why defence forces are needed, how they function and to stimulate an interest in a career as an officer in the Services.

The CCF is believed to receive about £11 million in funding each year.

The Role of the ACF

The role of the Army Cadet Force (ACF) is to inspire young people to achieve success with a spirit of service to the Queen, country and their local community, and to develop the qualities of good citizenship, responsibility and leadership.

Some reports suggest that Army cadets make up between 25%-30% of Regular Army recruits. There are about 1,674 ACF detachments based in communities around the UK. The ACF is run by over 8,000 adults drawn from the local community who manage a broad programme of military and adventurous training activities designed to develop character and leadership. The Army Cadets are administered by the MoD. The total budget provided to the Army Cadets is believed to have been in the region of £40 million during 2010-1011.

Early 2011 figures suggest a total of 47,000 Army Cadets.

CHAPTER 16 – MISCELLANEOUS

THE SERVICES HIERARCHY

Officer Ranks

Army	*Navy*	*Air Force*	*NATO Code*
Field Marshal	Admiral of the Fleet	Marshal of the RAF	OF-10
General	Admiral	Air Chief Marshal	OF-9
Lieutenant-General	Vice-Admiral	Air Marshal	OF-8
Major-General	Rear-Admiral	Air Vice Marshal	OF-7
Brigadier	Commodore	Air Commodore	OF-6
Colonel	Captain	Group Captain	OF-5
Lieutenant-Colonel	Commander	Wing Commander	OF-4
Major	Lieutenant-Commander	Squadron Leader	OF-3
Captain	Lieutenant	Flight-Lieutenant	OF-2
Lieutenant/2Lt	Sub-Lieutenant	Flying/Pilot Officer	OF-1
Officer Cadet	Midshipman		OF(D)

Non Commissioned Ranks

Army	*Navy*	*Air Force*	*NATO Code*
Warrant Officer 1	Warrant Officer 1	Warrant Officer	OR-9
Warrant Officer 2	Warrant Officer 2		OR-8
Staff/Colour Sergeant	Chief Petty Officer	Flight Sergeant/Ch Tech (1)	OR-7
Sergeant	Petty Officer	Sergeant	OR-6
Corporal	Leading Rate	Corporal	OR-4
Lance Corporal			OR-3
Private Cl 1 -3	Able Rating	Leading Aircraftsman (2)	OR-2
Private Cl 4/Junior		Aircraftsman	OR-1

Note: (1) Chief Technician (2) May include Junior Technician and Senior Aircraftsman

UK Armed Forces Pay 2011 – 2012

The following table shows the average pay based on pay rates for 2011-2012.

Other ranks are allocated to either higher or lower pay spines in accordance with their trade. These are Army rates. For other service rates consult the table of ranks above.

Rank	*Pay from 1 April 2011*
Private/Lance Corporal (Level 4)	£19,779 – £21,773
Corporal (Level 4)	£29,161 – £31,065
Sergeant (Level 4)	£31,892 – £34,890
WO2 (Level 4)	£35,565 – £39,648
WO1 (Level 4)	£40,938 – £44,448
Lieutenant	£21,810 – £32,703
Captain	£37,916 – £45,090
Major	£47,760 – £57,199
Lieutenant Colonel	£67,032 – £77,617
Colonel	£81,310 – £89,408
Brigadier	£97,030 – £100,964

From 1 April 2011 a Private soldier deploying on operations will receive:

♦ Basic pay plus a £5,281 tax free operational allowance.
♦ A minimum of £1,218 in Longer Separation Allowance over a six month tour.

This could bring the minimum pay for the average unmarried Private soldier deploying on his/her first operation up to at about £25,060.

The table does not include the specialist pay rates for medical officers, chaplins, pilots etc.

Modes of Address

Where appropriate officers and soldiers are addressed by their generic rank without any qualifications, therefore Generals, Lieutenant Generals and Major Generals are all addressed as 'General'. Colonels and Lieutenant Colonels as 'Colonel', Corporals and Lance Corporals as ' Corporal'. Staff Sergeants and Colour Sergeants are usually addressed as 'Staff' or 'Colour' and CSMs as Sergeant Major. It would almost certainly be prudent to address the RSM as 'Sir'.

Private Soldiers should always be addressed by their title and then their surname. For example: Rifleman Harris, Private Jones, Bugler Bygrave, Gunner Smith, Guardsman Thelwell, Sapper Williams, Trooper White, Kingsman Boddington, Signalman Robinson, Ranger Murphy, Fusilier Ramsbotham , Driver Wheel, Craftsman Grease or Air Trooper Rotor. However, it should be remembered that regiments and corps have different customs and although the above is a reasonable guide it may not always be correct. You are almost certain to enrage someone!

Regimental Head-Dress

The normal everyday head-dress of NCOs and Soldiers (and in some regiments of all ranks) is the beret or national equivalent. The norm is the dark blue beret. Exceptions are as follows:

a. Grey Beret	The Royal Scots Dragoon Guards
	Queen Alexandra's Royal Army Nursing Corps
b. Brown Beret	The King's Royal Hussars
	The Royal Wessex Yeomanry
c. Khaki Beret	All Regiments of Foot Guards
	The Honourable Artillery Company
	The Royal Anglian Regiment
	The Duke of Lancaster's Regiment
	The Yorkshire Regiment
d. Black Beret	The Royal Tank Regiment
e. Rifle Green Beret	The Rifles
	The Brigade of Gurkhas
	Adjutant General's Corps
f. Maroon Beret	The Parachute Regiment
g. Beige Beret	The Special Air Service Regiment
h. Light Blue Beret	The Army Air Corps
i. Scarlet Beret	Royal Military Police
j. Cypress Green Beret	The Intelligence Corps

The Royal Regiment of Scotland wear the Tam-O-Shanter (TOS) and the Royal Irish Regiment wear the Corbeen.

THE MoD'S CIVILIAN STAFF

The three uniformed services are supported by the civilian staff of the MoD. On 1 April 2011 there were approximately 85,000 civilian personnel employed by the MoD. This figure has fallen from 316,700 civilian personnel in 1980 and is a reduction of over 20 per cent since April 2004

During early 2011 MoD civilian staff were employed in the following budgetary areas:

Navy (Fleet)	4,800
Army (Land Forces)	16,500
RAF (Air Command)	8,700
Defence Equipment & Support	16,200
Central	19,800 (1)
Locally Engaged Civilians Overseas	10,200 (2)
Unallocated to Budgetary Areas	100 (approx)

Notes:

(1) Includes CJO, CSIT, DE and Trading Funds (DSTL, Meteorological Office, Hydrographic Office, DSG). (2) The overwhelming majority of this figure are locally entered civilians supporting BFG (British Forces Germany).

Earlier in the decade the UK MoD stated that " The Department remains committed to a process of civilianisation. Increasingly, it makes no sense to employ expensively trained and highly professional military personnel in jobs which civilians could do equally well. Civilians are generally cheaper than their military counterparts and as they often remain longer in post, can provide greater continuity. For these reasons, it is our long-standing policy to civilianise posts and so release valuable military resources to the front line whenever it makes operational and economic sense to do so".

In general, MoD Civil Servants work in a parallel stream with their respective uniformed counterparts. There are some 'stand alone' civilian agencies of which the QinetiQ is probably the largest.

THE DEFENCE ESTATE

The Ministry of Defence (MoD) is one of the largest landowners in the UK with a diverse estate of some 240,000 hectares (1 per cent of the UK land mass) and is valued at over £15 billion. Typically, approximately £1.5billion per year is spent on maintenance and new construction. Some of these costs are offset against income from tenants and other land users.

Defence Estates (DE) is the MoD Agency responsible for the management of the defence estate and provides services to support all aspects of a large and very diverse estate.

The estate is made up of:

- Built Estate which occupies around 80,000 hectares and is made up of naval bases, barracks/camps, airfields, research and development installations, storage and supply depots, communications facilities, around 49,000 Service Families Accommodation and town centre careers offices.
- The Rural Estate occupies around 160,000 hectares which includes 21 major armed forces training areas 39 minor training areas, small arms ranges, test and evaluation ranges and aerial bombing ranges.
- Significant overseas estate in Germany, Cyprus, the Falkland Islands and Gibraltar with major overseas training facilities in Canada, Norway, Poland and Kenya.
- There are 179 Sites of Special Scientific Interest (SSSIs) across the rural estate that is managed by the MoD, the largest number in government ownership.

- There are currently around 650 listed buildings and 1,057 scheduled monuments across both the built and rural estate. The defence estate includes the largest proportion of statutorily protected buildings held by the government, 43% of all government heritage properties.
- The size, diversity and nature of the estate is dictated entirely by the Services requirements to fulfil the Defence Mission. The UK estate also includes facilities for US forces based in the UK.

THE UNITED KINGDOM DEFENCE INDUSTRY

Despite uncertainties over future defence strategy and pressure on defence spending, the United Kingdom's Defence Industry has proved to be a remarkably resilient and successful element of our national manufacturing base.

Despite the rationalisation which is still taking place within the defence sector it is generally accepted that defence employment still provides a significant element of the broader UK economy via salaries paid throughout the supply chain.

Historically, the UK defence industry has possessed the capability and competence to provide a wide range of advanced systems and equipment to support our own Armed Forces. This capability, matched with their competitiveness, has enabled UK companies to command a sizeable share of those overseas markets for which export licence approvals are available. At home, UK industry has consistently provided some 75% by value of the equipment requirements of the Ministry of Defence. In simple terms, in recent years UK industry has supplied £9 – £10 billion worth of goods and services for our Armed Forces annually while a further £2 -4 billion worth of business has accrued to the UK defence industry from sales to approved overseas customers.

The United Kingdom's defence companies are justifiably proud of their record in recent years in the face of fierce overseas competition. Reductions in the UK's Armed Forces and the heavy demands on our remaining Service personnel, who face an unpredictable international security environment, make it inevitable that considerable reliance will be placed upon the support and surge capacity offered by our comprehensive indigenous defence industrial base. Without this effective industrial base, the ability of UK to exert independence of action or influence over collective security arrangements would be constrained. It is essential that government policies ensure that industry retains the necessary capabilities to support our forces in a changing world.

As importantly, the defence industry is not only a major employer but it is also the generator of high technology that is readily adaptable to civilian use in fields such as avionics and engine technology. The future of the UK's defence industry will almost certainly have to be properly planned if it is to remain an efficient and essential national support organisation in times of crisis. A look at MoD payments to contractors during FY 2009-2010 identifies some of the larger manufacturers.

Major Contractors Listing by Holding Company

Over £500 million

Babcock International Group PLC

Finmeccanica SpA

BAE Systems PLC

Lockheed Martin Corporation

Thales SA

QinetiQ Group PLC

EADS NV

Hewlett Packard Company

Rolls-Royce Group PLC

£250 – £500 million

> Aspire Defence Holdings
>
> BT Group PLC
>
> General Dynamics Corporation
>
> Jacobs Engineering Group Inc
>
> Man SE
>
> Serco Group PLC
>
> VT Group PLC

£100 – £250 million

> 3I Group PLC
>
> The Boeing Company
>
> Turner & Co (Glasgow) Ltd
>
> Sodexo SA
>
> Scottish & Southern Energy PLC
>
> Morgan Crucible Company PLC
>
> Marshall of Cambridge (Holdings) Ltd
>
> Lend Lease Group
>
> Supreme Group Holdings Sarl
>
> Carillion PLC
>
> Interserve PLC
>
> KBR Inc
>
> Le Grand Annington Ltd

Note: Payments to the companies listed may include payments made to subsidiaries or contractors.

QINETIQ

(Formerly known as the Defence Evaluation & Research Agency)

From 1 April 1995, the Defence Evaluation & Research Agency (DERA) assumed the responsibilities of its predecessor the Defence Research Agency (DRA). DERA changed its title to QinetiQ on 2 July 2001.

The name QinetiQ has been derived from the scientific term, kinetic (phonetic: ki'ne tik), which means 'relating to or caused by motion'. This in turncomes from the Greek, kinetikos based on 'kineo' which means 'to move'.

Following the 2001 restructuring, certain functions of DERA, encompassing the majority of the organisation's capabilities for defence and security and amounting to approximately three quarters of DERA, were formed into QinetiQ Limited, an entity which is a wholly-owned subsidiary of QinetiQ Group plc. In February 2006 QinetiQ was listed on the London Stock Exchange with a market capitalisation of £1.3 billion.

A quarter of QinetiQ has been retained within the MoD as the Defence Science and Technology Laboratory (DSTL) to manage the research programme and the International Research Collaboration, along with other sensitive areas such as CBD (Chemical & Biological Defence), Porton Down.

The Group employs over 14,000 people of which some 6,400 are in North America, and operates over 40 UK sites with major technology facilities at Farnborough, Boscombe Down and Malvern.

Since 2004 QinetiQ has acquired 13 companies in North America including five during FY 2008-2009 and the company is expanding into Australia.

QinetiQ 's global revenue was £1,366 million in the year to 31 March 2008 with a similar figure expected for FY 2009. The US business now accounts for over 45 per cent of group sales.

About 60 per cent of the group's UK employees are graduates and more than 700 hold PhDs. More than half of the employees in the UK are focussed on research, invention, development and application of new technology. There are strategic partnerships with 13 UK universities, and 30 QinetiQ staff have visiting professorships.

QinetiQ is organised into six major operational divisions:

Integrated Services (formerly Complex Managed Services)

- ♦ Test and evaluation
- ♦ Public sector strategic partnering, infrastructure rationalisation and operation
- ♦ Integrated acquisition support
- ♦ Asset management (e.g. logistics, calibration, technology upgrade, obsolescence management and disposal)

Sensors & Electronics

- ♦ Spectrum solutions
- ♦ Sensors, processing and integration
- ♦ Marine & acoustics
- ♦ Optronics

Knowledge and Information Systems

- ♦ Command & intelligence systems
- ♦ Information assurance
- ♦ Communications
- ♦ Technical consulting
- ♦ Human sciences
- ♦ Space

Future Systems and Technology

- ♦ Maritime
- ♦ Aerospace
- ♦ Vehicles, platforms and systems
- ♦ Weapons
- ♦ Energy
- ♦ Intelligence & control
- ♦ Materials
- ♦ Structures

North America

- ♦ Key focus on homeland security and defence markets.
- ♦ Major customers include US Department of Defence, Department of Homeland Security and DARPA (Defence Advanced Research Projects Agency).

There is another operational element in Australia

THE ROYAL MARINES

The Royal Marines (RM) are an elite Corps and specialists in Amphibious Warfare – and wherever there is action, the Royal Marines are likely to be involved. They were prominent, for example, in the Falklands campaign, and they can be found wherever the UK Armed Services are actively involved e.g. Northern Ireland, the Balkans, Sierra Leone, Afghanistan and Iraq. The Royal Marines number approximately 8,000 men and, since the end of the Cold War, and especially in recent years, the Corps appears to have reverted to its traditional role of being ready for operations anywhere in the world.

All Royal Marines, except those in the Royal Marines Band Service, are first and foremost, commando soldiers. They are required to undergo what is recognised as one of the longest and most demanding infantry training courses in the world. This is undertaken at the Commando Training Centre Royal Marines at Lympstone in the UK's West Country, not far from Dartmoor.

The titular head of the Royal Marines is always a Major General – Commandant General Royal Marines (CGRM). There have been significant recent structural changes in the higher management of the Royal Navy recently and this has added to the responsibilities and raised the profile of CGRM.

The Royal Marines have small detachments in ships at sea and other units worldwide with widely differing tasks. However, the bulk of the manpower of the Royal Marines is grouped in battalion plus sized organisations known as Commandos (Cdo). There are 3 Commando Groups and they are part of a larger formation known as 3 Commando Brigade (3 Cdo Bde).

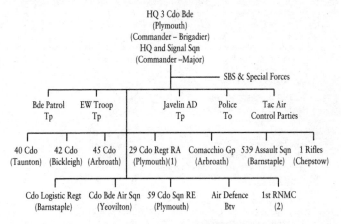

1st Battalion The Rifles – 3 Commando Brigade's Fourth Manoeuvre Unit

From 1 April 2008 1 Rifles have been attached to 3 Commando Brigade as a fourth manoeuvre unit. 3 Commando Brigade is now capable of providing both a brigade at high readiness for operations anywhere in the world and also an ability to support programmed operations.

1 Rifles will remain on the Army list under the Full Command of the Chief of the General Staff but serve under the operational command of the Commander in Chief Fleet and the Commander of 3 Commando Brigade Royal Marines. The battalion has been structured as a Light Role Battalion and personnel will continue to wear the Rifles cap-badge.

29 Cdo Regt RA has one battery stationed at Arbroath with 45 Cdo.

1st Bn The Royal Netherlands Marine Corps can be part of 3 Cdo Bde for NATO assigned tasks.

There are three regular Tactical Air Control Parties and one reserve.

539 Assault Squadron has hovercraft, landing craft and raiding craft.

Commando Organisation

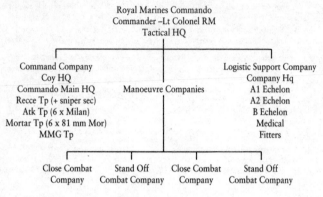

Note: There are 4 x Manoeuvre Companies:
- 2 x Close Combat Companies each with 3 x Fighting Troops (5 x officers and 98 other ranks).
- 2 x Stand Off Combat Companies one of which is tracked (armoured vehicle) and the other wheeled. Each Stand Off Combat Company has 1 x Heavy Machine Gun Troop with 6 x 0.5 HMG, 1 x Anti-Tank Troop with 6 x Milan and 1 x Close Combat Fighting Troop (5 x officers and 78 other ranks).

Total personnel strength is 692 all ranks. A troop (Tp) roughly equates to an army platoon and consists of about 30 men.

Locations.

Headquarters Royal Marines	(Portsmouth)
HQ 3 Commando Brigade Plymouth	(Stonehouse)
3 Commando Bde HQ & Signal Squadron	(Stonehouse)
3 Commando Bde Air Sqn	(RNAS Yeovilton)
40 Commando	(Taunton)
42 Commando	(Plymouth)
45 Commando	(Arbroath)
Commando Logistic Regiment	(Barnstaple))
539 Assault Sqn Plymouth	(Barnstaple)
Fleet Protection Group	(Clyde)
Commando Training Centre	(Lympstone)
Royal Marines Stonehouse	(Plymouth) .
Royal Marines Poole	(Poole)
Amphibious Training & Trials Unit	(Bideford)
1 Assault Group	(Poole)

Royal Marines Reserve (RMR)

The RMR consists of about 750 personnel based around the following locations:

RMR London: The detachment is in London and is located alongside the HQ. The remaining detachments are based in Cambridge, Chatham, Henley and Portsmouth.

RMR Merseyside: The Headquarters is in Liverpool were there is a detachment. The other detachments are based in Birmingham, Nottingham and Manchester.

RMR Scotland: HQ is in Glasgow with the remaining detachments based in Greenock, Edinburgh, Dundee, Aberdeen, Inverness and Belfast.

RMR Tyne: Location at Newcastle-on-Tyne. Hartlepool and Leeds.

RMR Bristol: The main detachment is in Bristol which is located alongside the HQ. The four remaining detachments are based in Poole, Plymouth, Cardiff and Lympstone.

Special Boat Service

This organisation is the Naval equivalent of the Army's SAS (Special Air Service). Personnel are all volunteers from the mainstream Royal Marines and vacancies are few with competition for entry fierce.

Generally speaking only about 30 per cent of volunteers manage to complete the entry course and qualify. The SBS specialises in mounting clandestine operations against targets at sea, in rivers or harbours and against occupied coastlines.

The SBS are a part of the UK Special Forces Group – see Chapter 12.

Fleet Protection Group (Comacchio Group) Royal Marines (FPGRM)

During 2001 Comacchio Group was renamed as the Fleet Protection Group Royal Marines (FPGRM) and the unit moved from RM Condor to HMNB Clyde. FPGRM has about 550 personnel and is structured around three Royal Marine elements, a Royal Naval Element (P Squadron) and a headquarters group.

The Group currently performs a variety of tasks some of which include:

Fleet Standby Rifle Troop (FSRT) – The FSRT provides teams that operate in support of the Royal Navy operations across the globe. These tasks can include counter narcotics, counter terrorist and counter piracy operations. FSRT personnel are highly trained specialists held at high readiness for deployment and equipped with the latest 'state of the art' systems and equipment. Before being accepted for the FSRT personnel are required to spend some time with the FPGRM serving what can only be described as an 'operational apprenticeship'.

Security of Nuclear Weapons – This element provides security for nuclear weapons at Faslane and the Armament Depot at Coulport. In addition, security is provided for nuclear weapons in transit with reaction forces available to support the Ministry of Defence police if that should be required.

Force Protection – The Force Protection element provides additional security for Royal Naval and Royal Fleet Auxiliary vessels stationed outside the UK and where necessary vessels alongside in the United Kingdom. In some cases regular protection teams are reinforced by personnel from the Royal Naval Reserve.

All Royal Marines serving on board Royal Navy frigates belong to the Fleet Protection Group.

RAF REGIMENT

The RAF Regiment was raised on 1 February 1942 by a Royal Warrant of King George VI as a result of the requirement to protect air installations which were vulnerable to enemy air and ground attack. As of 2011, the strength of the RAF Regiment is around 2,200 airmen (including approximately 300 officers). In addition there are about 500 part-time reservists. Currently the RAF Regiment exists to provide defence for RAF installations, and to train all the RAF's combatant personnel to enable them to contribute to the defence of their units.

The Regiment is generally formed into Squadrons of 100 to 150 personnel.

As of 1 April 2011, RAF Regiment units were as follows:

Field Squadrons

No 1 Squadron	Honington	Field Squadron
No 2 Squadron	Honington	Field /Parachute Sqn
No 3 Squadron	Wittering	Field Squadron
No 15 Squadron	Honington	Field Squadron
No 34 Squadron	Leeming	Field Squadron
No 51 Squadron	Lossiemouth	Field Squadron
No 58 Squadron	Leuchars	Field Squadron
No 63 (QCS)	Uxbridge	Ceremonial /Field Sqn
No 27 Squadron	Honington	CBRN Defence

(RAF element of Joint CBRN Regiment)

| RAF Regiment Depot | Honington |
| RAF Force Protection HQ | Honington |

Note: Joint CBRN Regiment: No 27 Squadron RAF Regiment provides some of the 244 personnel of the Joint CBRN Regiment alongside two squadrons of the Royal Tank Regiment, all of whom are stationed at Honington.

In a restructuring announcement in March 2006 it was announced that rapidly deployable RAF Force Protection elements were being enhanced by integrating elements of the RAF Regiment, RAF Police, Intelligence and Support to deliver a full range of capability from policing and security (including dogs) to close combat. There are RAF Force Protection units at Coningsby, Leuchars, Leeming, Lossiemouth, Lyneham, Henlow and Wittering.

Specialist RAF Regiment training for gunners is given at the RAF Regiment Depot at Honington. On completion of training at the RAF College Cranwell officers also undergo further specialist training at RAF Honington and, in some cases, the Combined Arms Training Centre at Warminster in Wiltshire.

The RAF Regiment also mans the Queen's Colour Squadron which undertakes all major ceremonial duties for the Royal Air Force. These duties involve mounting the Guard at Buckingham Palace on an occasional basis, and providing Guards of Honour for visiting Heads of State. The Queen's Colour Squadron also has a war role as a field squadron.

Royal Auxiliary Air Force Regiment (RAuxAF Regt)

Airfield defence is further enhanced by squadrons of the RAuxAF Regt who are recruited locally and whose role is the ground defence of the airfield and its associated outlying installations. An RAuxAF Regiment Squadron has an all-up strength of about 120 personnel and costs approximately £500,000 a year to keep in service. As a general rule, a squadron has a headquarters flight, two mobile flights mounted in Land Rovers and two flights for static guard duties. RAuxAF Regt squadrons are as follows:

501 (Operational Support) RAuxAF	RAF Brize Norton	Force Protection
504 (Operational Support) RAuxAF	RAF Cottesmore	Force Protection
2503 Sqn RAuxAF Regt	RAF Waddington	Ground Defence
2620 Sqn RAuxAF Regt	RAF Marham	Ground Defence
2622 Sqn RAuxAF Regt	RAF Lossiemouth	Ground Defence
2623 Sqn RauxAF Regt	RAF Honington	Force Protection

Royal Auxiliary Air Force Regiment squadrons are generally based alongside regular units in order to maximise training opportunities and give the auxiliary personnel access to equipment held by the regular unit.

CODEWORDS AND NICKNAMES

A Codeword is a single word used to provide security cover for reference to a particular classified matter, eg 'CORPORATE' was the Codeword for the recovery of the Falklands in 1982. In 1990 'GRANBY' was used to refer to operations in the Gulf and 'Op HERRICK' is used for current UK operations in support of NATO forces in Afghanistan. 'Op ELLAMY' is the Codeword for UK participation in the military intervention in Libya during 2011. A Nickname consists of two words and may be used for reference to an unclassified matter, eg 'Lean Look' referred to an investigation into various military organisations in order to identify savings in manpower.

DATES AND TIMINGS

When referring to timings the British Army uses the 24 hour clock. This means that 2015 hours (pronounced twenty fifteen hours) is in fact 8.15pm. Soldiers usually avoid midnight and refer to 2359 or 0001 hours. Time zones present plenty of scope for confusion! Exercise and Operational times are expressed in Greenwich Mean Time (GMT) which may differ from the local time. The suffix Z (Zulu) denotes GMT and A (Alpha) GMT + 1 hour. B (Bravo) means GMT + 2 hours and so on.

The Date Time Group or DTG can be seen on military documents and is a point of further confusion for many. Using the military DTG 1030 GMT on 20 April 2007 is written as 201030Z APR 07. When the Army relates days and hours to operations a simple system is used:

a. D Day is the day an operation begins.

b. H Hour is the hour a specific operation begins.

c. Days and hours can be represented by numbers plus or minus of D Day for planning purposes. Therefore if D Day is 20 April 2012, D-2 is 18 April and D + 2 is 22 April. If H Hour is 0600 hours then H+2 is 0800 hours.

PHONETIC ALPHABET

To ensure minimum confusion during radio or telephone conversations difficult words or names are spelt out letter by letter using the following NATO standard phonetic alphabet.

ALPHA – BRAVO – CHARLIE – DELTA – ECHO – FOXTROT – GOLF – HOTEL – INDIA – JULIET – KILO – LIMA – MIKE – NOVEMBER – OSCAR – PAPA – QUEBEC – ROMEO – SIERRA – TANGO – UNIFORM – VICTOR – WHISKEY – X RAY – YANKEE – ZULU.

OPERATION BANNER – NORTHERN IRELAND

The 1st Bn The Prince of Wales' Own Regiment was the first unit to be deployed in Northern Ireland in August 1969 closely followed by The 1st Royal Green Jackets.

During the worst period of The Troubles between 1972 and 1973, 27,000 military personnel were stationed in Northern Ireland, the majority of them Army. These military personnel were supported by over 13,000 personnel from the Royal Ulster Constabulary.

Over the course of Operation Banner, 763 servicemen and women were killed as a direct result of terrorism. This includes 651 Army and Royal Marine personnel; one Royal Naval Serviceman; 50 members of the former Ulster Defence Regiment and later Royal Irish Regiment; 10 members of the Territorial Army and 51 military personnel were murdered outside Northern Ireland. Some 6,116 members of the Army and Royal Marines were wounded over the period.

At one stage there were 106 military bases or locations in Northern Ireland, however, since the first Provisional IRA cease-fire in September 1994, 80 per cent of these were closed. The closure of the bases was accelerated after the Good Friday Agreement of April 1998.

The process of steadily reducing military presence began on 1 August 2005 and Operation Banner officially ended on 31 July 2007. It was superseded on 1 August 2007 by Operation Helvetic, a garrison of no more than 5,000 military personnel in 10 locations, trained and ready for deployment worldwide.

The names of the UK service personnel who lost their lives during Operation Banner are listed on the Armed Forces Memorial, Staffordshire. The Memorial, which opened to the public in October 2007, remembers all those killed on duty in conflicts or on training exercises, by terrorist action or on peacekeeping missions — www.forcesmemorial.org

UK ARMED FORCES – FATAL CASUALTIES SINCE 1945

Korea: 765

Northern Ireland: 763 (includes military deaths on UK mainland and Germany attributed to Irish terrorism) (171 died in 1972)

Malaya: 340

The Falklands: 255

Palestine: 233

Iraq 2003-2009: 179

Cyprus: 105

Aden: 68

Egypt: 54

Balkans: 48

The Gulf 1990: 47

Yangtse River: 46

Oman & Dhofar: 24

Suez: 22

Borneo: 126

Kenya: 12

Sierra Leone: 1

As of 1 May 2011 a total of 320 UK Service personnel had been killed in Afghanistan since October 2001 as a result of enemy action (364 from all causes).

This list does not include those wounded (over 12,000) or those killed on "non-active" service duties, training or through accidents.

QUOTATIONS

Young officers and NCOs may find some of these quotations useful on briefings etc: There are two groups – Military and General.

Military

"You may not be interested in war, but war is interested in you."
Leon Trotsky – 1879 – 1940

"Before all else, be armed. "
Machiavelli 1469-1527

"All warfare is based on deception. "
Sun Tzu – about 600 BC

"Tactics without Strategy is just noise before defeat"
Sun-Tzu – about 600 BC

"I hate war but only a soldier who has lived it can, only as one who has seen its brutality, its futility and its stupidity. "
President Dwight D Eisenhower 1890-1969

"War is delightful to those who have no experience of it. "
Ersamus 1456-1536

"Any government has as much of a duty to avoid war as a ship's captain to avoid a shipwreck. "
Guy de Maupassant 1850-1893

"Never be sad about becoming an old soldier – there are thousands who wished they had the chance. "
Anon

"The human factor will decide the fate of war, of all wars. Not the Mirage, nor any other plane, and not the screwdriver, or the wrench or radar or missiles or all the newest technology and electronic innovations. Men – and not just men of action, but men of thought. Men for whom the expression 'By ruses shall ye make war' is a philosophy of life, not just the object of lip service."
Israeli Air Force Commander Ezer Weizman 1924 – 2005

"It is the soldier, not the priest, who protects freedom of religion; the soldier, not the journalist, who protects freedom of speech. History teaches that a society that does not value its warriors will be destroyed by a society that does."
Jack Kelly (US Columnist for the Pittsburg Post Gazette 2004)

"In 1944 Major Digby Tatham-Warter won the DSO commanding a company of 2 Para at Arnhem. when he led a bayonet charge wearing a bowler hat and carrying an umbrella. When he was told that it would be useless against German fire he replied "But what if it rains".

"Anyone wanting to commit American ground forces to the mainland of Asia should have his head examined."
General Douglas MacArthur 1880-1964

"They used to say professionals talk logistics and then tactics. Today, real professionals talk command, control and communications, then logistics and after that tactics."
General Sir David Richards to the House of Commons Defence Committee (February 2009)

"In 1920 King Amunullah of Afghanistan made a state visit to London. As his coach rolled down The Mall towards Buckingham Palace two Cockney bystanders watched proceedings:
First Cockney: 'ose that in the coach then?
Second Cockney: Its the King of Arfghanistan!
First Cockney: 'ose the King of the other Arf then?"

"Having lost sight of our objectives we need to redouble our efforts."
Anon

"During the Second World War Air Marshal Sir Arthur (Bomber) Harris was well known for his glorious capacity for rudeness, particularly to bureaucrats. "What are you doing to retard the war effort today" was his standard greeting to senior civil servants."

"The military value of a partisan's work is not measured by the amount of property destroyed, or the number of men killed or captured, but the number he keeps watching."
Confederate Cavalry Leader – John Singleton Mosby 1833-1916

"Tacitus (56-117AD) wrote of the conquest and occupation of Britain by his father-in-law Agricola. as follows: "He declared an Empire where there was none, and created a desert, and called it peace."

"Keep shouting Sir, we'll find you. Keep going down hill – Don't cross the river!"
LCpl Thomas Atkins

"It is foolish to hunt the tiger when there are plenty of sheep around."
Al Qaeda Training Manual 2002

"Information is something that you do something with. Data is something that just makes officers feel good! I keep telling them but nobody listens to me."
US Army Intelligence specialist – CENTCOM Qatar 2003

"If you torture data sufficiently it will confess to almost anything."
Fred Menger – Chemistry Professor (1937-)

"If you tell someone what needs doing, as opposed to how to do it, they will surprise you with their ingenuity."
General Patton 1885-1945

"An appeaser is one who feeds a crocodile in the hope it will eat him last."
Winston Churchill 1874-1965

"More delusion as a solution."
US State Department Official – Baghdad March 2005

"If you claim to understand what is happening in Iraq you haven't been properly briefed."
British Staff Officer at Coalition HQ 2004

"If you can keep your head when all about you are losing theirs and blaming it on you – you'll be a man my son."
Rudyard Kipling 1865-1936

"If you can keep your head when all about you are losing theirs – you may have missed something very important."
Royal Marine – Bagram Airfield 2002

"Admiral King commanded the US Navy during the Second World War. His daughter wrote – "He was the most even tempered man I ever met – he was always in a rage. In addition, he believed that civilians should be told nothing about a war until it was over and then only who won. Nothing more!"

"We trained very hard, but it seemed that every time we were beginning to form up in teams, we would be reorganised. I was to learn in later life that we tend to meet any new situation by reorganising, and a wonderful method it can be for creating an illusion of progress, while producing confusion, inefficiency and demoralisation."
Caius Petronius 66 AD

"A few honest men are better than numbers."
Oliver Cromwell 1599-1658

"The beatings will continue until morale improves."
Attributed to the Commander of the Japanese Submarine Force in 1944

"When other Generals make mistakes their armies are beaten; when I get into a hole, my men pull me out of it."
The Duke of Wellington 11759-1852

"Take short views, hope for the best and trust in God."
Sir Sydney Smith 1764-1840

"There is no beating these troops in spite of their generals. I always thought them bad soldiers, now I am sure of it. I turned their right, pierced their centre, broke them everywhere; the day was mine, and

yet they did not know it and would not run."
Marshal Soult 1769-1851 (French Army) – Commenting on the British Infantry at Albuhera in 1811

"There can be no government without an army,
No army without money,
No money without prosperity,
And no prosperity without justice and good administration."
Muslim scholar Ibn Qutayba – 9th Century

"More powerful than the march of mighty armies is an idea whose time has come."
Victor Hugo 1802 – 1885

"Its always best to leave a party before the fight starts."
John Sergeant – 19 November 2008

"No one is foolish enough to choose war instead of peace. In peace sons bury fathers – in war fathers bury sons."
Herodotus – about 440 BC

"What experience and history teach us is this – that people and governments have never learned anything from history, or acted upon any lessons they might have drawn from it."
Georg Hegel 1770-1831

"Better ten years of repression than one night of mob mayhem."
Old Muslim proverb

"Why plan when panicking is so much more fun."
UN administrator in the Congo during 2006 when pressed for his lack of planning for an imminent operation

"You can get a lot more done with a kind word and a gun than you can with a kind word alone."
Attributed to Al Capone

"This is the right way to waste money!"
PJ O'Rourke – Rolling Stone Magazine (Watching missiles firing during an exercise)

"This is just something to be got round – like a bit of flak on the way to the target."
Group Captain Leonard Cheshire VC 1917-1992 – Speaking of his incurable illness in the week before he died.

"Pale Ebenezer thought it wrong to fight,
But roaring Bill, who killed him, thought it right."
Hiliare Belloc 1873-1952

"Everyone wants peace – and they will fight the most terrible war to get it."
Miles Kington – BBC Radio 4th February 1995

"War is a competition of incompetence – the least incompetent usually win."
General AAK Niazi (Pakistan) – after losing Bangladesh in 1971.

"In war the outcome corresponds to expectations less than in any other activity."
Titus Livy 59 BC – 17AD

"Nothing is so good for the morale of the troops as occasionally to see a dead general."
Field Marshal Slim 1891-1970

"It makes no difference which side the general is on."
Unknown British Soldier

"At the end of the day it is the individual fighting soldier who carries the battle to the enemy; Sir Andrew Agnew commanding Campbell's Regiment (Royal Scots Fusiliers), giving orders to his infantrymen before the Battle of Dettingen in 1743 shouted; "Do you see yon loons on yon grey hill? Well, if ye dinna kill them, they'll kill you! "

"The only time in his life that he ever put up a fight was when we asked for his resignation."
A comment from one of his staff officers following French General Joffre's resignation in 1916.

"How can the enemy anticipate us when we haven't got a clue what we are doing?"
Pte Thomas Atkins (Basrah 2006)

"Never disturb your enemy while he is making a mistake."
Mrs Saatchi explained her 12 month silence after her husband started living with Nigela Lawson by quoting Napoleon's dictum

General Quotes

"All rumours are true, especially when your boss denies them."
Dogbert – Build a better life by stealing office supplies

"If a miracle occurs and your boss finally completes your performance appraisal, it will be hastily prepared, annoyingly vague and an insult to whatever dignity you still possess."
Dogbert – Clues for the clueless

"Put all your friends in private offices and all of your wretched slaves in cubicles"
Roman General Dogbertius Dilbert – Thriving on vague objectives

"Don't worry about people stealing an idea. If it's original you will have to ram it down their throats."
Howard Aiken 1900-1973 (Howard Aiken completed the Harvard Mark II, a completely electronic computer, in 1947).

Homer Simpson's advice to his son Bart:
Homer to Bart: "These three little sentences will get you through life":
Number 1: "Oh, good idea boss".
Number 2: (whispers) "Cover for me".
Number 3: "It was like that when I got here".

"Democracy means government by the uneducated, while aristocracy means government by the badly educated.
GK Chesterton 1874-1936

"From the naturalistic point of view, all men are equal. There are only two exceptions to this rule of naturalistic equality: geniuses and idiots".
Mikhail Bakunin 1814-1876

"The greatest evil is not done in those sordid dens of evil that Dickens loved to paint ... but is conceived and ordered (moved, seconded, carried, and minuted) in clear, carpeted, warmed, well-lighted offices, by quiet men with white collars and cut fingernails and smooth-shaven cheeks who do not need to raise their voices. We should remember that...Evil flourishes where good men do nothing".
CS Lewis 1898-1963

'We're menaced by what I might call 'Fabio-Fascism', by the dictator-spirit working away quietly behind the facade of constitutional forms, passing a little law here, endorsing a departmental tyranny there, emphasizing the national need for secrecy elsewhere, and whispering and cooing the so-called 'news' every evening over the (BBC) radio, until opposition is tamed and gulled.'
EM Forster 1979-1970

"The incompetent always present themselves as experts, the cruel as pious, sinners as excessively devout, usurious as benefactors, the small minded as patriots, the arrogant as humble, the vulgar as elegant and the feebleminded as intellectual.
Carlos Ruiz Zafon – (from The Angels Game 2006)

"Tell the truth and run"
Old Yugoslav Proverb

"One of the great things about books is sometimes there are some fantastic pictures."
Attributed to *US President George W Bush 3 January 2000*

"The credit belongs to one who strives valiantly and errs often, because there is no effort without error or shortcoming. Even if such a person fails, he fails while daring greatly, so his place shall never be with those cold and timid souls who know neither victory nor defeat".
US President Theodore Roosevelt (1858-1919)

"All you need in this life is ignorance and confidence. Success is then assured."
Marl Twain 1835-1910

"In this country nobody really seems to know anything about anything anymore".
From the New York Times during the financial crisis of September 2008

"Avoid 'toxic colleagues' who stop you doing your job by whinging and complaining and diverting you from getting things done. Keep away from people who try to belittle your ambition. Small people always do that, but the really great make you feel that you too, can achieve something great".
Mark Twain 1835-1910

"The more corrupt a state; the more numerous its laws"
Tacitus AD 89

"Clear language, reflects clear thought."
George Orwell (1903-1950)

"It's like the old hooker said. I really enjoy the work – it's the stairs that are getting me down"
Elaine Stritch – Actress 2003

"The primary function of management is to create the chaos that only management can sort out. A secondary function is the expensive redecoration and refurnishing of offices, especially in times of the utmost financial stringency".
Theodore Dalrymple 'The Spectator' 6 November 1993.

"Success is generally 90% persistence".
Anon

"It is only worthless men who seek to excuse the deterioration of their character by pleading neglect in their early years".
Plutarch – Life of Coriolanus – Approx AD 80

"They say hard work never hurt anybody, but I figured why take the chance".
US President Ronald Regan 1911-2004

"To applaud as loudly as that for so stupid a proposal means that you are just trying to fill that gap between your ears".
David Starkey – BBCRadio 4 (Feb 1995)

"Ah, these diplomats! What chatterboxes! There's only one way to shut them up – cut them down with machine guns. Bulganin, go and get me one!"
Joseph Stalin 1878-1953 – As reported by De Gaulle during a long meeting.

"Whenever I hear about a wave of public indignation I am filled with a massive calm".
Matthew Parris – The Times 24th October 1994

"It is a general popular error to imagine that the loudest complainers for the public to be the most anxious for its welfare."
Edmund Burke 1729-1797

"The men who really believe in themselves are all in lunatic asylums."
GK Chesterton 1874-1936

"What all the wise men promised has not happened and what all the dammed fools said would happen has come to pass".
Lord Melbourne 1779-1848

"Awards are like haemorrhoids: in the end every asshole gets one".
Frederick Raphae (author born 1931)

"When we have finally stirred ourselves to hang them all, I hope that our next step will be to outlaw political parties outside Parliament on the grounds that, like amusement arcades, they attract the least desirable members of our society."
Auberon Waugh 1939-2001 (in The Spectator 1984)

Extracts from Officer's Annual Confidential Reports

"Works well when under constant supervision and cornered like a rat in a trap."

"He has the wisdom of youth, and the energy of old age."

"This Officer should go far – and the sooner he starts, the better."

"This officer is depriving a village somewhere of its idiot."

"Only occasionally wets himself under pressure."

"When she opens her mouth, it seems that this is only to change whichever foot was previously in there."

"He has carried out each and every one of his duties to his entire satisfaction."

"He would be out of his depth in a car park puddle."

"This young man has delusions of adequacy."

"When he joined my ship, this Officer was something of a granny; since then he has aged considerably."

"This Medical Officer has used my ship to carry his genitals from port to port, and my officers to carry him from bar to bar."

"Since my last report he has reached rock bottom, and has started to dig."

"She sets low personal standards and then consistently fails to achieve them."

"His men would follow him anywhere, but only out of curiosity."

"This officer has the astonishing ability to provoke something close to a mutiny every time he opens his mouth".

"His mother should have thrown him away and kept the stork".

"I cannot believe that out of 10,000 sperm his was the fastest".

"The most complementary thing that I can say about this officer is that he is unbearable".

Finally

Drill instructor to an embarrassed officer cadet who appears to be completely incapable of identifying left from right – "Tell me Sir, as an outsider, what is your opinion of the human race?

Overheard at the RMA Sandhurst

EXTRACTS FROM THE DEVIL'S DICTIONARY 1911

Accuracy: A certain uninteresting quality generally excluded from human statements.

Armour: The kind of clothing worn by a man whose tailor is a blacksmith.

Colonel: The most gorgeously apparelled man in a regiment.

Education: That which discloses to the wise and disguised from the foolish their lack of understanding.

Enemy: A designing scoundrel who has done you some service which it is inconvenient to repay.

Foe: A person instigated by his wicked nature to deny one's merits or exhibit superior merits of his own.

Foreigner: A villain regarded with various degrees of toleration, according to his conformity to the eternal standard of our conceit and the shifting ones of our interest.

Freedom: A political condition that every nation supposes itself to enjoy in virtual monopoly.

Friendless: Having no favour to bestow. Destitute of fortune. Addicted to utterance of truth and common sense.

Man: An animal so lost in rapturous contemplation of what he thinks he is as to overlook what he ought to be. His chief occupation is the extermination of other animals and his own species.

Overwork: A dangerous disorder affecting high public functionaries who want to go fishing.

Peace: In international affairs a period of cheating between two periods of fighting.

Plunder: To wrest the wealth of A from B and leave C lamenting a vanished opportunity.

Republic: A form of government in which equal justice is available to all who can afford to pay for it.

Resign: A good thing to do when you are going to be kicked out.

Revelation: Discovering late in life that you are a fool.

Robber: Vulgar name for one who is successful in obtaining the property of others.

Zeal: A certain nervous disorder affecting the young and inexperienced.

ABBREVIATIONS

The following is a selection from the list of standard military abbreviations and should assist users of this handbook.

AWOL	Absent without leave
accn	Accommodation
ACE	Allied Command Europe
Adjt	Adjutant
admin	Administration
admin O	Administrative Order
ac	Aircraft
AD	Air Defence/Air Dispatch/Army Department
ADA	Air Defended Area
ADP	Automatic Data Processing
AFCENT	Allied Forces Central European Theatre
AIFV	Armoured Infantry Fighting Vehicle
Airmob	Airmobile
ATAF	Allied Tactical Air Force
armr	Armour
armd	Armoured
ACV	Armoured Command Vehicle
AFV	Armoured Fighting Vehicle
AMF(L)	Allied Mobile Force (Land Element)
APC	Armoured Personnel Carrier

APDS	Armour Piercing Discarding Sabot
ARV	Armoured Recovery Vehicle
AVLB	Armoured Vehicle Launched Bridge
AP	Armour Piercing/Ammunition Point/Air Publication
APO	Army Post Office
ARRC	Allied Rapid Reaction Corps
ATGW	Anti Tank Guided Weapon
ATWM	Army Transition to War Measure
arty	Artillery
att	Attached
BE	Belgium (Belgian)
BEF	British Expeditionary Force (France – 1914)
BGHQ	Battlegroup Headquarters
BiH	Bosnia and Herzogovina
bn	Battalion
bty	Battery
BK	Battery Captain
BC	Battery Commander
BG	Battle Group
bde	Brigade
BAOR	British Army of the Rhine
BFG	British Forces Germany
BFPO	British Forces Post Office
BMH	British Military Hospital
BRSC	British Rear Support Command
C3I	Command, Control, Communications & Intelligence.
cam	Camouflaged
cas	Casualty
CCP	Casualty Collecting Post
CCS	Casualty Clearing Station
CASEVAC	Casualty Evacuation
cat	Catering
CAD	Central Ammunition Depot
CEP	Circular Error Probable/Central Engineer Park
CEPS	Central European Pipeline System
CET	Combat Engineer Tractor
CGS	Chief of the General Staff
CinC	Commander in Chief
CIMIC	Civil Military Co-operation
COMMS Z	Communications Zone
CVD	Central Vehicle Depot
CW	Chemical Warfare
COS	Chief of Staff
civ	Civilian
CP	Close Protection/Command Post
CAP	Combat Air Patrol
c sups	Combat Supplies
CV	Combat Vehicles
CVR(T) or (W)	Combat Vehicle Reconnaissance Tracked or Wheeled
comd	Command/Commander
CinC	Commander in Chief
CPO	Command Pay Office/Chief Petty Officer
CO	Commanding Officer

coy	Company
CQMS	Company Quartermaster Sergeant
comp rat	Composite Ration (Compo)
COMSEN	Communications Centre
coord	Co-ordinate
CCM	Counter Counter Measure
DAA	Divisional Administrative Area
def	Defence
DF	Defensive Fire
DPA	Defence Planning Assumptions
DK	Denmark
dml	Demolition
det	Detached
DISTAFF	Directing Staff (DS)
div	Division
DAA	Divisional Administrative Area
DMA	Divisional Maintenance Area
DS	Direct Support/Dressing Station
DTG	Date Time Group
ech	Echelon
EME	Electrical and Mechanical Engineers
ECCM	Electronic Counter Measure
emb	Embarkation
EDP	Emergency Defence Plan
EMP	Electro Magnetic Pulse
en	Enemy
engr	Engineer
EOD	Explosive Ordnance Disposal
eqpt	Equipment
ETA	Estimated Time of Arrival
EW	Early Warning/Electronic Warfare
ex	Exercise
FRG	Federal Republic of Germany
FGA	Fighter Ground Attack
fol	Follow
fmm	Formation
FUP	Forming Up Point
FAC	Forward Air Controller
FEBA	Forward Edge of the Battle Area
FLET	Forward Location Enemy Troops
FLOT	Forward Location Own Troops
FOO	Forward Observation Officer
FR	France (French)
FRT	Forward Repair Team
FUP	Forming Up Place
GDP	General Defence Plan
GE	German (Germany)
GR	Greece (Greek)
GOC	General Officer Commanding
GPMG	General Purpose Machine Gun
HAC	Honourable Artillery Company
hel	Helicopter
HE	High Explosive

HEAT	High Explosive Anti Tank
HESH	High Explosive Squash Head
HVM	Hyper Velocity Missile
Hy	Heavy
IFF	Identification Friend or Foe
II	Image Intensifier
IGB	Inner German Border
illum	illuminating
IO	Intelligence Officer
INTSUM	Intelligence Summary
ISTAR	Intelligence, surveillance, target acquisition and reconnaissance
IRG	Immediate Replenishment Group
IR	Individual Reservist
IS	Internal Security
ISAF	International Security Assistance Force (Kabul)
ISD	In Service Date
IT	Italy (Italian)
IW	Individual Weapon
JFHQ	Joint Force Headquarters
JHQ	Joint Headquarters
JSSU	Joint Services Signals Unit
KFOR	Kosovo Force (NATO in Kosovo)
LAD	Light Aid Detachment (REME)
L of C	Lines of Communication
LLAD	Low Level Air Defence
LO	Liaison Officer
Loc	Locating
log	Logistic
LRATGW	Long Range Anti Tank Guided Weapon
LSW	Light Support Weapon
MAOT	Mobile Air Operations Team
MBT	Main Battle Tank
maint	Maintain
mat	Material
med	Medical
mech	Mechanised
MFC	Mortar Fire Controller
MNAD	Multi National Airmobile Division
NE	Netherlands
MO	Medical Officer
MP	Military Police
MPSC	Military Provost Staff Corps
MOD	Ministry of Defence
mob	Mobilisation
MovO	Movement Order
msl	missile
MT	Military Tasks
MV	Military Vigilance
NAAFI	Navy, Army and Air Force Institutes
NADGE	NATO Air Defence Ground Environment
NATO	North Atlantic Treaty Organisation
NCO	Non Commissioned Officer
nec	Necessary

NL	Netherlands
NO	Norway (Norwegian)
NOK	Next of Kin
ni	Night
NORTHAG	Northern Army Group
NTR	Nothing to Report
NBC	Nuclear and Chemical Warfare
NYK	Not Yet Known
OP	Observation Post
OC	Officer Commanding
OCU	Operational Conversion Unit (RAF)
OIC	Officer in Charge
OOTW	Operations Other Than War
opO	Operation Order
ORBAT	Order of Battle
pax	Passengers
POL	Petrol, Oil and Lubricants
P info	Public Information
PJHQ	Permanent Joint Head Quarters
Pl	Platoon
PO	Portugal (Portuguese)
PUS	Permanent Under Secretary
QGE	Queens Gurkha Engineers
QM	Quartermaster
RAP	Rocket Assisted Projectile/Regimental Aid Post
RJDF	Rapid Joint Deployment Force
RTM	Ready to Move
RCZ	Rear Combat Zone
rec	Recovery
R & D	Research and Development
rebro	Rebroadcast
recce	Reconnaissance
Regt	Regiment
RHQ	Regimental Headquarters
RMA	Rear Maintenance Area/Royal Military Academy
rft	Reinforcement
RSA	Royal School of Artillery
RSME	Royal School of Mechanical Engineering
RTU	Return to Unit
SACUER	Supreme Allied Commander Europe
SATCOM	Satellite Communications
SDR	Strategic Defence Review
SFOR	Stabilisation Force (NATO in Bosnia)
2IC	Second in Command
SH	Support Helicopters
SHAPE	Supreme Headquarters Allied Powers Europe
sit	Situation
SITREP	Situation Report
SIB	Special Investigation Branch
SMG	Sub Machine Gun
SLR	Self Loading Rifle
smk	Smoke
SNCO	Senior Non Commissioned Officer

SP	Spain (Spanish)
Sqn	Squadron
SP	Self Propelled/Start Point
SSM	Surface to Surface Missile
SSVC	Services Sound and Vision Corporation
STA	Surveillance and Target Acquisition
STOL	Short Take Off and Landing
tac	Tactical
tk	Tank
tgt	Target
TOT	Time on Target
TCP	Traffic Control Post
tpt	Transport
tp	Troop
TCV	Troop Carrying Vehicle
TLB	Top Level Budget
TU	Turkish (Turkey)
TUL	Truck Utility Light
TUM	Truck Utility Medium
UAV	Unmanned Air Vehicle
UCAV	Unmanned Combat Air Vehicle
UK	United Kingdom
UKMF	United Kingdom Mobile Force
UNCLASS	Unclassified
UNPROFOR	United Nations Protection Force
UXB	Unexploded Bomb
US	United States
U/S	Unserviceable
VCDS	Vice Chief of the Defence Staff
veh	Vehicle
VOR	Vehicle off the Road
WE	War Establishment
wh	Wheeled
WIMK	Weapon Mounted Installation Kit
WIMP	Whinging Incompetent Malingering Person
WMR	War Maintenance Reserve
WO	Warrant Officer
wksp	Workshop
X	Crossing (as in roads or rivers)

Charles Heyman (Editor)

A former infantry officer, Charles Heyman served in the British Army between 1962 and 1986, with tours of active service in Borneo, Cyprus, Malaysia and Northern Ireland. Between active service tours he served as a Regimental Officer (commanding a Combat Team in Germany) and as a General Staff Officer in the Headquarters of the 1st British Corps. Before leaving the British Army in 1986 he spent two years as a lecturer in Defence Studies at the Royal Air Force College (Cranwell).

Since leaving the British Army Charles Heyman has been specialising in threat and general military and security analysis. Initially working as a consultant for various NATO Defence Ministries, by the early 1990s he was leading research teams for Jane's Information Group. From 1995 until 2003 he was the editor of *Jane's World Armies* and from 1994 to 2000 the editor of *Jane's Police and Security Handbook*. In addition, from 1995 until 2004 he was the Senior Defence Analyst for Jane's Consultancy Group and took part in over 200 defence related consultancy projects.

Charles Heyman has extensive experience in the Balkans, and during the recent campaigns in Iraq and Afghanistan he was a regular contributor to the BBC World Service, Sky News, National Public Radio in the USA and the Australian and Canadian Broadcasting Corporations. During the past five years he has written articles for a variety of newspapers that include *The Times*, *The Scotsman*, *Sunday Express* and the *Sydney Morning Herald*. He remains the author of the Armed Forces of the United Kingdom and The British Army Guide published by Pen & Sword. During recent NATO operations in Libya he was a regular contributor for both the BBC and Sky News.

He is a member of the International Institute for Strategic Studies (IISS).

E Mail – Charles.Heyman@Yahoo.co.uk

This publication was produced by R&F (Defence) Publications
Editorial Office Tel 07889 886170
E Mail: charles.heyman@yahoo.co.uk
Website: www.armedforces.co.uk

Editor: Charles Heyman

Other publications in this series are:
The Royal Air Force Pocket Guide 1994-95
The Armed Forces of the United Kingdom 2010-2011 (Volume 6)
The Armed Forces of the European Union 2011–2012
The Territorial Army – Volume 1 1999

Further copies can be obtained from:
Pen & Sword Books Ltd
47 Church Street
Barnsley S70 2AS

Telephone: 01226-734222 Fax: 01226-734438

12th Edition November 2011

HMSO Core Licence Number CO2W0004896
Parliamentary License Number P2006000197
PSI Licence Number C2006009533